# Plan Graphics for the Landscape Designer

## with Section-Elevation and Computer Graphics

## Second Edition

Tony Bertauski

*Trident Technical College*

**PEARSON**

Prentice
Hall

Upper Saddle River, New Jersey
Columbus, Ohio

**Library of Congress Cataloging-in-Publication Data**

Bertauski, Tony.
    Plan graphics for the landscape designer : with section-elevation and computer graphics /
    Tony Bertauski.—2nd ed.
       p. cm.
    Includes index.
    ISBN 0-13-172063-5
     1. Landscape architectural drawing. 2. Computer graphics. I. Title.

  SB472.47.B47 2007
  712.022′2—dc22
                                                          2005057486

**Editor in Chief:** Vernon Anthony
**Associate Editor:** Jill Jones-Renger
**Editorial Assistant:** Yvette Schlarman
**Production coordination:** David Welsh, Carlisle Publishing Services
**Production Editor:** Holly Shufeldt
**Design Coordinator:** Diane Ernsberger
**Cover and Insert Designer:** Jeff Vanik
**Cover Art:** Created by Tony Bertauski
**Production Manager:** Matt Ottenweller
**Marketing Manager:** Jimmy Stephens
**Senior Marketing Coordinator:** Liz Farrell
**Marketing Assistant:** Les Roberts

This book was set in Giovanni book by Carlisle Publishing Services. It was printed and bound by Edwards Brothers Malloy. The cover was printed by Edwards Brothers Malloy.

Pearson Education Ltd.
Pearson Education Singapore Pte. Ltd.
Pearson Education Canada, Ltd.
Pearson Education—Japan

Pearson Education Australia Pty. Limited
Pearson Education North Asia Ltd.
Pearson Educatión de Mexico, S.A. de C.V.
Pearson Education Malaysia Pte. Ltd.

11 12 1 14 15  V069  18 17 16 15 14

ISBN 0-13-172063-5

# Contents

# Introduction

With the advancement of computers, drafting skills have dropped in demand. Design software has made it quick and easy to draw a design and make revisions. This is certainly the case with large, commercial landscape designs that often go through many changes. Software has made making changes to a design a very simple, quick process that if drafted by hand would require long hours of redrawing.

However, there are still many landscape designs drawn by hand and embraced by many landscape architects and designers as an art form. Drawing is closely related to art, which itself is a designing process. Thus, learning an artistic approach to creating a design helps support one's understanding of the design process.

Students learn to draw to develop a successful landscape design that will communicate to the client effectively as well as artistically. Landscape design has a loose, aesthetic appeal that is often used for installation and construction.

Many students come to an introductory landscape design class knowing very little about the design process, not to mention how to draw. To assume that they know what a T-square is and how to use it would be a mistake. Because many of the tools and techniques are simple, they are often overlooked for explanation. An introductory class has to start with the very basics so that students can build on the fundamentals in advanced classes. These skills are taught by instructors providing demonstrations and students completing exercises. However, a thoroughly illustrated guide would help students work without the assistance of the instructor, catch up on assignments they have missed, as well as for reference.

Much of the feedback I have gotten from students is that they lack a good drawing text for class. The text that had been used explained the design process with great clarity, but not how to draw a design. Much of the drawing instructions are provided in the lab by the instructor with personal feedback. However, a text that students can refer to would greatly improve assignments outside of class in addition to preparing students for the next class. In essence, what many students wanted was a clear guide showing how the tools work, how to create symbols and textures, and a stepwise approach from start to finish in the design process.

This book starts at the beginning of the landscape design process and proceeds with a simplicity that will help beginning students. This book serves as a reference for symbols and textures, and provides students with the skills to create an aesthetic plan drawing that communicates effectively.

# New in This Edition

Since the first edition, I have made note of techniques or concepts that students have difficulty grasping, areas I've felt need to be expanded, clarified, or included. For instance, how should existing trees be represented? How large should a symbol be drawn? How much should the plat be enlarged? To answer these questions, I've added text and illustrations within each chapter, as well as:

- Updated tool photos with improved quality. Also, the section on prints/copies was updated.

- Reorganized the entire section on line weights and added new illustrations.

- Expanded the section on determining symbol size.

- Included new sections on how to address existing plant symbols and drawing miscellaneous symbols.

- Updated illustrations on ground plane textures.

- Added a new section on label placement preferences.

- Expanded information on building plant lists and enlarging plats to change scale.

This edition includes a new appendix of student drawings at the end of the book illustrating many good (and some bad) techniques. This is to give you a concise section of examples that implement the content of this text.

To access supplementary materials online, instructors need to request an instructor access code. Go to **www.prenhall.com**, click the **Instructor Resource Center** link, and then click **Register Today** for an instructor access code. Within 48 hours after registering you will receive a confirming e-mail including an instructor access code. Once you have received your code, go to the site and log on for full instructions on downloading the materials you wish to use.

I've learned so much from landscape designers over the years as well as from my students. I'm always open to new, fresh ideas about how to draw or present a concept to a client. It's a never-ending process, after all. I would like to expand my learning sphere beyond my own classroom, so if you have any comments, ideas, or drawings you would like to share, please e-mail them to me at tbert204@yahoo.com. I cannot guarantee a reply, but I would love to hear or see them.

Best of luck!

# Acknowledgments

The author would like to thank those who made this book possible, including the following reviewers: Anne Spafford, North Carolina State University; Karen Midden, Southern Illinois University; and Patricia Lindsey, North Carolina State University. Also Doug Hihn, Monet's Gardens in Charleston, for all the time, insight, and drawings he volunteered. Thom Hood, Good Earth Inc., who has been unselfish with his time for input. All the students who have given invaluable feedback and drawings. Mack Fleming and Sharon Coke of the Horticulture Program at Trident Technical College, who have been integral to its success. Tom Riccardi at Visual Impact software for allowing the use of software. And my wife, Heather, who has always supported this project; and my kids, Ben, the builder, and Maddy, the storyteller, who have kept things fun.

# 1  The Landscape Design Process and Presentation Graphics

## Objectives

- Understand the role of presentation graphics in the landscape design process
- Indentify the different phases of the landscape design process
- Understand the ultimate goal of landscape design

## Landscape Designers' Communication Tools

Before discussing graphics in a landscape design, let's examine the purpose of the designer's drawings. A landscape designer has to sketch ideas, draw plans, and in some cases create elevated drawings in order to get his or her ideas across clearly to the audience. The majority of designing typically occurs in the form of the plan drawing. A **plan drawing** is a two-dimensional drawing of the design that appears like a bird's-eye view looking from directly overhead. Above all else, the plan drawing serves as a tool to communicate the designer's ideas.

A copy of the plan drawing will be given to the client and the installation contractor. The **client** is the person(s) paying for the design services; the **landscape contractor** is the company implementing the ideas. The landscape contractor may or may not be affiliated with the designer. Therefore, the plan drawing has to be clear and concise as well as accurate.

Sketches, section drawings, or computer images may accompany the plan drawing. These are pictures of the design used to communicate the vertical elements of the design. Clients will often understand visual aspects with sketches and elevations better than plan drawings.

## Presentation Graphics

In addition to clarity and accuracy, plan drawings are used to sell the project to the client. The landscape contractor, on the other hand, just wants a clearly labeled plan to follow.

A well-organized plan drawing is easier to read and looks professional. Presentation graphics present a concept with few words. A professional plan relays the overall design to the observer quickly and effectively with symbols and textures. Anyone, regardless of background, can look at a fully developed plan drawing and get a feel for the type of plants and the texture of construction materials (Figure 1-1).

Plan drawings that rely heavily on verbal descriptions take more time and effort to understand, and the potential to convey the overall design concept is compromised. Compare this statement to advertisements. How do billboards or magazine inserts communicate? Graphics that present the message, rather than a lengthy description, get the message to us quickly and effectively. The graphically developed plan drawing is efficient in the same way.

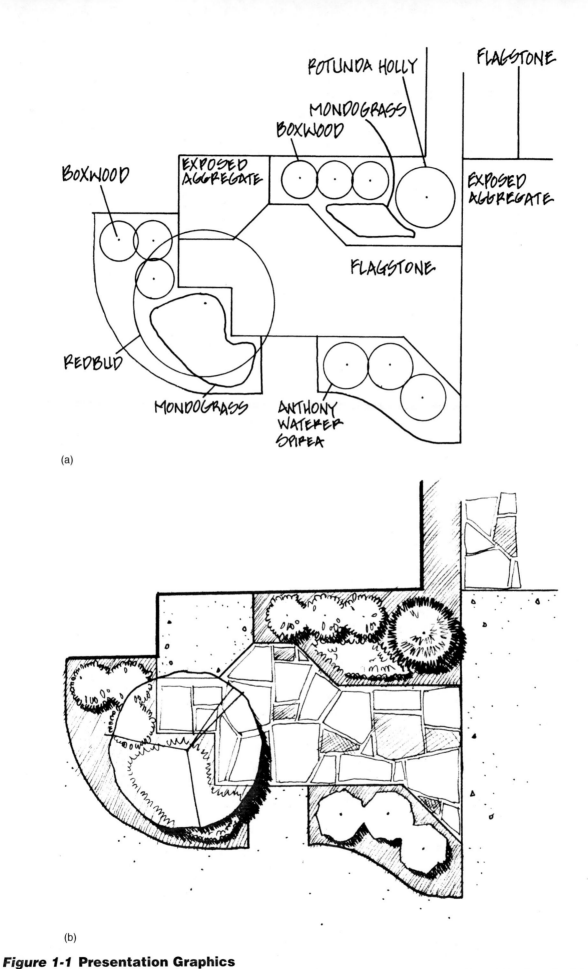

**Figure 1-1 Presentation Graphics**

Presentation graphics improve the readability of the design. (a) Plans graphically undeveloped; (b) plans developed.

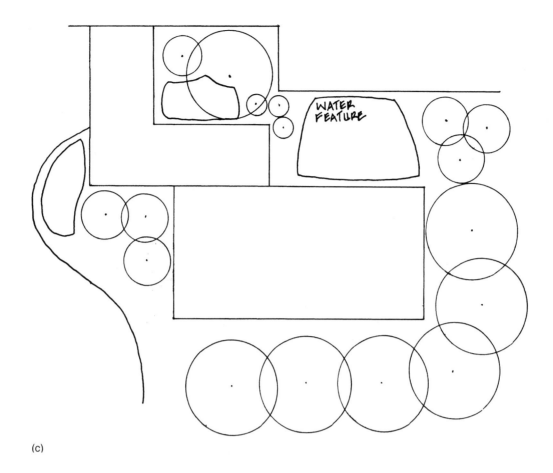

(c)

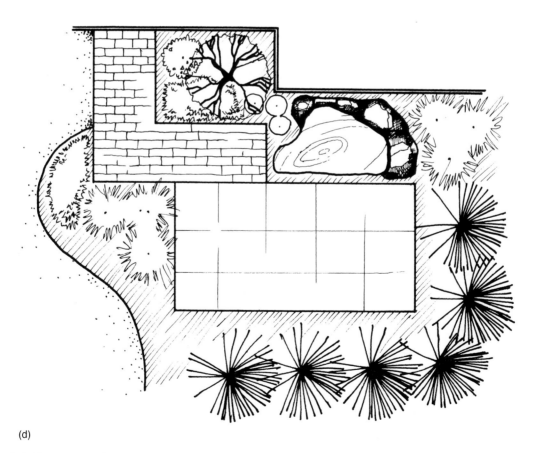

(d)

**Figure 1-1 Presentation Graphics (continued)**
Presentation graphics improve the readability of the design. (c) Plans graphically undeveloped; (d) plans developed.

## Does Every Plan Have to Be Presentation Graphics?

The degree of graphical development is based on the designer's need. Certainly, presentation graphics take more time to complete and will not be feasible for every project. For instance, a small-scale freelance designer may simply sketch ideas with plan circles and lines on tracing paper for a steady client or a small job where he or she doesn't need to sell the project. On the other hand, if the project is intended for proposal or bid that will be presented to an owner or a board of directors, the designer will want to leave a professional impression on the audience and spend the extra time on graphics and color.

It certainly is up to the discretion of the designer, but the advantage of learning presentation graphics is having a skill that makes the designer more marketable. Also, efficiency will develop over time and even quick drawings will improve dramatically.

This text will be addressing the development of plan drawings intended for presentation and therefore will provide instruction to create a presentable format and artistic graphics.

## Graphics Only Aid Presentation

Keep in mind that, although presentation graphics are visually interesting, the ultimate goal is *NOT to draw a pretty picture*. As a landscape designer, the goal is to create a design that addresses the analysis, one that is functional with properly selected plants, in addition to one that is visually appealing. Any artist can draw a stunning portrait of a landscape design. But with little background in horticulture, this drawing may be functionally deficient, with shade plants growing in full sun. *A good drawing does not necessarily make a good design.*

However, presentation graphics can help sell the design and the designer's reputation. People are often excited by a great drawing and often associate a good design with drawing ability. These presentation graphics look good in a portfolio and appear professional. They are also more effective at communicating the overall design.

> ***Tip Box:*** **Presentation Graphics Not a Substitute for Good Design**
>
> The ultimate goal is *NOT to draw a pretty picture*. A successful design is one that is functional as well as aesthetic.

# Design Process

Although this text will focus on the development of presentation graphics, it is important to have a brief overview of the design process: the steps a designer takes in order to arrive at the final drawings. Whereas other texts go into great detail on the theory of design, this text will dwell mostly on drawing. The purpose of this section is simply to familiarize you with the process of drafting and sketching and when presentation graphics are utilized.

## Client Interview

The design process begins with meeting the client, which may be a couple looking to landscape their residence or a group of people wishing to landscape a commercial project. The interview allows the designer to find out the wishes of the client. It's also an opportunity to present a portfolio of design work to the client to gain their trust and confidence. The portfolio will contain a collection of drawings and pictures of past work. Obviously, drawings that are well developed are more likely to communicate to the client a sense of professionalism and pride in the designer's work. At this point in the design, presentation graphics can help sell the design to the client, especially if it is being bid against other designs. There are several types of plan drawings that occur during the design process and not all of them are intended for presentation. Sketches are rough drawings that help the designer work through the design process and are not typically intended for presentation.

## Site Inventory and Analysis

Following the interview is the **site inventory** and **analysis** (Figure 1-2). Inventory is observing and recording what is already on site. From this information, the strong and weak points of the landscape are analyzed. The analysis establishes what changes must be made to be functionally sound, such as screening out unsightly areas or facilitating circulation. All of these ideas are worked out through *rough sketches and outlines.*

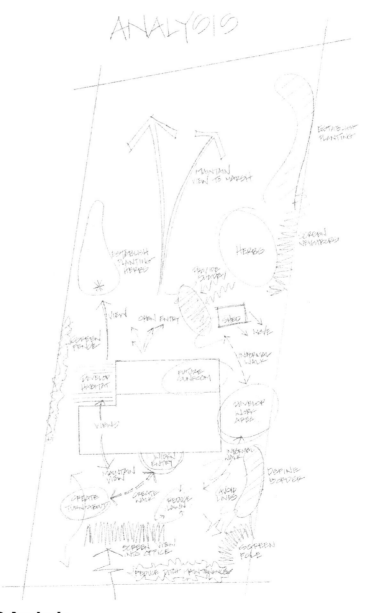

*Figure 1-2* **Analysis**
A graphical analysis illustrates strong and weak points to develop a plan of action.

# Concept Plan

The **concept plan** is sometimes referred to as a **functional diagram** or **bubble diagram** (Figure 1-3). The concept plan uses the inventory and analysis to organize the ground plane. This step establishes the functionality of the design and provides the backbone on which the rest of the design will be built. It takes various approaches to a site by organizing beds, screens, turf, sidewalks, entertainment areas, and so on. These ideas are typically *rough sketches*.

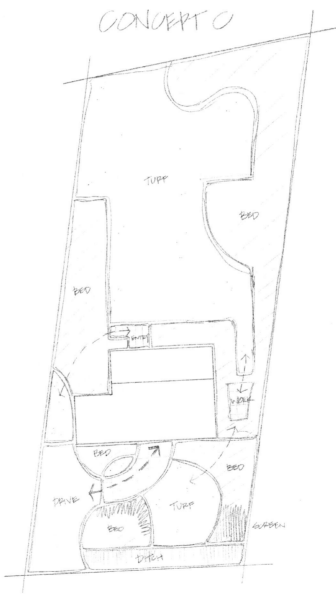

***Figure 1-3* Concept Plan**
A concept plan organizes the ground plane.

## Preliminary Design

The ideas from the analysis and concept plan are brought together to form a **preliminary design** (Figure 1-4). The preliminary design is a more detailed approach from the analytical/concept phases. Plants and hardscapes (non-living material) are drawn to scale and begin to form the design. It focuses on objects, not specific plant material, to form the elements of the design.

The preliminary design is used to get feedback and approval to continue on with the master plan. In some cases, it is *developed for presentation* to sell the design. In this case, presentation graphics help to communicate the design concept and appeal visually. Smaller companies that design/build may not include this step in the presentation. In this case, a preliminary may be a sketch to help work through ideas to get to the master plan.

## Master Plan

The **master plan** is the final detailed plan drawing (Figure 1-5). The term **master plan** can vary, depending on the designer. In some cases, it is a detailed design without any specific labels to communicate the overall design concept. In this case, the designer would use a planting plan (see next section) to label symbols for installation. In other cases, the master plan is also used as the planting plan. A planting plan is used by the landscape contractor to install the design.

If the designer uses the preliminary design as the presentation, then the master plan may sometimes be less graphically developed. However, the master plan will be presented to the clients if the preliminary has not.

## Other Plans and Drawings

There may be other plans included in a design. **Planting plans** are plan drawings that consist of simple symbols and labels that give exact plant placement. Keep in mind that some designers, especially freelancers and smaller companies, combine the master plan with the planting plan. **Layout plans** show the measurements for ground plane areas, such as beds and sidewalks.

**Construction details** (Figure 1-6) are drawings that specify construction techniques. These serve as legal documents for installation and construction. They may include, but are not limited to, planting techniques of trees and shrubs, spacing of groundcover plants, paver construction, fence detail, or post installation. These serve more as a legal document for contractors to follow during installation.

**Grading plans**, or **contour plans** or **topography maps** (Figure 1-7), show the slope of the land. **Contour lines** are used to show existing and proposed changes to the project. Contour changes are mostly used to affect surface drainage but may also be used for visual effect, such as retaining walls or planting berms.

**Irrigation plans** (Figure 1-8) are a schematic of layout and parts for the irrigation system.

Other drawings include **sketches**, **sections**, or **perspectives** (Figure 1-9a and Figure 1-9b) of the proposed design to help the client better visualize the ideas. In Chapter 10, computer graphics demonstrate how **imaging software** (Figure 1-10a and Figure 1-10b) can be used to develop three-dimensional photographs of the project site. This is a great advantage; unlike sketches, sections, and perspectives, the realism of the drawing does not depend on the designer's ability to draw. Instead, an actual photo of the design is presented.

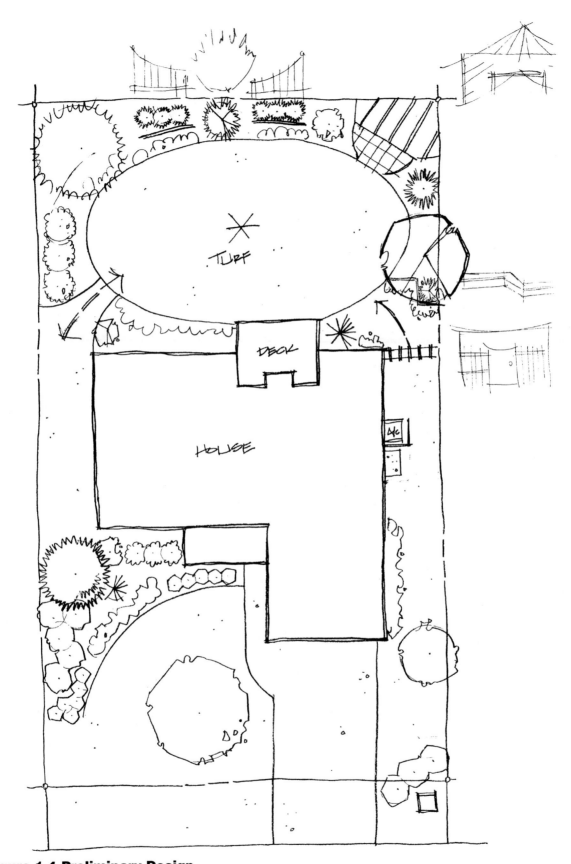

### *Figure 1-4* Preliminary Design

Following the analysis and concept plan. The preliminary plan arranges plants' symbols in an organized ground plane without necessarily labeling anything.

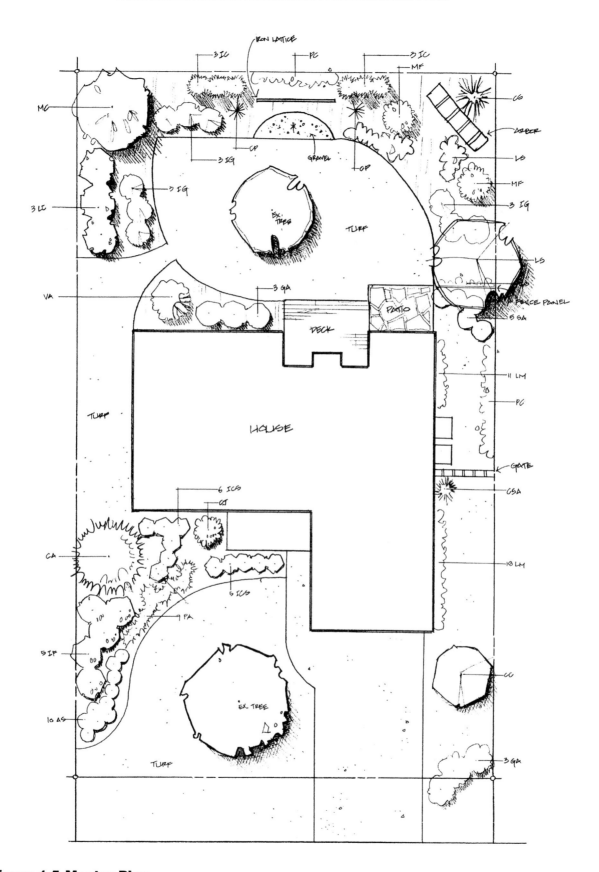

***Figure 1-5* Master Plan**
Completely detailed plan of all plant and hardscape material.

GROUNDCOVER SHALL BE POT OR CONTAINER GROWN

REMOVE CONTAINER PLANTS AND SCARIFY ROOTS BEFORE PLACING IN POSITION

SEE PLANT SCHEDULE FOR GROUNDCOVER SPACING

FINISH GRADE

3" MULCH INSTALLED BEFORE PLANTS

SCARIFY ROOTS BEFORE PLANTING

PLANTING BED 6" DEPTH

GROUNDCOVER PLANTING DETAIL
NO SCALE

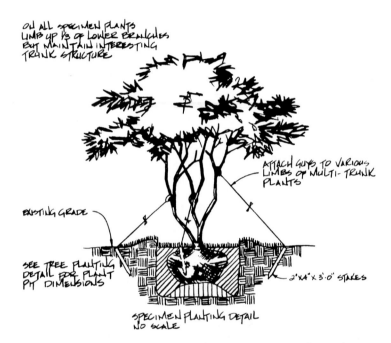

ON ALL SPECIMEN PLANTS LIMB UP 1/3 OF LOWER BRANCHES BUT MAINTAIN INTERESTING TRUNK STRUCTURE

ATTACH GUYS TO VARIOUS LIMBS OF MULTI-TRUNK PLANTS

EXISTING GRADE

SEE TREE PLANTING DETAIL FOR PLANT PIT DIMENSIONS

2"X4"X3'-0" STAKES

SPECIMEN PLANTING DETAIL
NO SCALE

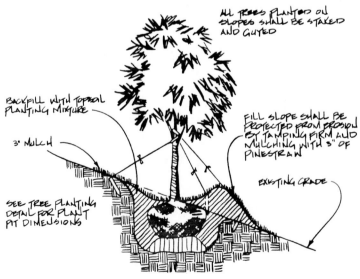

ALL TREES PLANTED ON SLOPES SHALL BE STAKED AND GUYED

BACKFILL WITH TOPSOIL PLANTING MIXTURE

3" MULCH

FILL SLOPE SHALL BE PROTECTED FROM EROSION BY TAMPING FIRM AND MULCHING WITH 3" OF PINESTRAW

EXISTING GRADE

SEE TREE PLANTING DETAIL FOR PLANT PIT DIMENSIONS

TREE SLOPE PLANTING
NO SCALE

### Figure 1-6 Construction Detail
Specify installation techniques.

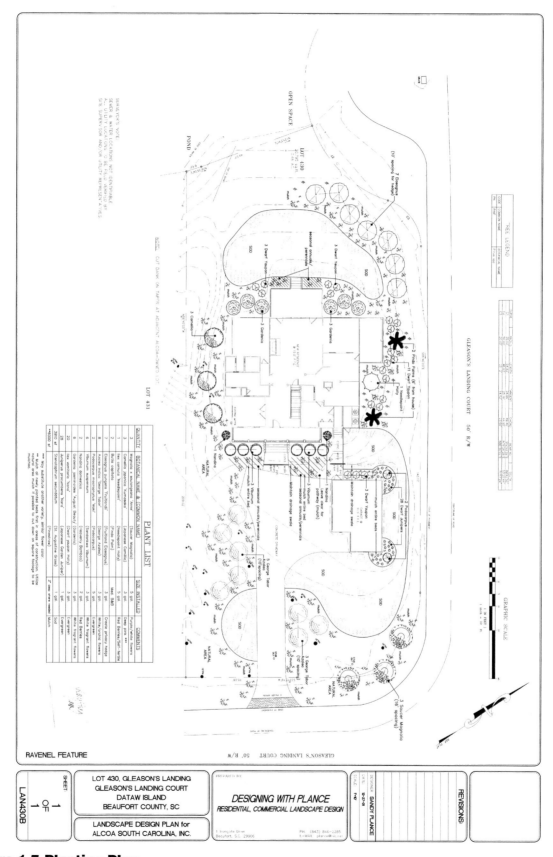

***Figure 1-7* Planting Plan**
Used by the landscape contractor to install the design. *(Drawn in AutoCAD by Sandy Plance)*

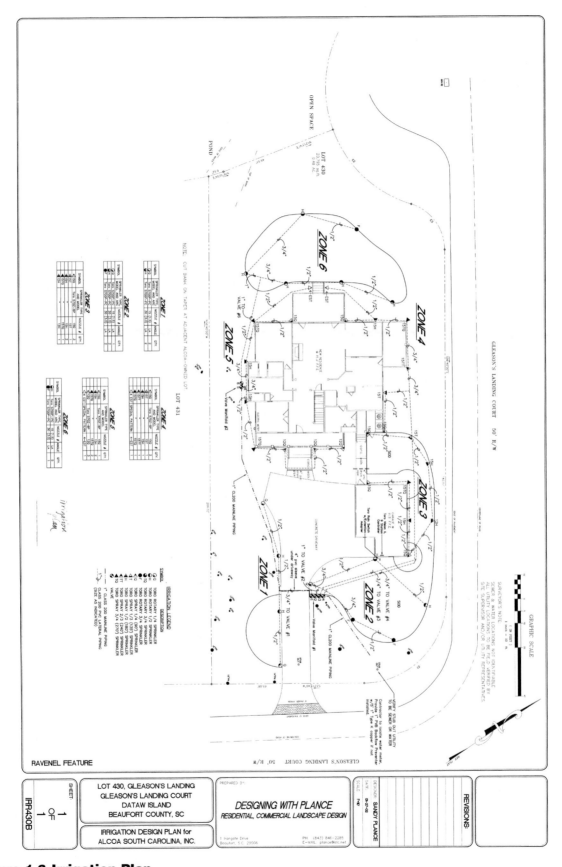

**Figure 1-8 Irrigation Plan**
Separate plan to specify the irrigation installation. (*Drawn in AutoCAD by Sandy Plance*)

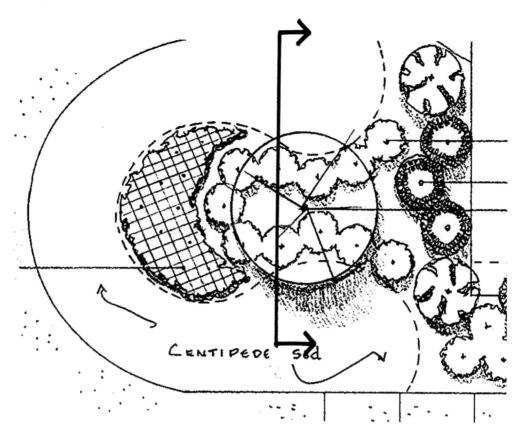

***Figure 1-9a* Plan Drawing and Cut Line**
The section view is indicated by the cut line.

***Figure 1-9b* Section-Elevation**
This is the designer's interpretation of the plan drawing. This elevated view gives the client an idea of the plan.
*(Drawn by Sarah Thornby)*

***Figure 1-10a* Before Imaging**
This is the original picture.

***Figure 1-10b* After Imaging**
This is the designer's interpretation of the plan using imaging software. *(Created by Nate Dubosh)*

# Summary

How the graphics are developed depends on the design process. In some instances, drawings help the designer work through ideas to achieve a final design. These drawings are merely for the designer to organize ideas. Other drawings serve as blueprints and legal documents for installation. Drawings that are presented to clients can help the designer communicate the design concept and ultimately sell the design. Well-drawn plans promote a sense of professionalism and build a positive reputation. However, the drawing is not the ultimate goal of the design process but, rather, the design itself.

# Key Words

**Analysis:**   strong and weak points of the landscape are assessed.

**Bubble diagram:**   see *concept plan*.

**Client:**   person, couple, or committee rendering the services of a landscape designer.

**Concept plan:**   organization of the ground plane that establishes the functionality of the design.

**Construction details:**   drawings that specify construction techniques.

**Functional diagram:**   see *concept plan*.

**Imaging software:**   utilizing a picture to create a computer-rendered version of design.

**Irrigation plans:**   used to lay out and specify irrigation system.

**Landscape contractor:**   company that installs design.

**Layout plans:**   show the measurements for the layout of the ground plane.

**Master plan:**   detailed final plan drawing where all plants are labeled and hardscape material specified.

**Perspective:**   a sophisticated drawing to illustrate vertical elements in a *realistic* approach utilizing vanishing points.

**Plan drawing:**   two-dimensional drawing of the design that is similar to a bird's-eye view from directly overhead.

**Planting plans:**   plan drawing that shows exact plant placement.

**Preliminary design:**   refinement of the concept plan; plants and hardscapes are drawn to scale and form elements of the design; it focuses on objects, not specific plant material.

**Section:**   technique to illustrate vertical elements of design by establishing a cut line (see Chapter 9).

**Site inventory:**   observing and recording what is already on site.

**Sketches:**   rough drawings to illustrate the vertical elements of design.

# 2 Tools

## Objectives

- Learn the drafting tools and materials used to draw plan drawings
- Understand the basic tools required for the beginning design student
- Learn tips and techniques for using drafting tools

Although much of the landscape plan is freehand drawing, **drafting tools** are necessary to be efficient and accurate. Drafting tools make it easy to draw horizontal and vertical lines, circles, and duplicate angles; locate points on the plan; and efficiently erase mistakes. Also, since the master plan, planting plan, or layout plan will be used to locate material during installation, it is equally important that the plan be drawn to scale so that it reads correctly like a blueprint.

While there are many great tools for drafting, beginning students don't need to purchase all of them to get started. This chapter will present basic tools used to draw landscape designs. Please note that **essential tools** will be noted as *required* for beginning students to get started, while other tools will be noted as **additional tools** that can be *helpful* but are not necessarily required for the beginning student.

## Drawing Surface (Essential)

Any table will do the job for a **drawing surface** as long as it has two important characteristics. The first is a *smooth surface* with no cuts or bumps. Inconsistencies in the drawing surface will show in the paper and ruin lines (Figure 2-1). The second is a *straight edge* to slide a T-square along and draw horizontal lines (Figure 2-2). If the drawing surface has a square corner (90 degrees) with straight edges across the top and down the side, then the T-square can be used to draw vertical lines that are perpendicular to the horizontal lines.

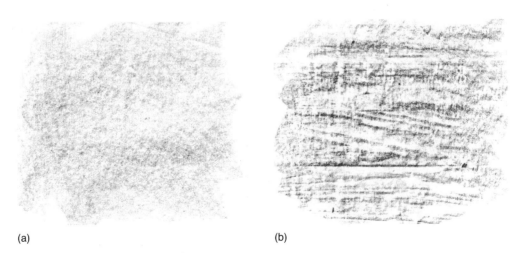

(a)                                              (b)

***Figure 2-1* Drawing Surface**
Coloring over the drawing surface with an art stick reveals the smoothness, which can affect the quality of drawing. (a) Drafting table; (b) kitchen table.

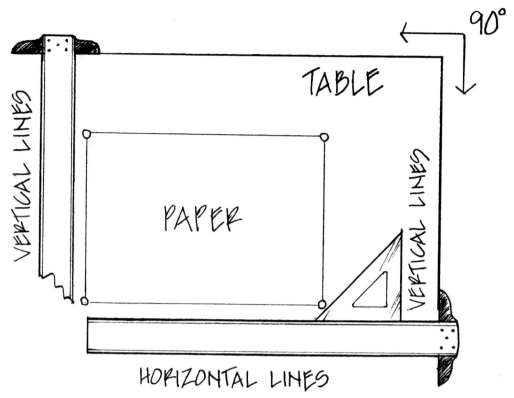

**Figure 2-2 Table Edge**
Square corners and straight edges are important to draw horizontal and vertical lines with
a T-square and triangle.

**Figure 2-3 Drafting Table**
Smooth drawing surface and adjustable height and angle.

Drafting tables are preferred by many designers because tools can be stored in the tray
at the bottom edge of the table and the desktop can be raised, lowered, or tilted for comfort
(Figure 2-3). Some drafting tables will have a **drafting mat** used to cover the drawing surface to protect it. **Drafting desktops** that are portable are also an option (Figure 2-4).

**Figure 2-4 Portable Drafting Table**
Drawing surface can be easily transported.

# Paper (Essential)

There are several kinds of drafting paper (Figure 2-5). **Tracing paper**, sometimes called **trash paper, onionskin,** or **bumwad,** is a thin, translucent paper used to sketch ideas. It is a *low-quality paper* that comes in white, yellow, or buff and is often placed over the site plan to work out different designs in the initial phases such as an analysis or a concept plan. It is sold in rolls 12″ to 36″ wide. It is the least expensive paper and lots of it should be kept on hand.

**Figure 2-5 Paper**
*Trash,* or *tracing,* paper used to work out ideas and take notes; *vellum* paper, high-quality paper used for lead drawings; *Mylar,* high-quality film used for ink drawings.

*High-quality paper* is preferred for the final draft because it has better reproduction quality and longevity. **Vellum paper**, or **rag vellum**, is translucent and can be placed over previous drawings to trace. It is more expensive than tracing paper and can be purchased in individual sheets or in rolls. *Vellum is primarily used for lead drawings* because ink does not erase easily.

**Mylar** is high-quality paper that is actually drafting *film*. It is heavier than vellum and has better longevity and reproduction quality. It often comes with a glossy side and a rough (matte) side. Drawing is done on the rough finish. *Mylar is expensive and is primarily used for ink drawings* because it can be easily erased with an ink eraser. *Plastic lead* can be used on Mylar with minimal smudging.

---

### *Tip Box:* High-Quality Paper

*Vellum* is primarily used for lead drawings.

*Mylar* is expensive and is primarily used for ink drawings.

---

**Grid paper** has non-photo blue lines laid out in squares over the paper. The grid can be used to draw to scale because the size of the boxes is consistent. For instance, the boxes may be 1/8" wide and tall, which would be convenient if the scale of the plan were 1/8" = 1'. The lines should not show up on a print. Some designers like to use grid paper in preliminary drawings because it is quicker to assess the scale.

**Bond paper** is standard-weight paper, like that used in home printers. It is primarily used for copies rather than the actual drawing.

---

### *Tip Box:* Carrying Tubes (Figure 2-6)

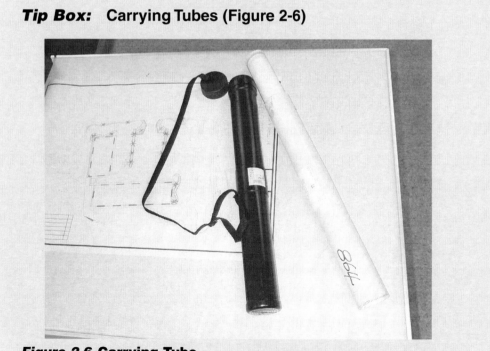

**Figure 2-6 Carrying Tube**
Roll up drawing for easy transport. Use a professional carrying tube with strap or a simple postal tube.

Drawings are easily transported in **carrying tubes,** in which they can be rolled and inserted.

**Professional tubes** are made of plastic and have a carrying strap. An inexpensive solution is to use a cardboard **postal tube**.

---

---

**Tip Box:** Rolling Drawing Facing Out (Figure 2-7)

**Figure 2-7 Title Roll Drawing**
Roll the drawing *facing out*. This way, when the plan is unrolled it will not continue to roll up. To avoid smudging, wrap a blank paper around the outside once the drawing is rolled.

---

# Prints

A **blueprint**, by definition, is "any carefully designed plan." **Blueprinting**, however, as it was originally done, produced a negative copy of the original with white lines on a *blue background*, thus the name blueprint. The original blueprinting process is no longer used to produce copies.

Although losing favor, **diazo** production is still done, but much less frequently. Diazo copies utilize ultraviolet light and ammonia vapor to produce **blueline** or **blackline** prints that are true reproductions with the prospective line color on a white background. The color of the line was mostly a preference of the designer.

However, the title of **blueprinter** is now being replaced by **reprographer** because **reprographics**—the digital reproduction of plans—is the most common form of printing. Reprographics, also referred to as **xerographics** (*xero-* means "dry" and *graphy-* means "write"), is preferred because, even though the equipment is expensive, it is more efficient and there is no need for dangerous chemicals. The original drawing is scanned into the computer system and then printed at any dimension or saved as a digital file.

Copies, often referred to as prints, are given to client and contractor. The original should be kept by the designer in storage and not handled on site. Copies are often obtained at a **blueprinting company** that specializes in reproducting architectural plans, although printing technology has improved enough that quality prints can be obtained at commercial copy stores, such as Kinkos and Copy Max. In most cases, a copy will be done on bond paper but, when quality paper is needed, blueprinting companies can print on vellum or Mylar as well.

---

***Tip Box:*** **Test Print**

Take your plan drawing to make a **test print** to test how your lines show up on the print versus the original.

---

# Tape (Essential)

**Drafting tape** and **drafting dots** are used to anchor the corners of paper onto the design table (Figure 2-8). Dots come in a box that dispenses them from one end as the paper is pulled from the other.

A small roll of **masking tape** can be used as well, although it tends to be very sticky and can rip the corners. Another disadvantage to using tape is it tends to roll over as the T-square is pulled over it. If the tape is too sticky and ripping the corner of the paper, dull the adhesive side more by rubbing each piece in the palm of your hand or on your forehead with the oil from your skin.

---

***Tip Box:*** **Dulling Sticky Tape**

To dull excessively sticky tape and avoid tearing the corners of the paper, rub the adhesive side in the palm of your hand or on your forehead.

---

***Figure 2-8* Drafting Dots**
Tape (bottom) or dots (top) used to anchor the corners of drawing.

# T-Square (Essential)

The **T-square** provides a *horizontal line* by placing the head of the T-square on the edge of the drafting table and sliding it up and down (Figure 2-9). Consistent horizontal and vertical lines can be quickly drawn with this tool. By placing the head of the T-square across the top of the table, it can be used to draw *vertical lines*.

*Wooden* T-squares have 1/2" Plexiglas strips for the drawing edge. *Steel* T-squares have ruler measurements engraved on the straight edge and are commonly used by engineers.

The T-square is especially helpful when the plan is removed from the table. When the plan is again laid down on the table, it can be reoriented to the original work.

## Holding the T-Square

When drawing a line on the T-square, hold the head firmly against the table with the nondrawing hand (Figure 2-10).

## Squaring the Paper

In order to draw horizontal lines parallel with the bottom and top of the paper, the paper must be squared to the T-square (Figure 2-11). First set the T-square on the drafting table with the head firmly against the side edge. Now place the paper on the straight edge so that it conforms along the entire length. Now tape the corners of the paper in place. Be sure to smooth out all bubbles and wrinkles when taping down the paper.

Drafting tables can have a **parallel rule**, which looks and acts like a T-square attached to the table but that slides up and down cables (Figure 2-12).

# Triangles (Essential)

There are two standard **triangles: 45/45-degree** and **30/60-degree** (Figure 2-13). Triangles are made of transparent material to see the paper below. They are very handy as a straight-edge because of their smaller size, and they provide a 90-degree corner to draw square corners.

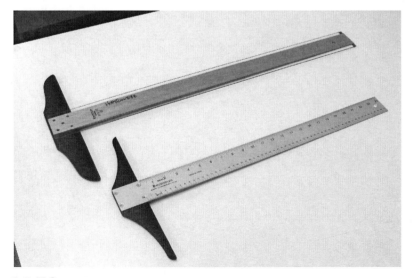

***Figure 2-9* T-Square**
Steel and wooden T-squares.

*Figure 2-10* **Holding T-Square**
Hold the head firmly with the nondrawing hand.

*Figure 2-11* **Squaring Paper**
Square the paper to the T-square so that the lines are drawn parallel to the edge of the paper.

***Figure 2-12* Parallel Rule**
Horizontal bar attached to the drafting table that slides up and down like an attached T-square.

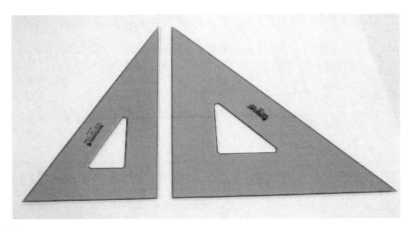

***Figure 2-13* Triangles**
(a) 45-degree triangle and (b) 30/60-degree triangle for drawing angles and straight lines.

They can be used in conjunction with the T-square to draw *vertical lines* (see Figure 2-2). With the T-square in place, put the square corner of the triangle on the T-square for a vertical line. The triangle can also be used to draw consistent lines at an angle, a 30-, 45-, or 60-degree angle. There are also *adjustable triangles* that can be set to various angles.

# Lead (Essential)

For the beginner, the great advantage to using lead is that it is very forgiving. Mistakes can be easily corrected. The disadvantage is weak reproduction, especially if lines are too light. Beginning students should test-print their drawings to learn how to draw line weights with good reproduction quality.

**Lead** comes in *degrees of hardness and softness*. **H lead** is *hard lead* that draws thin, lighter lines. A number will come before H to give the degree of hardness. The higher the number, the harder the lead. The advantage to harder lead is that it requires infrequent sharpening and does not smudge. 4H is used for guidelines and 2H is often used to draw details and sometimes letters. H (without a number) is often used for general drawing.

**B lead** is *softer lead* that draws thicker, darker lines. The higher the number, the softer the lead. It is used for heavy weight lines. Because it is softer, it requires frequent sharpening and smudges easily. HB is used to draw shadows and create contrast. HB is sometimes used for general drawing. Occasionally, 2B is used, but it should be used with caution because it smudges easily.

---

> ### *Tip Box:* Commonly Used Leads
> 4H, 2H, H, HB, and sometimes 2B are the pencil leads must commonly used.

---

## Types of Lead

**Standard leads** are made of *graphite*. **Plastic leads** are used to draw on Mylar film to avoid smudging.

# Pencils (Essential)

Any of the following tools can be used to draw with lead.

**Drawing pencils** are a convenient way to draw (Figure 2-14). They are wooden pencils without an eraser at the end. They are inexpensive and easy to handle.

**Lead-holders** operate like a mechanical pencil but hold larger sticks of lead that can be sharpened to a fine point and draw very sharp lines (Figure 2-15). Lead-holders are versatile because leads can be switched easily.

**Mechanical pencils** hold various thicknesses of lead (from 0.5 mm to 0.9 mm) and do not need to be sharpened (Figure 2-16). Because the lead is thin, it tends to break when too much pressure is applied, especially when it is smaller than 0.5 mm.

## Non-Photo Blue Pencil (Additional)

The lines from a **non-photo blue pencil** show up on a reprographic print. However, be careful. It can be used to draw guidelines for lettering or to make comments on the original plan.

# Pencil Sharpener (Essential)

Keeping pencil lead sharp is important, so have a quality pencil **sharpener** on hand. Lead-holders require a **lead pointer** (Figure 2-17).

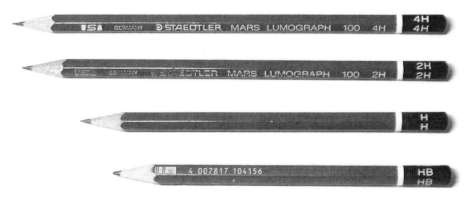

**Figure 2-14 Pencils**
Various leads are used to draw lighter or darker lines.

*Figure 2-15* **Leads**
Used to load into lead-holders.

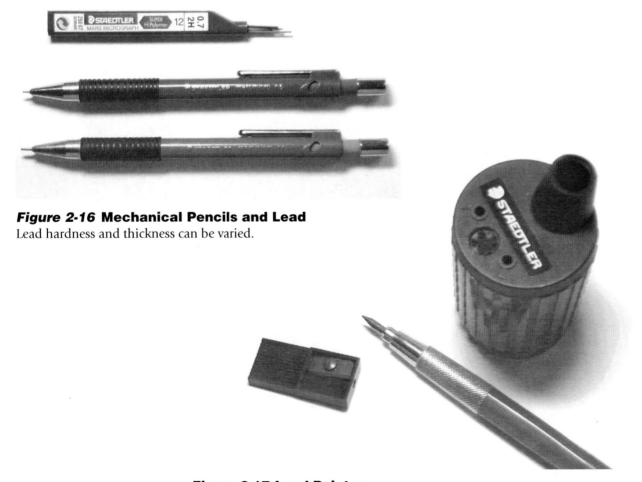

*Figure 2-16* **Mechanical Pencils and Lead**
Lead hardness and thickness can be varied.

*Figure 2-17* **Lead Pointer**
Used to sharpen lead loaded into lead-holder.

# Sandpaper Paddle (Additional)

The **sandpaper paddle** has sheets of fine sandpaper that can be used to sharpen lead (Figure 2-18).

# Erasers

## Essential Erasers

With any eraser, be careful when erasing lines drawn with soft lead because they smear and cause a smudge spot that is hard to remove (see *eraser shield*). **Plastic erasers**, which are commonly white, are frequently used to erase lead (Figure 2-19a). As lead builds up on plastic erasers, it can be washed off to prevent it from smudging the paper. Also, cutting the eraser with a knife can sharpen the edges. **Pink erasers** work well but may not be as effective and tend to harden over time.

## Additional Erasers

A **stick eraser** is a round, 1/4"-diameter stick. It can be used in handheld dispensers for more control. An **electric eraser** utilizes a stick eraser that spins at high speed (Figure 2-19b). It is very efficient. Not only do electric erasers save wear on your hand but they will reduce smudging lines that can happen with block erasers. **Ink erasers** have embedded solvent to erase ink. They often come in a blue or yellow color and work well as a handheld block eraser or as a stick eraser in an electric eraser. **Kneadable erasers** are like putty (Figure 2-19a). They can be used to prepare a soft line to be erased by a hard eraser by lifting the lead from it, which would otherwise smudge. Kneadable erasers are great tools to take weight off lines. By dabbing them onto a line that has been drawn too dark, they will lift off lead and lighten the line without erasing it. *However, be careful! This can cause inconsistent line weights.*

**Figure 2-18 Sandpaper Paddle**
Sharpens lead.

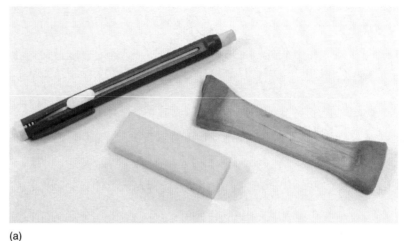

(a)

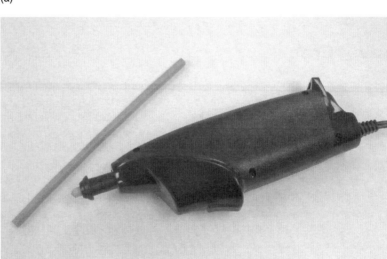

(b)

***Figure 2-19*** **Erasers**
(a) Various erasers (starting right, moving clockwise): kneadable, plastic, and stick. (b) Electric eraser. Stick eraser is rotated at high speed.

# Eraser Shield (Additional)

A thin, flexible metal template with various holes—called an *eraser shield*—is used to mask other lines that are not being erased (Figure 2-20). This can be valuable when erasing a line that is very close to other lines. Without the shield, other lines will be smudged. Although it is not required for beginners, it is so inexpensive it is worth having in the set.

# Markers and Ink (Additional)

*Markers* and *ink* may be used in addition to lead, although they are not required for the beginning student. They provide *excellent line quality*. The contrast of black lines on white paper creates a very clean and legible document. *Be sure the ink is dry before moving tools across it*. It will smudge and ruin a drawing.

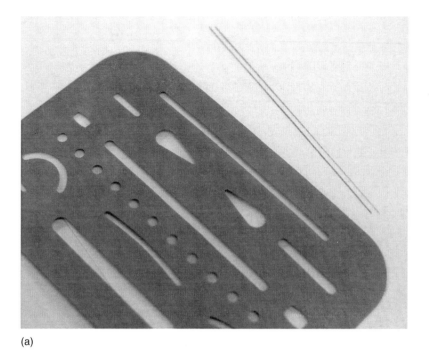

(a)

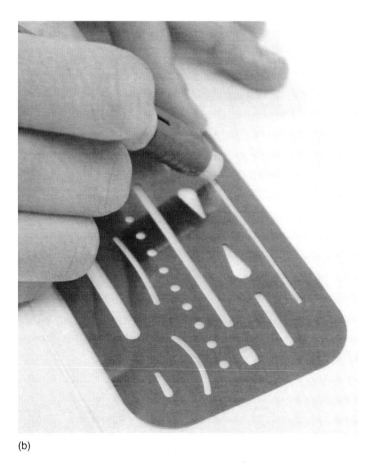

(b)

***Figure 2-20* Eraser Shield**
Thin plate to cover lines not intended to erase.

# Markers

**Round tips** are great for heavyweight lines. **Chisel tip markers** are great for drawing wide lines (Figure 2-21).

**Professional marker sets** have markers with a tip on both ends (Figure 2-22). One end has a fine tip that can be used for detail. The other end is a chisel tip that can be used to draw wide (1/4") lines or narrow lines only 1/8" wide. Some professional markers come with interchangeable tips to change the line width.

# Ink

**Technical pens** have tips made of metal and an ink reservoir (Figure 2-23). Today's pens utilize ink cartridges rather than filling a reservoir, thus avoiding the mess of refilling. Pens are held upright and lightly when drawing. In the past they have been relatively expensive but have become much more affordable and easier to use. The line widths are measured in millimeters. Sets have very narrow tips, such as 0.2 mm, and wider tips, about 1.0 mm. The various widths of tips are used to get different line weights by using different line widths (Figure 2-24).

**Pigment liners** are fiber-tip markers that come in a set that has a variety of line widths. Similar to technical pens, they are relatively inexpensive and disposable. Unlike technical

***Figure 2-21* Marker Tips**
Round tip (left) and chisel tip (right).

***Figure 2-22* Professional Marker**
Fine writing tip (left end) and chisel tip (right end).

pens, the tips of liners tend to flatten on one side and should be rotated when drawing to keep lines of consistent width. A five-pen set can be purchased with a range of tips from .005mm to .08mm.

# Circle Template (Essential)

A **circle template** is used to draw circles of various sizes (Figure 2-25). All the circles on the template have a measured diameter. The usual range of circle templates is from 1/16″ to

(a)

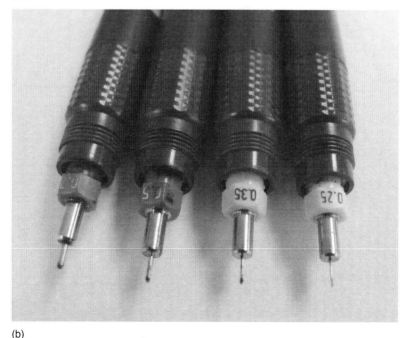

(b)

***Figure 2-23* Technical Pens and Pigment Liners**
(a) Pens are refilled with ink. (b) Each technical pen has a different tip to specify line width, measured in millimeters.

(c)

***Figure 2-23* Technical Pens and Pigment Liners (continued)**
(c) Pigment liners are disposable pens.

***Figure 2-24* Drawing with Technical Pens**
Technical pens should be held at a 90-degree angle to the paper.

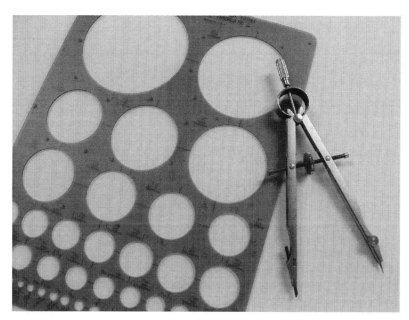

*Figure 2-25* **Compass and Circle Template**
Tools used to draw circles.

21/2", although larger circle templates can be purchased. It is a very valuable tool for drawing circles quickly and to scale.

*Tip Box:*  **Drawing Bedlines**

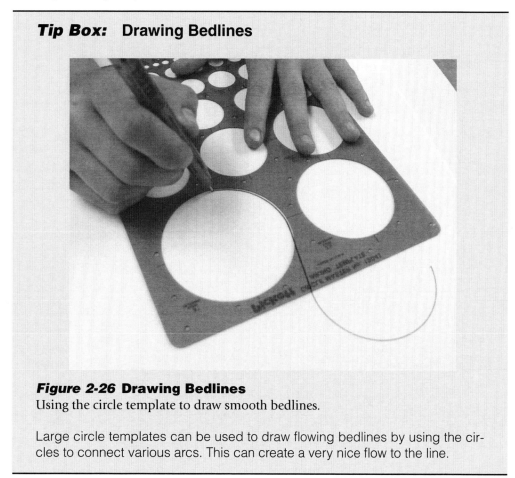

*Figure 2-26* **Drawing Bedlines**
Using the circle template to draw smooth bedlines.

Large circle templates can be used to draw flowing bedlines by using the circles to connect various arcs. This can create a very nice flow to the line.

# Compass (Essential)

A **compass** is used to draw large circles. It consists of one leg that has a sharp point that sticks into the middle of the circle and another leg with lead at the end. When the compass is spun around on the point, the lead draws the circle (Figure 2-27).

The width between legs is adjustable, often by means of an adjustment knob near the top. Circles can be drawn to scale by adjusting the distance between the point and the lead

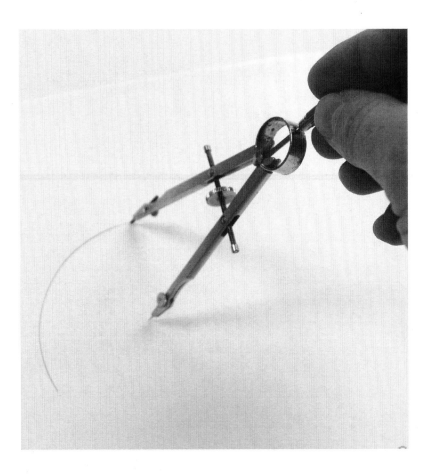

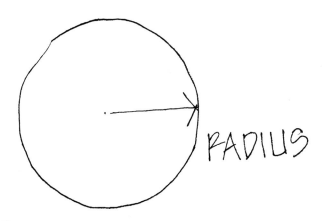

***Figure 2-27* Compass**
Use sharp end to anchor compass in the center of the circle.

to equal the *radius* of the circle (Figure 2-27, bottom). By holding the compass legs to the scale, the right adjustment can be made.

A **compass extender** is an attachment that can be used to draw larger circles. It simply clips onto the leg of the compass to widen the arc.

---

### Tip Box: Sharpening Compass Lead

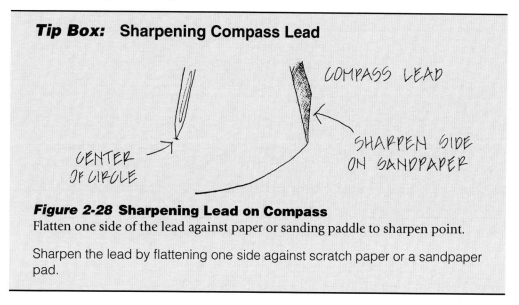

**Figure 2-28 Sharpening Lead on Compass**
Flatten one side of the lead against paper or sanding paddle to sharpen point.

Sharpen the lead by flattening one side against scratch paper or a sandpaper pad.

---

# Scale (Essential)

A **scale** is a ruler that has units that represent feet in the plan drawing (Figure 2-29). It is critical to use it properly, so that the plan drawing is accurate. There are two types of scales: *architect* and *engineer*.

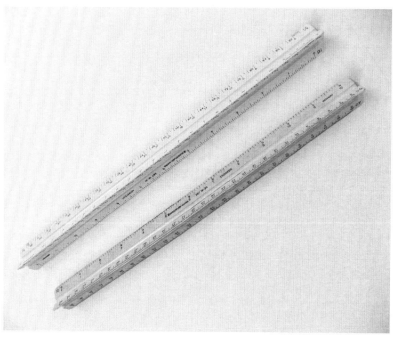

**Figure 2-29 Scales**
Engineer (top) and architect (bottom).

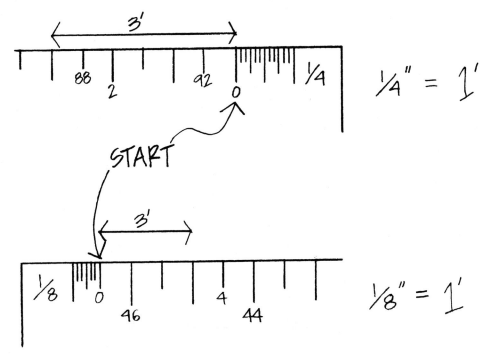

**Figure 2-30 Architect Scale**
Units of an inch; 1/8" = 1'.

An **architect scale** is based on *units of an inch* (Figure 2-30). For instance, the plan may be drawn so that every 1/4" is equal to 1'. Many designs drawn with an architect scale use 1/8" scale, although it will depend on the scope of the project and size of the paper.

An architect scale can be confusing to use at first because it utilizes unit measurements running in both directions. The nice thing about working with increments of an inch is that a ruler can be used in case an architect scale is not available.

The architect scale has increments of an inch starting on the left side of the scale and running to the right, as well as increments of an inch starting on the right and running to the left. For instance, you will find the 1/8" measurement on the left side of the scale. Every increment is 1/8" wide, but only every fourth increment is numbered. If you start at the "0" mark and count every line going to the right, you will find the "4" is on the fourth 1/8" increment. On the right side opposite of 1/8" is the 1/4" scale. Notice it is double the increment of 1/8". Since it is double 1/8", every other line will be used as the 1/4" increment. To use the 1/4" scale, start at the "0" and go left along the scale. Notice that every other line is longer and numbered running left.

When measuring lines that are less than 1', the incremental block that comes before the "0" is used (Figure 2-31). If drawing a 3.25' line using a 3/4" scale, the line would go three 3/4" increments from the "0"; then the remaining 0.25' would be drawn to the increments to the left of the "0."

An **engineer scale** is based on *unit increments in an inch* (Figure 2-32). The 10-scale has 10 evenly spaced increments per inch, the 20-scale has 20 increments per inch, and so on. In most cases, it is used so that every increment is equal to a foot. Therefore, if using a 10-scale, where every inch has 10 increments, the scale is 1" = 10".

Unlike the architect scale, the engineer scale starts only on the left side of the scale and runs to the right. Thus, there are only 6 scales: 10, 20, 30, 40, 50, and 60.

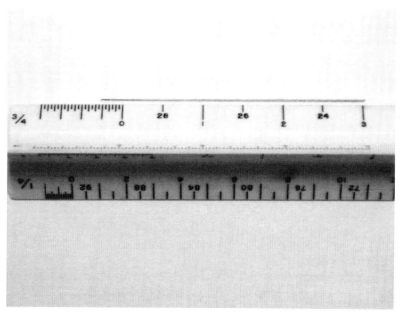

***Figure 2-31* Architect Scale**
Using the smaller increments next to the "0" mark to measure lines that are part of a foot. The image represents a 3.25' line.

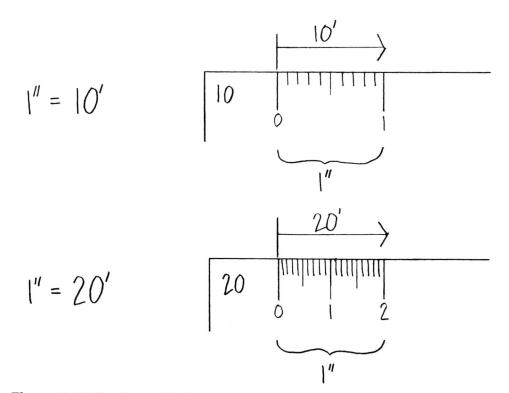

***Figure 2-32* Engineer Scale**
Units in an inch; 1" = 10'.

---

*Tip Box:*  **Common Scale**

When using an architect scale, 1/8" scale (1/8" = 1') is commonly used. For an engineer scale, the 10-scale (1" = 10') is common. However, this will depend on the scope of the project and size of the paper.

---

*Tip Box:*  **Drawing Circles to Scale (Figure 2-33)**

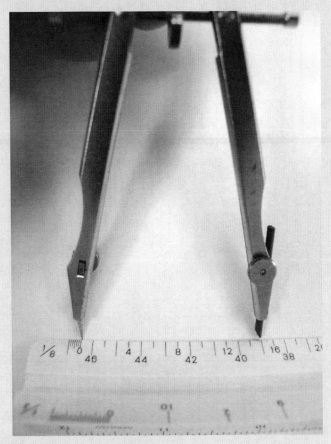

**Figure 2-33 Scale and Compass**
Adjusting the compass to draw circles to scale. If the scale were 1/8" = 1', then this compass would draw a circle radius of 15' (30' diameter).

Hold the compass up to the scale to adjust the radius (half the diameter of the circle).

# Ames Lettering Guide (Additional)

The **Ames lettering guide** is a template that can be slid across a T-square to create guide-lines (Figure 2-34). A bottom and top guideline, and sometimes a midline, is drawn so that letters appear consistent in size and direction.

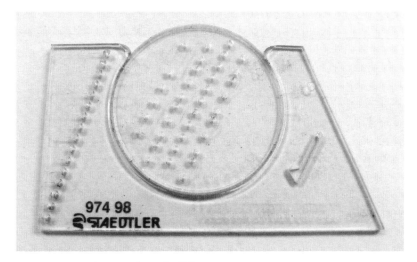

**Figure 2-34 Ames Lettering Guide**
Used to draw guidelines for writing letters at consistent size.

# Dry Cleaning Pad (Additional)

What looks like a rosin bag is actually a bag filled with bits of eraser. Use the **dry cleaning pad** to dust your paper before drawing to *reduce smudging of lines* (Figure 2-35). Some designers do not care to use a dry cleaning pad because those bits of eraser can affect line quality and even show up on the print.

# Brush (Additional)

A **brush** is used to remove eraser bits and other debris from the paper without smudging lines (Figure 2-36). Using your hand to brush off paper has a tendency to smudge lines. Some prefer to use a clean rag, although the brush is less likely to smudge.

**Figure 2-35 Dry Cleaning Pad**
Eraser bits sprinkled over the drawing reduce smudging.

*Figure 2-36* **Brush**
Removes debris without smudging.

# Protractor (Additional)

A **protractor** is used to measure and draw angles (Figure 2-37). This is vital when increasing the scale of property lines. By duplicating the angles, the information is transferred accurately.

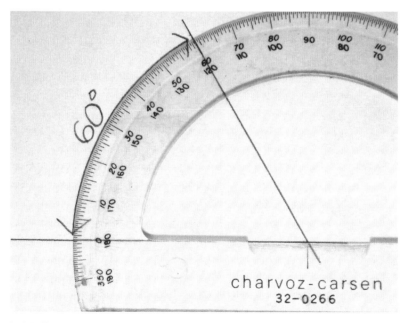

*Figure 2-37* **Protractor**
Measures angles.

# Curves (Additional)

A **flex curve** is a flexible plastic stick that can be shaped to set curves (Figure 2-38). It is usually 12" to 18" long, sometimes with a ruler printed on the side that can be used to measure linear feet of a curving line. It can be used to draw flowing bedlines or connect points. A **French curve** is made of hard, clear plastic and has various arcs that can be used (Figure 2-39).

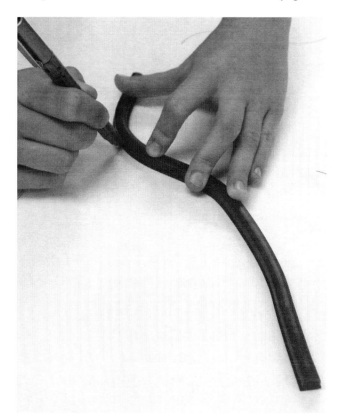

***Figure 2-38*** **Flex Curve**
Used to draw curves.

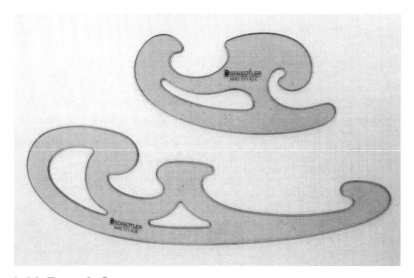

***Figure 2-39*** **French Curve**
Hard plastic templates used to draw curves.

# Parallel Glider (Additional)

A **parallel glider** is a straightedge set on rubber wheels that grip tightly to the paper and can pull the edge consistently across for parallel lines (Figure 2-40).

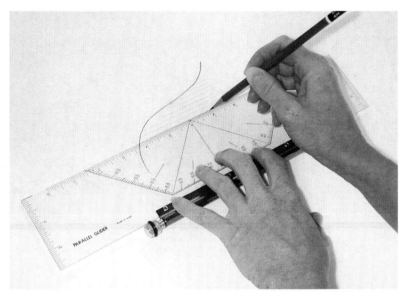

***Figure 2-40* Parallel Glider**
Straightedge on wheels for consistent parallel lines.

# Summary

There are numerous tools the landscape designer can purchase. Many of these tools are essential to drawing an accurate plan, which is critical to producing a plan drawing that will be used to lay out and install plants and other materials. This chapter has presented tools that are used in drafting the plan and has noted which ones should be considered *essential* for the beginning student, without which drafting would be very difficult. Other tools are described as *additional*, meaning that, although helpful in drafting, they are not essential to drafting. Lead is the easiest medium of drawing for beginning students because it is very forgiving. Exercises and sketching are done on tracing paper, while final plans are done on higher-quality paper, such as vellum or Mylar (film). There are a number of tools that help maintain crisp, quality lines and reduce smudging, such as a dry cleaning pad and brush. There are several tools that aid drafting quality by providing consistent straight lines, such as drafting tables, T-squares, triangles, and parallel gliders. Circles are drawn with a circle template and compass, while curves are drawn with the aid of a flex curve and French curve. The plan is kept accurate by the use of scales, which use units to represent length in feet. And, finally, it is important to be familiar with prints to test the reproduction quality of your drawing, since copies are presented to the client and handled in the field.

# Key Words

**30/60 degree:**   drafting triangle with 30-degree, 60-degree, and 90-degree corners.

**45/45 degree:**   drafting triangle with two 45-degree corners and one 90-degree corner.

**Additional tools:**   *helpful* but not necessarily required for the beginning student.

**Ames lettering guide:**   template that can be slid across a T-square to create lettering guidelines.

**Architect scale:**   scale based on units of an inch.

**B lead:**   designates soft lead that draws thick, dark lines that are more prone to smudging; the higher the number, the softer the lead.

**Blackline:**   see *diazo.*

**Blueline:**   see *diazo.*

**Blueprint:**   any carefully designed plan or the original blueprinting process (see also *blueprinting*).

**Blueprinting:**   original blueprinting process produced a negative copy of the original with white lines on a blue background.

**Blueprinting company:**   specializes in reproducing architectural plans.

**Bond paper:**   standard weight "computer" paper.

**Brush:**   used to remove eraser bits and other debris from the paper without smudging lines.

**Bumwad:**   see *tracing paper.*

**Carrying tubes:**   used to transport drawings.

**Chisel tip markers:**   tip that is wide and narrow, "chisel shaped"; can draw wide or narrow lines.

**Circle template:**   used to draw circles of various sizes.

**Compass:**   used to draw large circles; it consists of one leg that has a sharp point that sticks into the middle of the circle and another leg with lead at the end.

**Compass extender:**   attachment that can be used to draw larger circles.

**Diazo:**   utilizes ultraviolet light and ammonia vapor to produce blueline or blackline prints that are true reproductions with the prospective line color on a white background.

**Drafting desktops:**   portable drawing surfaces.

**Drafting dots:**   used to anchor the corners of paper onto the design table.

**Drafting mat:**   used to cover the drawing surface to protect it and a drawing when not in use.

**Drafting tables:**   preferred by designers, they can be raised, lowered, or tilted for comfort.

**Drafting tape:**   see *drafting dots.*

**Drafting tools:**   instruments and materials used to efficiently create an accurate landscape plan.

**Drawing pencils:**   wooden pencils without an eraser at the end.

**Drawing surface:**   has two important qualities—smooth surface and a straight edge.

**Dry cleaning pad:**   bag filled with bits of eraser used to dust your paper before drawing to reduce lines from smudging.

**Electric eraser:**   utilizes an eraser stick that spins at high speed and erases very efficiently.

**Engineer scale:**   scale based on unit increments in an inch.

**Eraser shield:**   a thin, flexible metal template with various holes used to mask other lines that are not being erased.

**Essential tools:**   *required* for beginning students.

**Flex curve:**   flexible plastic stick that can be shaped to set curves.

**French curve:**   template made of hard, clear plastic that has various arcs.

**Grid paper:**   has non-photo blue lines laid out in a grid pattern that can be used to assess scale; grid lines will not show on a print.

**H lead:**   designates hard lead that draws thin, light lines that are less prone to smudging; the higher the number, the harder the lead.

**Ink erasers:**   have embedded solvent to erase ink.

**Kneadable erasers:**   erasers like putty; can be used to prepare a soft line to be erased by a hard eraser.

**Lead:**   typically graphite used in pencils that come in degrees of hardness and softness.

**Lead pointer:**   used to sharpen lead-holders.

**Lead-holders:**   drawing utensils that hold larger sticks of lead that can be sharpened to a fine point and draw very sharp lines.

**Masking tape:**   used to anchor corners of paper to a drawing surface.

**Mechanical pencils:**   hold various thicknesses of lead (from 0.5 mm to 0.9 mm) that do not need to be sharpened.

**Mylar:**   high-quality paper that is actually drafting film; it is heavier than vellum and has better longevity and reproduction quality.

**Non-photo blue pencil:**   lines will not show up on a print.

**Onionskin:**   see *tracing paper*.

**Parallel glider:**   straightedge set on rubber wheels that grip tightly to the paper and can pull the edge consistently across for parallel lines.

**Parallel rule:**   looks and acts like a T-square attached to the drafting table but slides up and down cables.

**Pigment liners:**   fiber-tip markers that come in a set that has a variety of line widths; similar to technical pens, they are relatively inexpensive and disposable.

**Pink erasers:**   erasers that tend to harden over time.

**Plastic erasers:**   commonly white, are frequently used to erase lead; they have good longevity.

**Plastic leads:**   are used to draw on Mylar film to avoid smudging.

**Print:**   a copy that is made for presentation or color development.

**Postal tube:**   cardboard carrying tube.

**Professional marker sets:**   have a tip on both ends; one end has a fine tip that can be used for detail; the other end is a chisel tip that can be used to draw wide (1/4") lines or narrow lines only 1/8" wide.

**Professional tubes:**   sturdy, plastic carrying tubes with straps.

**Protractor:**   used to measure and draw angles.

**Rag vellum:**   see *vellum paper*.

**Reprographer:**   company that produces prints, or copies.

**Reprographics:**   the production of a digital copy; the original is scanned into the system and then printed at any dimension or saved as a digital file.

**Round tips:**   markers with a rounded point.

**Sandpaper paddle:**   sheets of fine sandpaper used to sharpen lead.

**Scale:**   used to draw lines that represent length in feet on the plan.

**Sharpener:**   used to sharpen drawing pencils.

**Standard leads:**   graphite drawing leads.

**Stick eraser:**   handheld dispenser that holds a round, 1/4"-diameter eraser stick.

**Technical pens:**   have tips made of metal and an ink reservoir; the line widths are measured in millimeters.

**Test print:**   copy of a drawing to measure the quality of reproduction.

**Tracing paper:**   low-quality translucent paper used to sketch ideas.

**Trash paper:**   see *tracing paper*.

**Triangles:**   used to draw angles or, in conjunction with a T-square, vertical lines.

**T-square:**   provides a horizontal or vertical line when head firmly placed on the edge of the drafting table.

**Vellum paper:**   high-quality paper used for a final draft; it has better reproduction quality and longevity than tracing paper.

**Xerographic:**   See *reprographics.*

# 3 | Line

## Objectives

- Understand the characteristics of line quality
- Learn techniques for controlling line quality
- Learn how to reduce line smudging
- Understand how line weights are used in the plan drawing
- Learn how to create different line weights

Plan drawings are an organization of lines that create a legible document. Lines make up the house, property lines, symbols, textures, and labels. The line drawing should first and foremost read clearly and present little confusion. It is important that all details pertaining to material, installation, and layout can be easily read by the client or contractor. Second, the line drawing should be presentable. A clean, crisp drawing appears professional.

# Line Quality

## Consistency

For **consistency**, lines should be an equal width and value from the beginning of the line to the end (Figure 3-1). These two qualities are affected by the following:

*Speed of hand.* The faster the drawing hand moves, the thinner and lighter the line appears (Figure 3-2). If the speed of the hand varies on a long line, it will be inconsistent in width and value.

*Drawing tip.* The tip of pencils and some markers can become flattened on one side and create inconsistent line width.

**Figure 3-1 Line Consistency**
Keep line width consistent from the beginning to the end of the line by keeping the lead sharp and rotating the pencil to avoid a flat side developing on the lead.

***Figure 3-2* Speed of Hand**
As the drawing hand moves faster, the line becomes thinner and lighter.

## Pencil

Sharpen lead often. Sharp lead creates lines that have crisp edges. When lead gets dull, line edges are vague, similar to a crayon.

Once sharpened, the tip of lead is brittle and can break easily. Slightly dull the tip on a piece of scratch paper or a sandpaper board to round the edges and knock down the tip.

Sharpen lead frequently to keep line width consistent. Without frequent sharpening, lines will begin thin and eventually widen as the tip wears down.

Lead tips also begin to develop a flat side, which can disrupt line consistency. Rotate lead point by frequently by regripping and turning pencil.

---

### *Tip Box:* Consistent Lines

Slightly dull the tip of lead after sharpening. Also, rotate the pencil while drawing to avoid developing a flat side.

---

## Ink

Because the line width is based on the size of the ink tip, line quality is excellent. The line width remains consistent and solid from beginning to end as long as speed of hand is consistent. Disposable markers (pigment liners) that have a soft tip will develop a flat side if they are not occasionally rotated while using. The steel tips of technical pens, however, will not flatten and maintain constant line width.

# Solid Lines

Have confidence in your **solid lines**. Do not be nervous and end up with tentative lines (Figure 3-3). Also, do not sketch a line with several short strokes. You will end up with poor-quality lines that appear sloppy.

For relatively short lines, draw with quick, crisp strokes. This creates a line with solid character. Focus on the beginning and end of the line to get straight lines that have the weight on the ends (Figure 3-4). For long lines, use a straightedge to create a solid, straight line.

## Redrawing Lines?

Once a line is drawn, many students draw back over it in an attempt to improve the line quality. In most cases, this creates a double line: a darker line with the original line curving around it (Figure 3-5).

**Figure 3-3 Line Quality**
Keep lines solid and crisp. Sketchy lines do not read well on a plan drawing.

**Figure 3-4 Line Emphasis**
For relatively short lines, focusing on the beginning and end of the line with a short stroke will help create a sharp line.

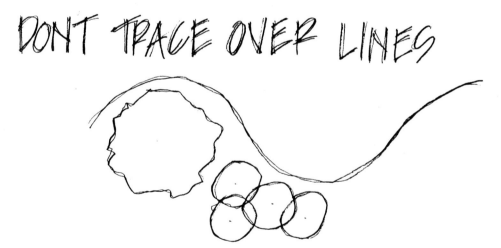

**Figure 3-5 Tracing Lines**
Avoid tracing over lines to "improve" them. If the lines need to be redrawn, then erase the originals.

The desire to redraw the line is usually due to lack of confidence in drawing ability. Students want to "improve" the drawing by tracing over it. Be confident! Go with the first stroke! If the original line is poor, erase it before redrawing. Otherwise, stick with the original.

There are some cases where lines can be drawn over without the double-line effect. These are usually short lines or touch-up improvements. *However, as a rule, avoid drawing over lines.*

# Straight Lines

Use a straightedge, such as a triangle or T-square, to draw **straight lines** (Figure 3-6). This is important for long lines, such as property lines or driveways.

Either draw sharp, straight lines across the edge of the straightedge or use the straightedge to draw a light guideline to trace over freehand. Long freehand lines can exhibit a nice, loose quality.

# Corners

Where **corners** are drawn, lines should meet in order to establish a well-defined, solid connection (Figure 3-7). The lines can even slightly cross over, emphasizing the object and lending a loose quality. Do not overly cross corners and make them confusing or distracting.

# Smudging

**Smudging** takes the crisp quality from lines. Lines can be ruined from your drawing hand and equipment being dragged across them. Lead lines tend to smudge as they are continually drawn over, with softer leads being more susceptible. Over time, the drawing will develop a gray haze, reducing the contrast between lines and white space as well as looking sloppy. Smudging lead can be avoided with a few simple techniques (Figure 3-8).

*Scratch paper.* Place a small piece of paper (or triangle or cloth) under your hand when drawing. This will prevent your hand from dragging on the paper as well as keeping the paper moisture-free.

*Dry cleaning pad.* Lightly dust the paper before drawing; the eraser crumbs will reduce smudging (be careful of bits that negatively affect the print quality).

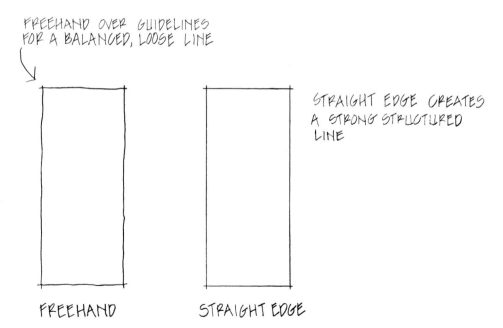

**Figure 3-6 Straight Lines**
Straight lines can be drawn across a straightedge or over a guideline that is drawn with a straightedge.

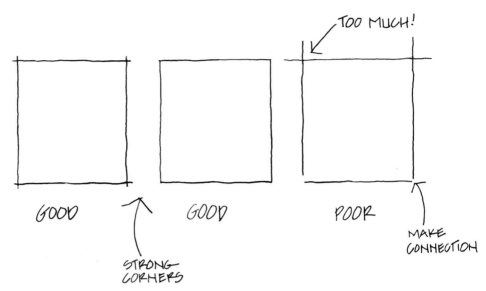

### Figure 3-7 Corners

Where lines meet to form a corner, they should always make the connection or slightly cross over.

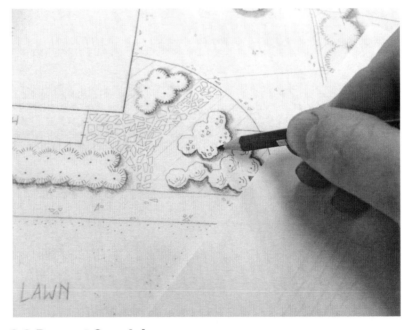

### Figure 3-8 Prevent Smudging

Keep lines from smudging by dusting the paper before drawing and placing your drawing hand on a piece of paper.

When using ink on a straightedge, such as a triangle, there is a tendency for the ink to bleed under the edge and smear when the triangle is lifted off the paper. Be sure you are using an ink triangle that has a beveled edge (Figure 3-9). The marker will run across the edge that is off the paper and prevent it from bleeding under.

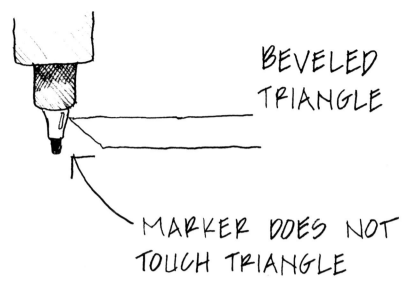

BEVELED TRIANGLE

MARKER DOES NOT TOUCH TRIANGLE

**Figure 3-9 Ink Triangle**
When using ink, the straightedge has to be elevated off the paper to avoid the ink from bleeding under the edge.

---

**Tip Box:** Avoid Smudging Lines with Equipment (Figure 3-10)

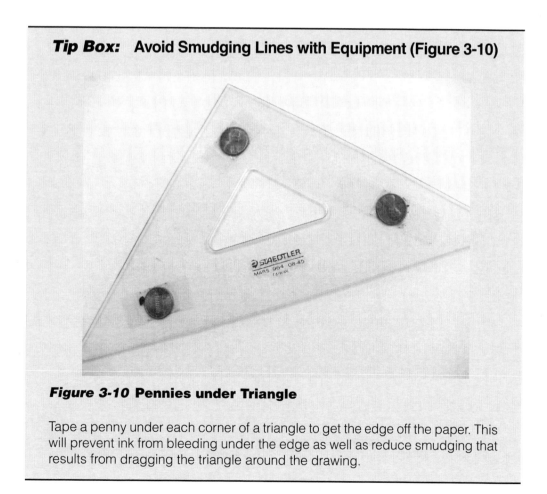

**Figure 3-10 Pennies under Triangle**

Tape a penny under each corner of a triangle to get the edge off the paper. This will prevent ink from bleeding under the edge as well as reduce smudging that results from dragging the triangle around the drawing.

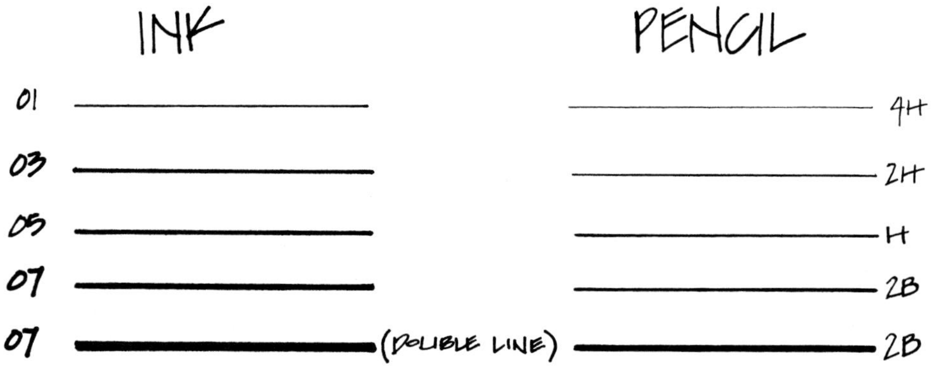

INK                              PENCIL

01  ——————————          —————————— 4H

03  ——————————          —————————— 2H

05  ——————————          —————————— H

07  ——————————          —————————— 2B

07  ——————————(DOUBLE LINE)—————————— 2B

**Figure 3-11 Line Weight**
Line weight is determined by the darkness and thickness of the line.

# Line Weight

The width and darkness of a line define line weight (Figure 3-11). The more weight a line has, the higher degree of presence it exhibits. **Heavyweight** lines are dark and thick. A softer lead (B lead) will draw darker and wider lines. With ink, a wider line is achieved with larger tips, since the darkness of lines does not change. **Lightweight** lines are lighter and thinner. Use harder leads (H leads) and smaller ink tips to get lighter weights.

**Tip Box:** Line Weight Variety (Figure 3-12)

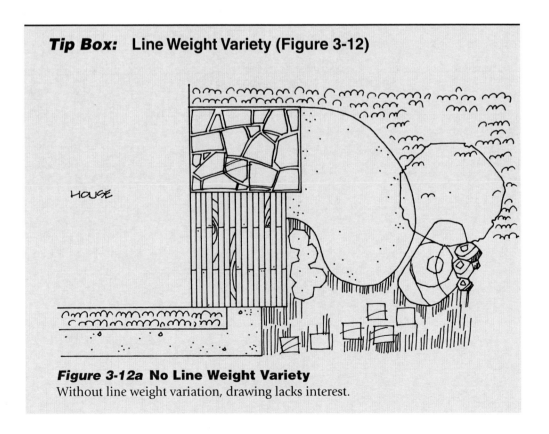

HOUSE

**Figure 3-12a No Line Weight Variety**
Without line weight variation, drawing lacks interest.

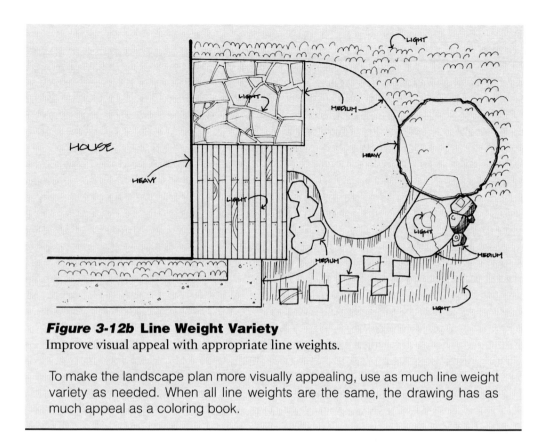

**Figure 3-12b Line Weight Variety**
Improve visual appeal with appropriate line weights.

To make the landscape plan more visually appealing, use as much line weight variety as needed. When all line weights are the same, the drawing has as much appeal as a coloring book.

# Heaviest Weight

- *Round tip marker.* The heaviest weight lines in the drawing will be the border and title block (if used) to help frame and focus attention to the plan. Use a round tip marker to draw the border and title block (or use predrawn border paper).

# Heavy Weight

- HB lead (double line)
- 0.7-mm ink (double line)

The next heaviest line should be on the floorplan of the house. Some designers like to use heavier weights on immovable objects, such as walls. Regardless of preference, heavy weight on the house lends a balance to the drawing, since the house is the focus of the surrounding landscape.

Also, a heavyweight line (although not as heavy as the house) can be used on the canopy of an overhead tree symbol (Figure 3-13). Objects that are closer in space to the observer appear with more detail and greater contrast. By giving more line weight to tree canopies, it gives the impression those symbols are farther off the ground.

# Medium Weight

- H or HB lead
- 0.3-mm or 0.5-mm ink

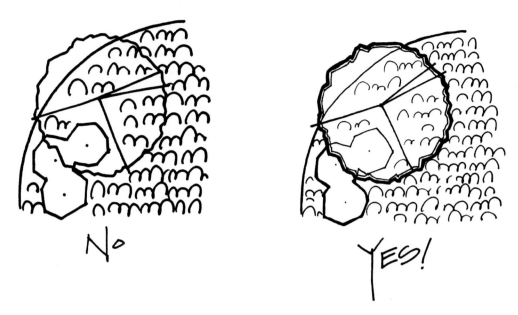

***Figure 3-13* Outlines**
Using a heavier line weight on objects and areas helps define them.

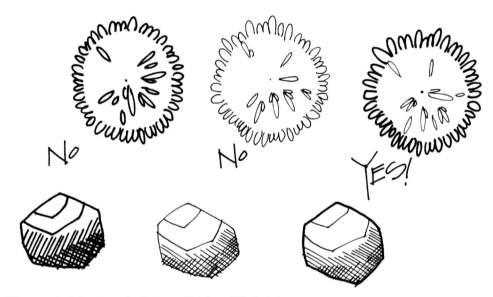

***Figure 3-14a* Symbol Detail Line Weight**
Light detail line weight supports the heavier defining outline of symbols.

Medium line weights should be used to emphasize the outlines of symbols, objects, and forms (Figure 3-14a). This will separate them from surrounding objects, providing more contrast between the line and white space of the paper.

Medium weight is also suggested for lettering and property lines.

Leaderlines in the label are a medium line weight (H lead or 0.3-mm ink at most). They are sometimes drawn with a lighter line weight to keep them from becoming so busy, since there are so many of them.

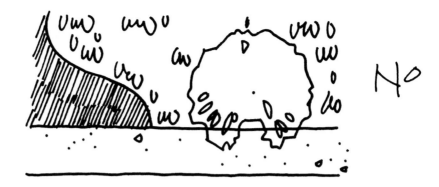

**Figure 3-14b Ground Detail Line Weight**
Detail on ground plane is lighter to support defining outlines.

## Light Weight

- 2H lead
- 0.1-mm or 0.3-mm ink

Lightweight lines are typically used to draw the detail in a plan (Figure 3-14a and b). This includes any type of texture on the ground plane or within the outline of a symbol. There are exceptions that will be noted in later chapters. Lighterweight details helps emphasize the defining outline, as well as add line weight variety to the drawing for more visual interest.

Another use for lightweight lines is underneath the canopy of overhead tree symbols (Figure 3-15). Since the outline of the overhead symbol is already heavier, drawing the detail underneath *lighter than the detail outside the symbol* further pops the tree symbol off the paper for additional visual interest. Keep in mind that these lines are lighterweight than the detail in the rest of the drawing, so a lighter line with a 2H lead or a 0.1-mm ink can be used (as long as 0.3-mm is used for the rest of the detail).

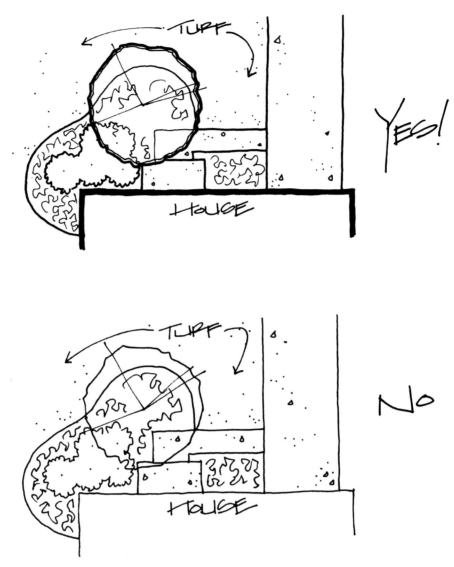

**Figure 3-15 Line Weight under Symbol**
Light line weight for lines drawn under symbol for clarity and to visually "lift" symbol.

---

**Tip Box:**  **Lifting Line Weight**

Kneadable erasers are helpful lifting weight from lead lines (Figure 3-16). If you forget to draw detail lighter underneath an overhead symbol, dab it with a kneadable eraser a few times to lighten it.

---

## Lightest Weight

- 4H lead
- Ink should not be used

The lightest line weights on the drawing are the guidelines. Guidelines are used for lettering and drawing symbols. Only 4H lead is used, so that the guidelines will not show up on the print.

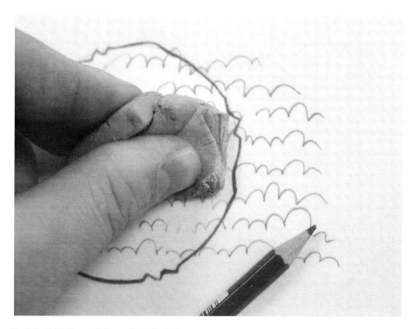

***Figure 3-16* Lifting Line Weight**
To lighten line weight, use a kneadable eraser.

# Summary

This chapter looked at two components of line: quality and weight. There are many factors that affect the quality of line drawing. Consistent, solid lines are important to present a crisp, clear drawing. Speed of hand and the condition of the drawing tip affect line width and value. Smudging lines also reduces line quality and can be reduced by keeping the paper clean, placing the drawing hand on scratch paper, and using a dry cleaning pad.

Line weight is measured by its width and value. Wide, dark lines are heavyweight, while thin, light lines are lighterweight. There should be a range of line weights used in the plan drawing and so that the plan reads more easily. Heavyweight lines help define areas and objects imply solidity to objects such as walls and fences. Lightweight lines are used in the detail of objects and areas in support of the heavy defining outlines.

# Key Words

**Consistency:** lines should be a consistent width and value from the beginning of the line to the end.

**Corners:** lines should meet or even slightly cross over, in order to establish a well-defined, solid connection.

**Heavyweight:** dark and wide.

**Lightweight:** light and thin.

**Smudging:** takes the crisp quality from lines; lines can be ruined from your drawing hand and equipment being dragged across them.

**Solid lines:** use crisp strokes to get crisp lines; avoid tentative and sketchy lines.

**Straight lines:** use a straightedge, such as a triangle or T-square, to draw straight lines.

# 4 Lettering

## Objectives

- Understand the role of lettering in presentation graphics
- Learn how to draw and use lettering guidelines
- Learn techniques for consistent and legible lettering
- Become familiar with various lettering styles

## The Art of Lettering

It is not enough to be able to draw attractive symbols and flowing bedlines for a finished drawing. Lettering your words with an artistic style is just as important to the overall appearance.

Every designer adds his or her own personal touch to lettering, but there is a quality to landscape design lettering that is common. First, there is looseness to the lettering style that is quite different from engineer drafting (Figure 4-1). Engineer drafting is often very regimented and precise. Each letter has specific guidelines on how it is spaced. It is a very formal style.

Landscape design lettering has a flowing quality that communicates a stylish flair, mimicking the flowing bedlines and staggered plantings (Figure 4-2). The letters may be more formal in appearance—being more square and exact—but still drawn loosely and quickly. Usually, landscape design lettering has an informal quality. It is often easy to spot someone who has design experience by the way he or she writes.

## Guidelines to Good Lettering

Even if you do not have good handwriting, there are a few rules you can follow that will improve your lettering.

### Words Are Printed

Printing creates very legible writing (Figure 4-3). Stylistic writing is appealing, but more importantly there should be no confusion as to what is written due to style. Cursive writing can appear too informal, as well as be difficult to read.

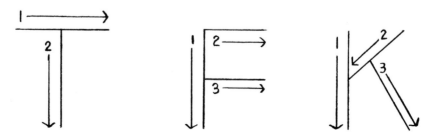

***Figure 4-1* Formal Drafting**
Letters conform to strict guidelines.

## PLANT LIST

| | | | | | |
|---|---|---|---|---|---|
| A | 13 | RED MAPLE | ACER RUBRUM | | |
| B | 4 | WILLOW OAK | QUERCUS PHELLOS | | |
| C | 3 | LEYLAND CYPRESS | X CUPRESSOCYPARIS LEYLANDII | | |
| D | 8 | 'NATCHEZ' CREPE MYRTLE | LAGERSTROEMIA INDICA 'NATCHEZ' | | |
| E | 3 | SWEET BAY MAGNOLIA | MAGNOLIA VIRGINIANA | | |
| F | 4 | PODOCARPUS | PODOCARPUS MACROPHYLLUS MAKI | 3 GALLON | |
| G | 32 | DWARF YAUPON HOLLY | ILEX VOMITORIA NANA | 3 GALLON | |
| H | 2 | DWARF HINOKI CYPRESS | CHAMAECYPARIS OBTUSA 'NANA GRACILIS' | 3 GALLON | |
| I | 10 | VARIEGATED PITTOSPORUM | PITTOSPORUM TOBIRA 'VARIEGATA' | 5 GALLON | |
| J | 8 | 'EAST PALATKA' HOLLY | ILEX X ATTENUATA 'EAST PALATKA' | 5 GALLON | |
| K | 7 | WAX MYRTLE | MYRICA CERIFERA | 5 GALLON | |
| L | 28 | 'HARBOR DWARF' NANDINA | NANDINA DOMESTICA 'HARBOR DWARF' | 2 GALLON | |
| M | 4 | TULIP POPLAR | LIRIODENDRON TULIPIFERA | | |
| N | 2 | SWEET GUM | LIQUIDAMBAR STYRACIFLUA | | |
| O | 1 | CHINESE ELM | ULMUS PARVIFOLIA | | |
| P | 10 | DWARF GARDENIA | GARDENIA JASMINOIDES 'RADICANS' | 3 GALLON | |
| Q | 200 | MONDO GRASS | OPHIOPOGON JAPONICUS | 4" | |
| R | 277 | ASIATIC JASMINE | JASMINUM ASIATICUM | 1 GALLON (2'O.C.) | |
| S | / | FLOWERING ANNUALS | PANSY, SNAPS, PETUNIA | 4" | |

NOTES:
PINE STRAW AROUND PLANTINGS (150 BALES)
SOD GRASS IN COURTYARD - ST. AUGUSTINE
SEED OTHER GRASS AREAS - ANNUAL RYE

**Figure 4-2 Landscape Design Lettering**
Has a stylish informality that lends aesthetic appeal to plan drawing.

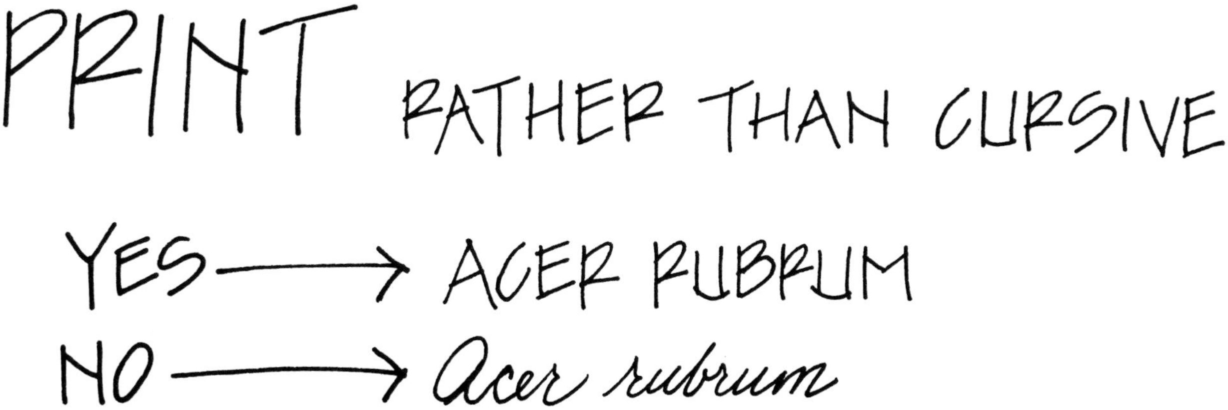

PRINT RATHER THAN CURSIVE

YES ⟶ ACER RUBRUM

NO ⟶ Acer rubrum

**Figure 4-3 Printed Letters**
Cursive writing can be difficult to read as well as sloppy.

## Lettering Guidelines

**Guidelines** will keep the letters consistent in size and level across the paper (Figure 4-4). A bottom guideline is used to keep lettering oriented in a straight line across the paper. The top guideline keeps letters consistent in height. A middle guideline is sometimes used for larger letters to keep the middle portions of the letters consistent.

GUIDELINES: GOOD SIZE AND LEVEL LINES
NO GUIDELINES: POOR SIZE AND WAYWARD LINES

**Figure 4-4 Guidelines**
Keep letters consistent in size and lines level across the paper.

(a)

(b)

(c)

(d)

**Figure 4-5 Lettering Guide**
(a) Draw the baseline on the T-square. (b) Place the lettering guide on the T-square; insert the pencil into the hole for the midline. Holes along the left edge are 1/8" apart. In this figure, letters will be drawn 1/2" tall, so the middle guideline is drawn with the pencil in the second hole, which is 1/4" above the baseline. (c) The top line is placed 1/2" above the baseline. (d) Lettering will follow the bottom and top lines for a level guide across the paper. The midline is a guide for letters that have middle points, such as *B*, *E*, and *F*.

## Drawing Guidelines

Use a 4H lead or non-photo blue pencil to draw guidelines, so that they do not show up on a print. There are a number of ways to draw guidelines, one is with an **Ames lettering guide** (Figure 4-5).

- Draw the baseline across the T-square.
- Without moving the T-square, place the Ames lettering guide on the T-square so that the square side, not the angled side, of the lettering guide is on the left side. Each hole represents 1/8" in height.
- Draw the top guideline at 1/2" by placing the pencil in the fourth hole and sliding the lettering guide across the T-square. (This creates guidelines for 1/2" letters.)

- Draw the middle guideline at 1/4" in the second hole and slide it across the T-square again.

Another approach to drawing guidelines may not be as accurate and easy as the preceding technique:

- Mark the top, middle, and bottom lines with a ruler.
- Line a T-square on each mark and draw the guidelines across.

---

### *Tip Box:*   Guideline Template

Create a **guideline template** with guidelines on a separate sheet of paper that can be slid under and seen through the drawing (Figure 4-6). You will not have to spend time drawing guidelines on the drawing.

**Figure 4-6 Guideline Template**
Create guidelines on a separate sheet of paper that can be slid underneath the drawing to avoid having to draw guidelines on the drawing.

Templates can be quickly printed from word processing programs by underlining a document of tabs (or spaces). Change the font size of the document to get different line spacing.

---

### Visible Guidelines

Guidelines are drawn lightly with a 4H lead, so that they will not appear on a copy. Some designers prefer to draw the guidelines darker, so that they *do appear on a copy*. Some feel that the appearance of guidelines lends a professional quality (Figure 4-7).

## Use an H Lead

This lead will give a good line weight without smudging easily.

*GUIDELINES THAT SHOW*

*GUIDELINES THAT DON'T SHOW*

**Figure 4-7 Visible Guidelines**
Some designers prefer to have the guidelines appear on the copy to lend a professional quality.

## Hold the Pencil Firmly

In the beginning, move your hand instead of your fingers to get crisp, solid lines. (This is a good starting technique; however, with more experience it gets easier to move your fingers.)

## Draw Solid, Bold Lines

Each line is drawn quickly with solid, crisp strokes (Figure 4-8). The emphasis of each stroke is on the start and finish of the line. *Avoid the wispy ends that trail off.* Do not think about the lines and *trying* to draw them. When the lines are drawn quickly, the lettering takes on an attractive looseness that maintains character.

Pay attention to the width of the line. It should be consistent from start to finish.

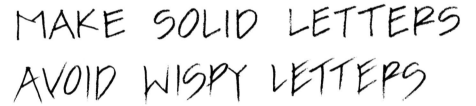

*MAKE SOLID LETTERS*
*AVOID WISPY LETTERS*

**Figure 4-8 Solid Lines**
Lines should be crisp, so lead must be sharpened often.

## Case Consistency

An important rule in good lettering is **case consistency** between all letters. Use either uppercase or lowercase letters, but do not mix them (with the exception of the first letter in the first word of a sentence) (Figure 4-9). Uppercase letters are quite often used exclusively, but either one is acceptable.

## Spacing Between Letters, Words, and Lines

Be consistent with spacing between letters and words. When consistency is present, the lettering takes on a rhythm that is appealing (Figure 4-10). There is no real rule of thumb for spacing between letters because the space varies for letter combinations. The spacing should appear balanced without looking crowded or spaced so wide as to cause confusion.

If lines are printed in a block, be sure there is about 1/8" that separates each line.

UPPER CASE ONLY

Lower case only (except first letter)

<u>Don'T</u> COMBINE Upper ANd loWer CASE

**Figure 4-9 Do Not Mix Upper- and Lowercase Letters**
Most designers use uppercase letters exclusively. Regardless, avoid mixing upper- and lowercase letters, which can look strange as well as cause confusion.

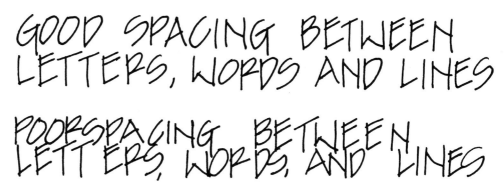

**Figure 4-10 Consistent Spacing Between Letters, Words, and Lines**
Consistent spacing between letters, words, and lines will create a good balance and appealing flow.

## Horizontal and Vertical Axes

A good way to ensure style consistency is to pay attention to the horizontal and vertical axes of the letters (Figure 4-11). Most designers letter with a 90-degree **vertical axis** (no slanting), while the **horizontal axis** has a slight upward slant; a **formal lettering** style has no slanting on the horizontal axis. Whatever writing style you use, every letter should conform to the same degree.

## Letter Size

Lettering is generally 1/4" tall. This height is done easily without a straightedge (Figure 4-12). Letters may be as tall as 1/2" in areas such as the title block. It will take practice and repetition to get good and consistent lettering. Once the lettering becomes effortless, it is a part of the design process that is fun.

Once you complete a few alphabets at the 1/2" height, draw guidelines for letters that will be 1" and 2" in height. You will notice that lettering with sharp, crisp lines becomes

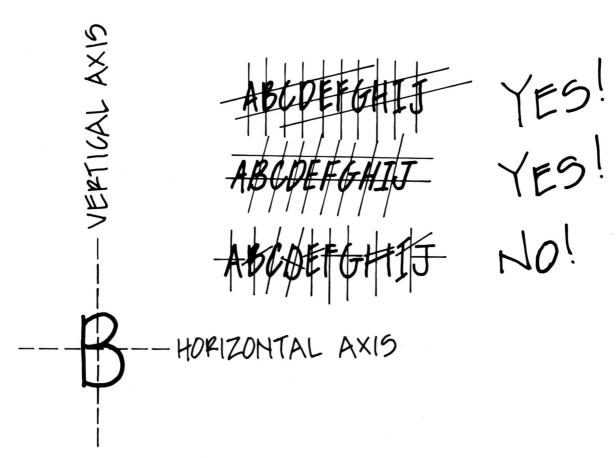

***Figure 4-11* Letter Axis**
Judge letter consistency by the vertical and horizontal axes of all the letters. No matter what angle your axis is drawn, every letter should be consistent.

ℐ GENERAL LETTERING ¼″ HIGH

***Figure 4-12* Letter Height**
Most letters in plan drawings are 1/4" in height. Title blocks ordinarily have letters as tall as 1/2".

more difficult on larger letters. In cases where you will be using large letters, use the straightedge of the triangle on the T-square to get quality lines (Figure 4-13).

## Hierarchy of Size

Although the majority of the plan is often lettered with 1/4" letters, the size is dictated by the scale of the project as well as the importance of the information. For instance, titles and subtitles are typically larger than the information around them to emphasize importance, in addition to making them easier to read.

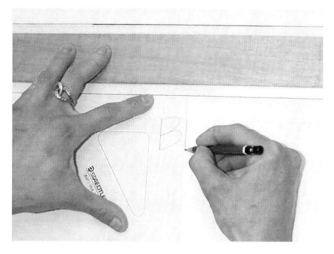

***Figure 4-13* Lettering with Straightedge**
Letters larger than 1/2" can be drawn with the aid of a straightedge.

---

***Tip Box:*** **Letter Height**

Most letters are 1/4" tall. Letters may be as tall as 1/2" in areas such as the title block.

---

## Word Placement

Labels and blocks of description should be consistent throughout the plan drawing (Figure 4-14). All labels are written on a horizontal plane to be consistent and legible. Short descriptions should be positioned on the plan drawing to be spatially balanced with the weight of the design.

Labeling will be one of the last things placed on the plan drawing. In some cases, it may be prudent to put trash paper over the plan drawing and roughly letter areas of description to be sure there is enough room. Consider world and label placements before drawing to avoid erasing and redrawing.

# Lettering Styles

The following are variations of lettering style. The most commonly accepted lettering style by landscape designers is the **informal style.** However, regardless of the lettering style, every letter is drawn with a series of separate lines. (Figure 4-15). By focusing on the individual lines, it is easier to create sharp, bold lines in each letter. In addition, it creates a loose style, in which the lines overlap slightly.

---

***Tip Box:*** **Preferred Lettering Style**

The most commonly accepted lettering style by landscape designers is the informal style, in which the horizontal axis slants slightly upward.

---

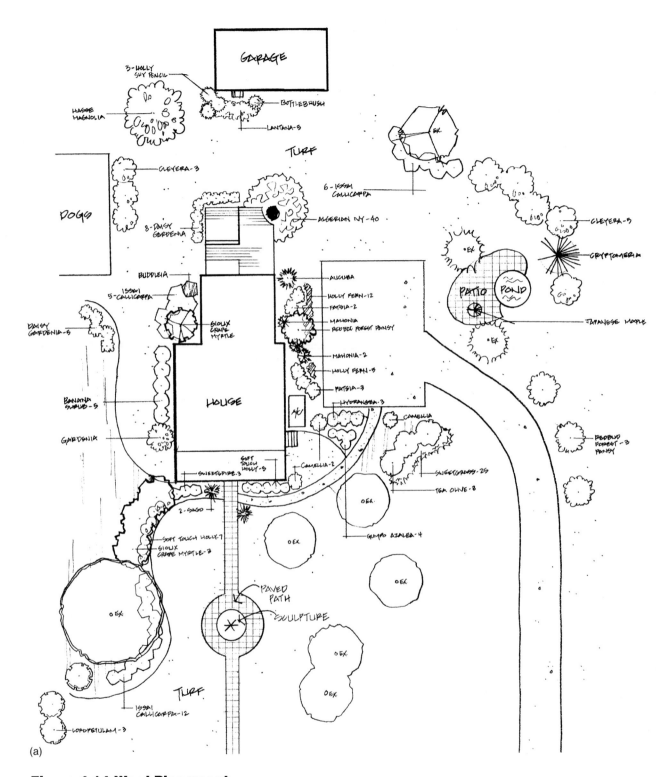

(a)

## *Figure 4-14* Word Placement
Labels and descriptions should be an integral part of the plan drawing, and they should complement the drawing as well as clarify it. (a) These labels are adequate in size and placement, blending with the graphics nicely. *(Drawn by Brad Goshorn)*

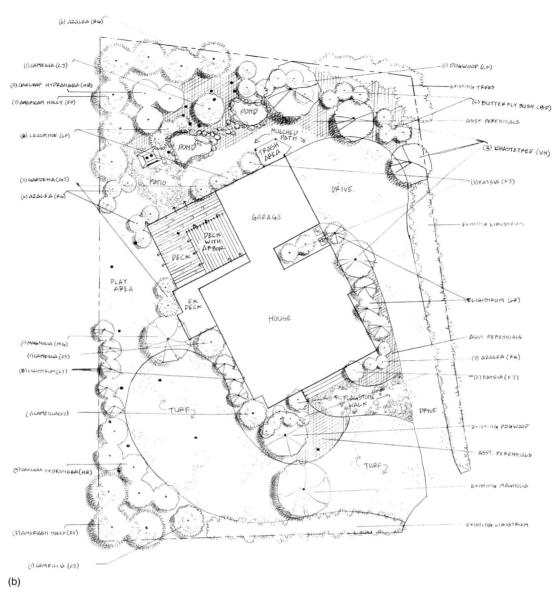

(b)

## *Figure 4-14* Word Placement

(b) The labeling in this design is erratic and distracting in an otherwise nice drawing. *(Drawn by Chris Ross)*

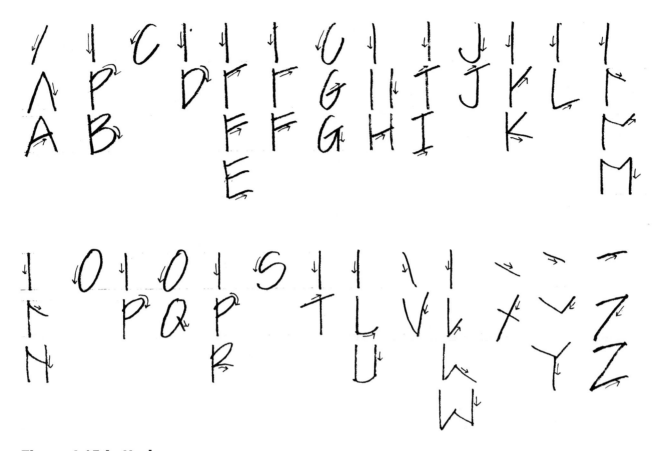

## Figure 4-15 Lettering

Crisp, solid lines are important in good-quality letters. Each stroke for these letters is shown in order from start (top) to finish (bottom). Each line should be completed with a brisk stroke, which results in a smooth, bold line.

## Informal Letters

Informal letters are upright with a 90-degree vertical axis, but the horizontal axis slants upward a few degrees (Figure 4-16). This is a very common style of lettering in landscape design.

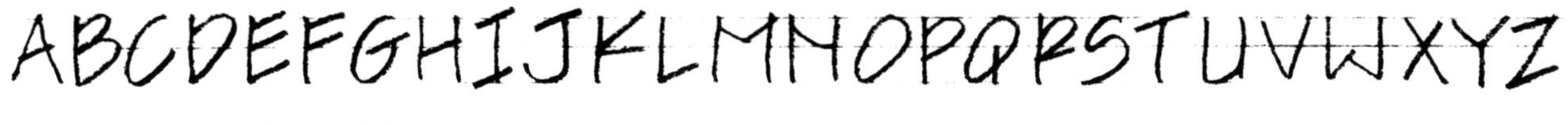

ABCDEFGHIJKLMNOPQRSTUVWXYZ

## Figure 4-16 Informal Letters

Vertical axis is straight and the horizontal axis slants slightly upward (90 degrees to horizontal).

## High-Gravity Letters

High-gravity letters are created by raising the midline so that the midpoint in all the letters sits higher (Figure 4-17). This style gives an interesting quality to either formal or informal lettering.

ABCDEFGHIJKLMNOPQRSTUVWXYZ

## Figure 4-17 High-Gravity Letters

Vertical axis is straight and the horizontal axis raised (90 degrees to horizontal).

## Low-Gravity Letters

**Low-gravity letters** are similar to high-gravity letters, but the midline is lowered (Figure 4-18).

ABCDEFGHIJKLMNOPQRSTUVWXYZ

***Figure 4-18* Low-Gravity Letters**
Vertical axis straight, horizontal axis lowered.

## Slanting Letters

**Slanting letters** are an informal style of lettering that slants the vertical axis a few degrees (Figure 4-19).

ABCDEFGHIJKLMNOPQRSTUVWXYZ

***Figure 4-19* Slanting Letters**
Vertical axis is slanting to the right and the horizontal axis is slanting upward, or 0 degrees.

## Stylistic Letters

This style is an informal, loose approach that often breaks the guidelines. The weighted ends and quick strokes lend to the appeal (Figure 4-20).

ABCDEFGHIJKLMNOPQRSTUVWXYZ

***Figure 4-20* Stylistic Letters**
Loose lettering style that often breaks the guidelines.

## Lowercase Letters

Lowercase letters are not used as much as uppercase letters. They maintain a loose style similar to uppercase letters (Figure 4-21).

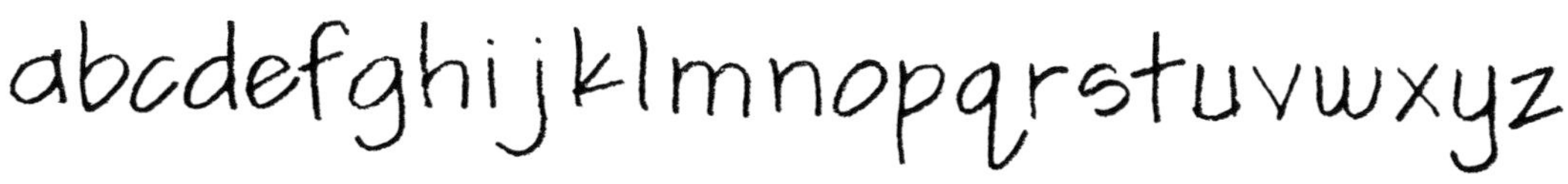

abcdefghijklmnopqrstuvwxyz

***Figure 4-21* Lowercase Letters**
Examples of lowercase.

## Numbers

Numbers adhere to the same guidelines as the lettering style (Figure 4-22).

1234567890

***Figure 4-22* Numbers**
Should follow the same style as lettering.

## Block Letters

Informal title blocks may use large **block letters** about 1" tall. Various details with light line weight add interest (Figure 4-23).

***Figure 4-23* Block Letters**
Large letters used in some title blocks.

# Summary

Lettering is an integral part of the artistic style of presentation graphics. Words are most often printed because printed words are more legible than cursive writing. Guidelines are used to keep words consistent in height and orientation on the plan. The horizontal and vertical character should be consistent for all letters regardless of style, although the most common style has a horizontal axis that slants slightly upward. Lettering strokes are solid, crisp lines rather than wispy ends that trail off. Typical height is 1/4" for most words, and placement of words should be in balance with the design.

# Key Words

**Block letters:**   informal title blocks may use large block letters about 1" tall.

**Case consistency:**   avoid mixing upper- and lowercase letters in a word and sentence (the exception being the first letter in a sentence).

**Formal lettering:**   lettering style has vertical axis at 90 degrees and horizontal axis at 0 degrees.

**Guideline template:**   set of guidelines that can be slid under the drawing; reduces the need to draw guidelines.

**Guidelines:**   keep the letters consistent in size and level across the paper.

**High-gravity letters:**   lettering style created by raising the midline so that the midpoint in all the letters sits higher.

**Horizontal axis:**   horizontal character of letters; most designers letter with a slightly upward slant.

**Informal letters:**   lettering style is upright with a 90-degree vertical axis, but the horizontal axis slants upward a few degrees.

**Informal style:**   lettering that does not conform to exact size and angles.

**Low-gravity letters:**   lettering style created by lowering the midline so that the midpoint in all the letters sits lower.

**Slanting letters:**   informal style of lettering that slants the vertical axis a few degrees.

**Vertical axis:**   vertical character of letters; most designers letter with a 90-degree vertical axis.

# 5 Symbols

## Objectives

- Understand the role of symbols in the design
- Learn the different types of symbols and the types of plants they represent
- Learn the basic approach to drawing symbols
- Understand how to scale symbols
- Learn the techniques to shadow symbols

Symbols are used to show the approximate size and placement of plant material. They also identify plant material with the help of labels. In cases where a plan drawing is not intended for presentation to a client, symbols appear as simple circles.

Designs that are drawn with simple circles have the advantage of being quick and easy to draw. The disadvantage may be in referring back to the plant list a great deal in order to identify plants. For presentations, these plans may be difficult to understand for clients with limited plant knowledge.

To prepare a plan drawing for presentation to a client, symbols developed with adequate detail will aid the communication of the overall design concept. Although it takes more time to draw, this development makes the plan easier to read. Symbols should reflect the quality, or character, of the plant material.

When symbols take on the quality of the plant, they reflect a clearer picture in the two-dimensional plan. In addition, symbol variation separates symbols from each other, and the observer can locate that same plant in other areas of the design (Figure 5-1).

It is also much easier to see the repetition of a plant or plants that have a similar quality. For instance, variations of a needle symbol may be sufficiently repeated throughout the design, which shows the repetitive use of a sharp quality and not necessarily the same plant (Figure 5-2).

# The Basic Elements of Symbols

Regardless of the symbol that you are creating, there are basic elements used to draw the plan.

## Center Dot

Every symbol has a **dot** placed in the center of the symbol to signify it as a single plant (Figure 5-3). This helps to identify individual plants, which is important when massing several plants together. It also shows the contractor installing the design exactly where the center of the plant is to be located.

Some designers differentiate dots, depending on whether the symbol represents a plant to be installed or removed or an existing plant (Figure 5-4).

## Scale

The diameter of the plant symbol illustrates the width of the canopy (Figure 5-5). The client must understand that the landscape will grow into the proposed design. Clients are sometimes surprised after installation because the plants in the ground are nowhere near the size (**scale**) in the plan drawing.

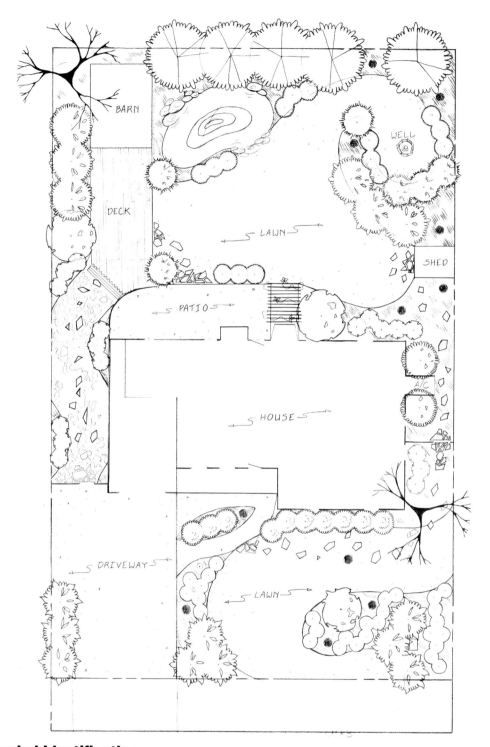

### *Figure 5-1* Symbol Identification

Notice in this unlabeled design how symbols help to identify plants throughout the design. See if you can recognize the same symbol in the design, indicating the same plant. *(Drawn by Gabrielle Justice)*

Plant placement in a landscape design is based on the mature size to allow the plants to grow into the space. One common mistake is overcrowding plants in order to create a finished landscape design after planting.

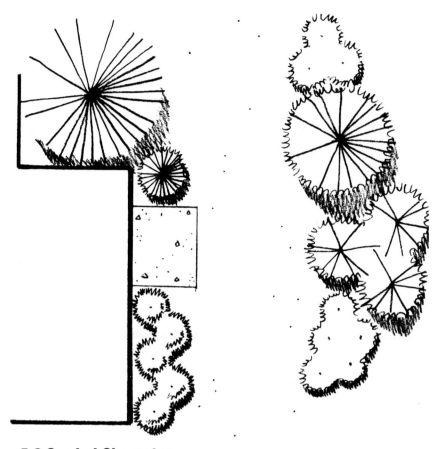

**Figure 5-2 Symbol Character**
This plan drawing shows that all the plants have needlelike qualities. Differences in scale and complexity in the symbols separate the plants but maintain the same quality.

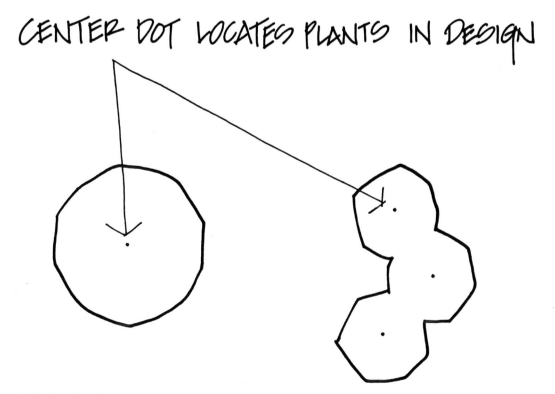

**Figure 5-3 Center Dot**
A dot is placed in the center of every symbol to locate individual plants. The center of the plant will be used to locate the plant during installation.

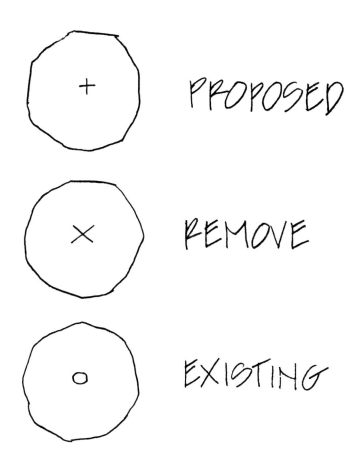

**Figure 5-4 Center Dots**
Some designers use various dots to designate whether the symbol represents a plant to be proposed or removed or an existing plant.

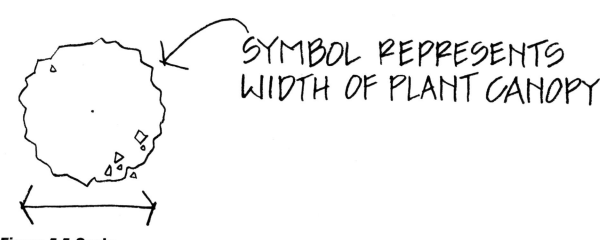

SYMBOL REPRESENTS WIDTH OF PLANT CANOPY

**Figure 5-5 Scale**
Symbols should accurately reflect the diameter of the plant.

**Tip Box:** **Drawing Symbols to Scale**

On a circle template, write the diameters of each circle that is 3′, 5′, 10′, 15′, and 20′ (Figure 5-6). This will be the scale you are working in and can be

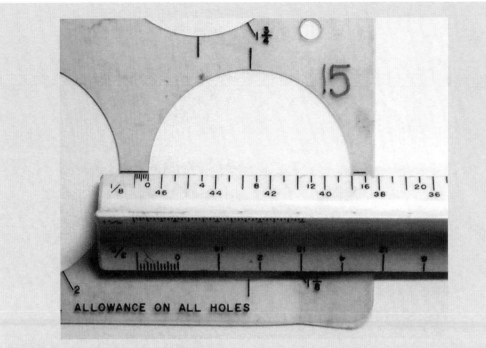

**Figure 5-6 Circle Template**
Quickly draw symbols to scale by noting on the circle template the size of each circle (in this case, using a common scale of 1/8″ = 1′).

changed for a different scale. This will be a quick reference during the preliminary design phase to draw guidelines for small to medium plants. Larger symbols will require a compass.

## Determine Size of Symbol

Drawing symbols to an accurate scale is vital. One of the most common oversights for beginning design students is not drawing symbols to accurate size. If the symbols on the plan are too small, the plan will be overcrowded when planted (Figure 5-7). Likewise, if symbols are too big, there will be too much space between plants. It doesn't matter if you are planting a 1-gallon or 5-gallon shrub, the symbol is still drawn the same size. It will take longer for the 1-gallon to reach that size, but it will eventually reach the mature width of the symbol.

---

### Tip Box:   Space Often Feels Bigger on Paper

When the plan is drawn on paper, many students feel there is more space than there actually is. In the beginning, it's always a good exercise to visit the site, draw the design on paper, then visit it again to see how realistic your spacings are.

---

### Symbols at Mature Width

Many designers draw symbols to represent plants at mature width (Figure 5-8). For example, the mature width of an Indian hawthorne is approximately 4′ to 6′ wide. Therefore, a symbol 5′ in diameter is sufficient. There are exceptions—most notably, large trees that would take several decades to reach mature size. It these cases, the symbols are drawn

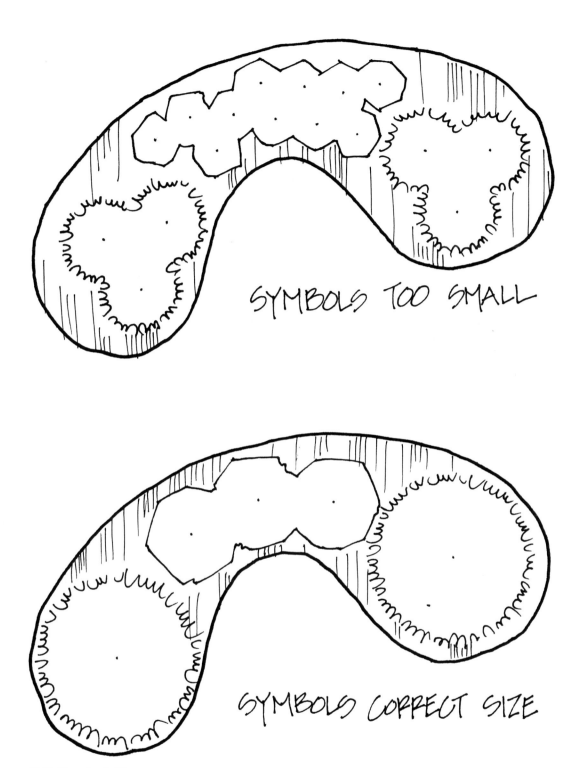

SYMBOLS TOO SMALL

SYMBOLS CORRECT SIZE

**Figure 5-7 Symbol Size**
If symbols are drawn smaller than mature size, design will quickly become overcrowded (top).

approximately 25% to 50% mature width (Figure 5-9). For instance, live oaks can grow over 100′ wide over a long period of time. Drawing a symbol 100′ in diameter would not be feasible in most plans. The exceptionally large symbol would dominate the drawing.

For the beginning designer, this method is not as clear-cut as it sounds. Although book references are helpful to research the mature size of plants, much of the growth depends on the climate zone it is growing in. Mature sizes are based on ideal growing

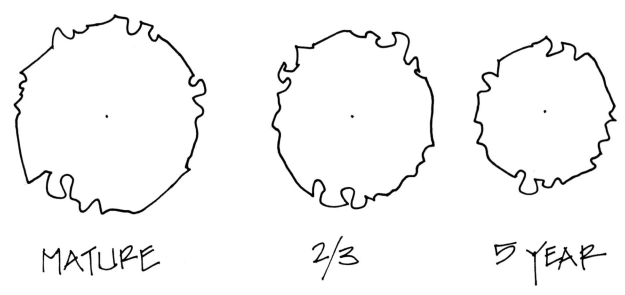

**MATURE**                    **2/3**                    **5 YEAR**

**Figure 5-8 Sizing Symbols**
Variations in symbol diameter to accurately depict size of plant.

conditions. Therefore, if the plant is growing under stressful conditions, it may not even come close to that size. For the beginning designer, references are the main resource, but, with experience, local knowledge of plant growth will be the determining factor. In fact, it is helpful to consult seasoned designers or plant nurseries if you are not familiar with plant maturities.

---

> ***Tip Box:*** **Large Tree Symbols Drawn 25% to 50% Mature Width**
>
> With visual interest in mind, symbols of large trees are often not drawn to mature width. Instead, they are drawn 25% to 50% mature width.

---

## Symbol Within Time Frame

Rather than use mature plant size, some landscape designers work with a certain window of time in mind. The symbols are drawn to a diameter of how wide they would grow under ideal conditions in five to seven years. This gives the client a reasonable amount of time to expect the design to develop into the plan drawing. This method relies on the designer's experience with plant material and growth rate.

---

> ***Tip Box:*** **Symbols Based on Time Frame**
>
> Another approach is to draw symbols based on growth over five to seven years.

---

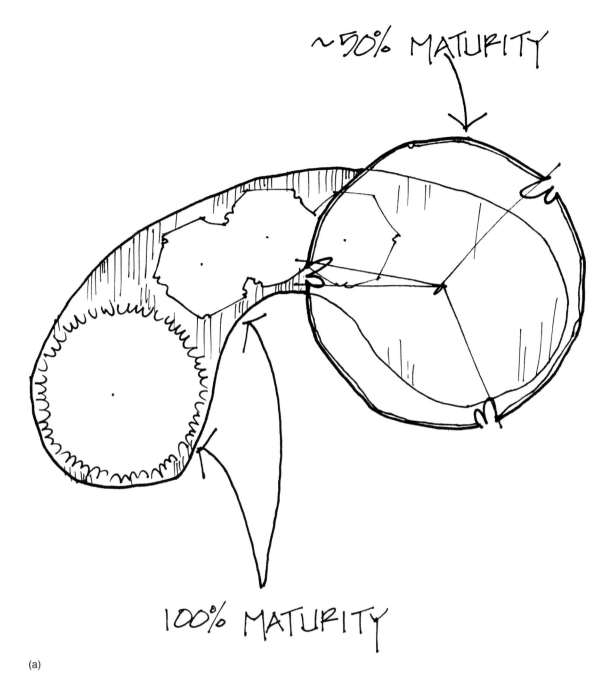

~50% MATURITY

100% MATURITY

(a)

### *Figure 5-9* Symbols for Large Trees

(a) Regardless of technique, large trees are often drawn smaller than mature diameter (25% to 50%).

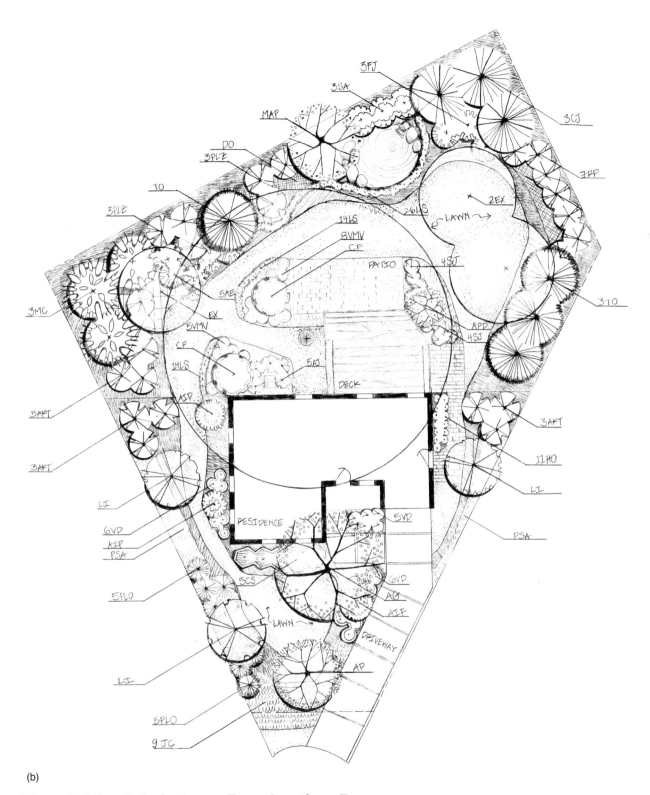

(b)

**Figure 5-9 Symbols for Large Trees (continued)**
(b) This design has an enormous symbol for the existing live oak. It is much too large and would be more visually balanced if smaller. *(Design by Courtney Smith)*

### Symbols at Two-Thirds Maturity

This is a simplified version of the time frame method, in which all symbols are drawn *two-thirds the mature diameter*. Spacing will be a little tighter, but it will allow for the plan to fill in quicker and account for slower-growing species. Fast-growing plants may require pruning.

### Symbols in the Preliminary Design

In the preliminary design, general plant sizes are used instead of specific plant species. How do you know how big to draw the symbol? As a general guideline, when not designing with specific plants in mind, the following can be used:

| Shrubs | Trees |
| --- | --- |
| Small: 3' | Small: 10' |
| Medium: 5' | Medium: 15' |
| Large: 7' | Large: 20' |

The preliminary is the first design idea for the project. Feedback is given and changes are made for the master plan (the final phase of the project). Once plants are chosen, symbols can be adjusted in size. Of course, this may change the number of plants in the grouping, but the purpose of the preliminary is to provide a starting point for making changes.

# Drawing Symbols

## Draw a Guideline for the Symbol

Use a 4H lead to draw a guideline of the symbol. The guideline should not show through on the print. This guideline will help you draw a well-balanced, spherical symbol. Symbols drawn without a guideline can end up odd-shaped (Figure 5-10).

## Draw the Outline of the Symbol

Use an H or HB lead to get darker lines and develop the outline of the symbol (Figure 5-11). The outline should be drawn directly over the guideline. Do not use the guideline as a baseline-like lettering. This draws attention to the guideline (should the guideline show on the print) and detracts from the outline (Figure 5-12).

The outline should always radiate from the center dot, like spokes on a wheel (Figure 5-13). It is difficult to draw a radiating outline on some portions of the symbol because of the angle at which your fingers and hand are moving. The three o'clock and nine o'clock positions always seem to be the most difficult because the fingers are moving sideways. On large symbols, you may find it helpful to move around the design table to position your drawing hand for a comfortable feel.

---

### *Tip Box:*  Difficult Drawing Angles

Physically moving around the design can help create comfortable drawing angles for your hand in order to draw good, consistent outlines.

---

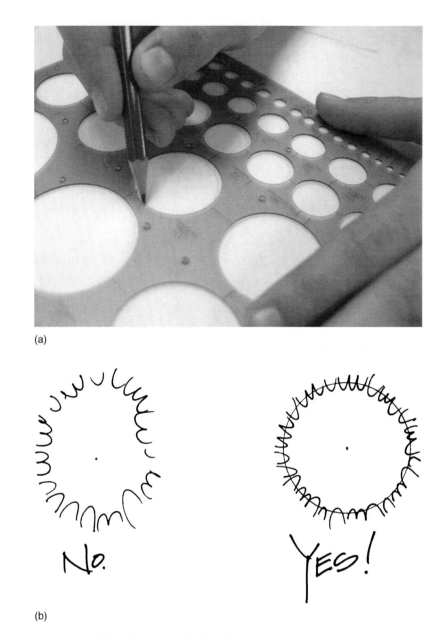

(a)

(b)

***Figure 5-10*** **Drawing Symbol Guideline**
Using a 4H lead, draw a guideline using a circle template or compass. The 4H lead will draw a light line that will not show on a copy.

## Create Symbol Detail

Detail is created with an H or 2H lead (Figure 5-14). The harder lead creates a lighter line that will add texture to the symbol, while the outline is a heavy, defining line.

# Symbols Reflecting Plant Material

Symbols are often drawn to reflect the plant's physical characteristic, the exception being the *generic* symbol.

**Figure 5-11 Drawing Symbol Outline**
Using an H or HB lead, draw the symbol outline directly over the guideline.

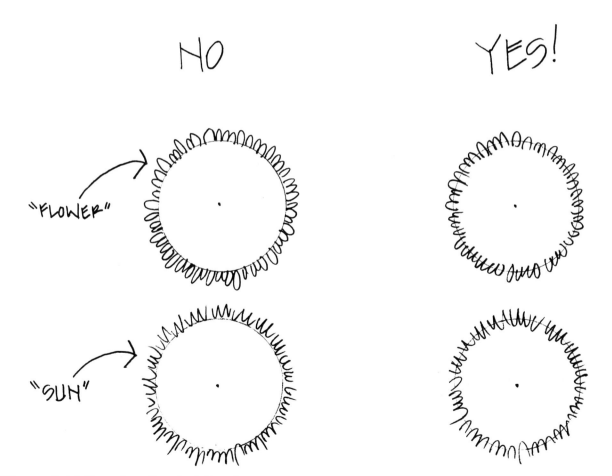

**Figure 5-12 Drawing Symbol Outline**
Draw directly on top of the guideline. This will hide the guideline. If the outline is drawn around the outside of the guideline, it will highlight the guideline.

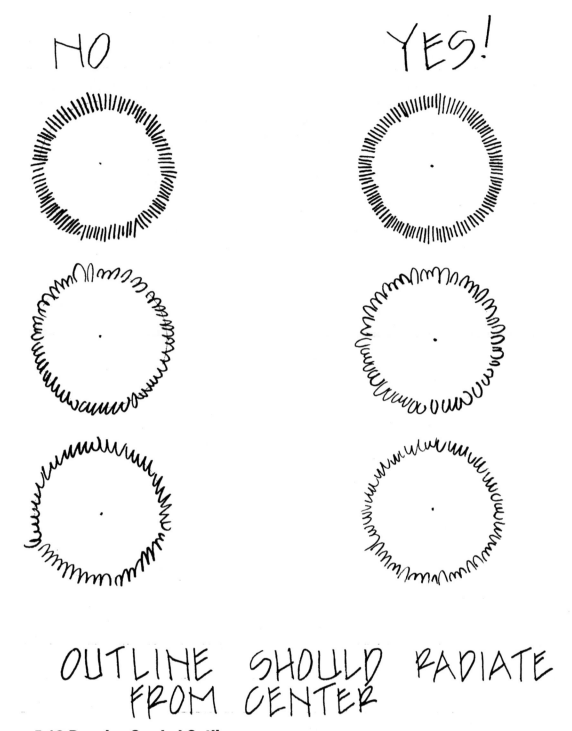

**Figure 5-13 Drawing Symbol Outline**
If the outline has dashes or loops, they should radiate from the center dot.

**Figure 5-14 Drawing Symbol Detail**
Using an H or 2H lead, create detail on the interior of the symbol.

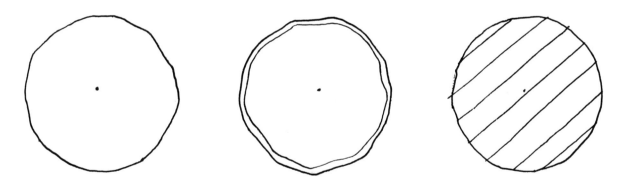

**Figure 5-15 Generic Symbols**
These are plain symbols that can represent any plant.

# Generic

The **generic symbol** is used to represent any type of plant (Figure 5-15). It is generally used for foundation plants (see the section "Specimen and Foundation Symbols"). It can be as simple as drawing a circle right over the guideline. This circle can be drawn with a template or freehand. A freehand symbol over the guideline is nice because it is a bit wavy, implying a certain randomness that plants naturally have.

***Figure 5-16* Broadleaf Plants**
Any plant that has a flat, wide leaf.

# Broadleaf

Any plant that has a flat, wide leaf is a **broadleaf** (Figure 5-16).

## Broadleaf Outlines (Figure 5-17)

**Looping Outline**   Over the guideline, draw a series of loops. The looping outline looks like a series of W's. Randomly draw each series at various lengths. Notice how some of the sections have five or six loops and some are simply a single loop.

**Irregular Outline**   There are many variations of this outline. An irregular outline is similar to a generic outline, but it provides greater emphasis on reflecting foliage in the outline. It does not necessarily follow a pattern, like the looping outline, but gives an informal, natural appeal.

**Umbrella Outline**   An umbrella outline is a good outline for medium to large symbols. Simply trace the guideline, but add three to five pairs of loops (looping toward the center) evenly spaced around the perimeter.

## Broadleaf Detail

**Foliage Detail**   You can create foliage detail on the interior of the symbol (Figure 5-18). Try to keep your detail loose and natural-looking. If you concentrate too hard on drawing it perfectly, you will begin to lose the natural appeal of the plants. Once you learn how to draw good random lines, you will find it takes much less time.

# BROADLEAF OUTLINES

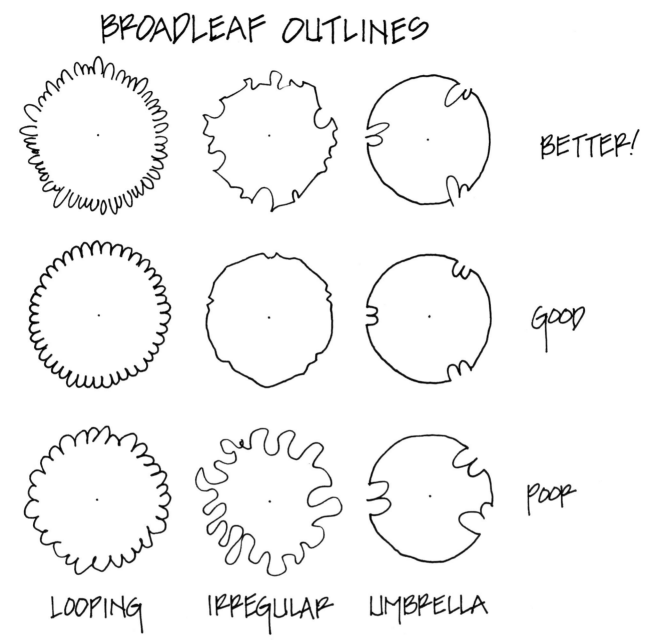

**Figure 5-17 Broadleaf Symbol Outlines**
Examples of looping, irregular, and umbrella outlines.

**Bananas:** Draw various bunches of leaves (bananas) to reflect foliage. Draw them in bunches of one, two, three, or four to get variety.

**Triangles and squares:** Use a variety of triangles and squares to give the detail a random feeling.

**Static:** Draw scribbly lines that conform to the shape of the circle. Be careful not to draw them too concentric or else the detail loses its randomness.

**Radial Detail**   Radial detail can be created with lines radiating from the center to add interest (Figure 5-19). Start at the center dot and draw a sharp line to the outline. Do not try to make the radiating line meet exactly with the outline. Instead, let it run outside the outline a bit. This will give it a good random feel.

# BROADLEAF DETAIL

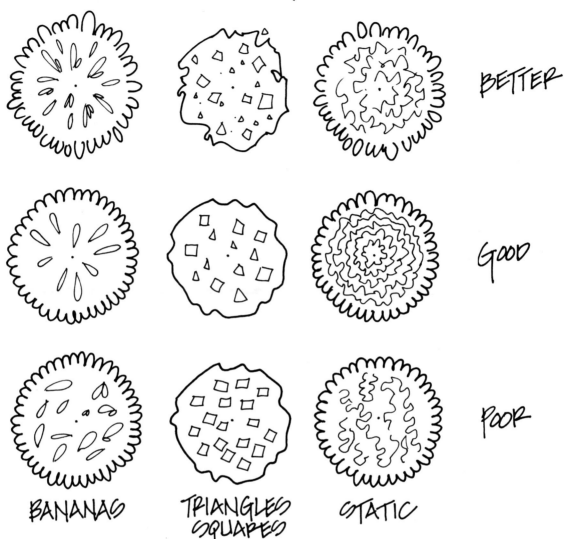

BETTER

GOOD

POOR

BANANAS     TRIANGLES SQUARES     STATIC

**Figure 5-18 Broadleaf Symbol Detail**
Examples of bananas, triangles and squares, and static detail.

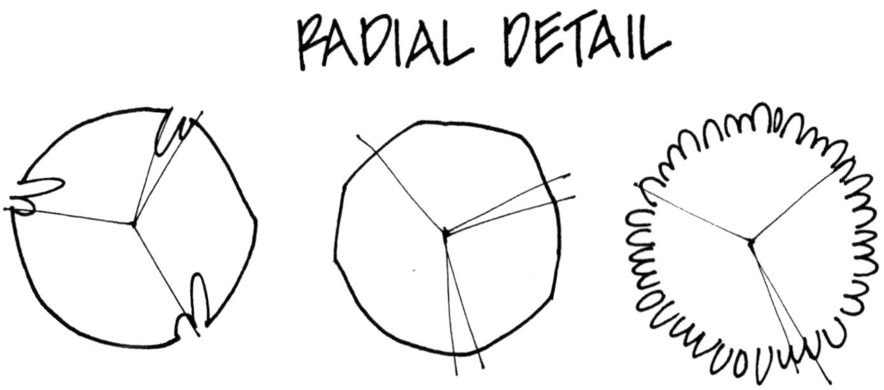

# RADIAL DETAIL

**Figure 5-19 Radial Detail**
These are lines, like spokes on a wheel, that add interest to symbols.

# Needle

*Needle* refers to any plant that has needlelike foliage (Figure 5-20). It can also include plants that have a prominent spiny nature. In the case of the rotunda holly, which has a broadleaf with sharp spines around the margin, a spiny, needlelike symbol is appropriate (Figure 5-21). Another example is a broadleaf that has stems covered with thorns.

***Figure 5-20* Needle Plants**
Any plant that has needlelike foliage, such as pine trees and yucca.

(a)

(b)

***Figure 5-21* Needle Characteristics**
Plants that have sharp qualities. (a) Rotunda holly has sharp spines along the margin of broadleaf. (b) Wintergreen barberry has long, sharp thorns.

## Needle Outlines (Figure 5-22)

**Dashing Outline**   In a dashing outline, short lines are drawn directly over the guide-line as if radiating directly from the center point.

**Spiking Outline**   The spiking outline is drawn like a random series of W's, an inverse outline of the looping broadleaf outline. Draw sections of W's with one to several loops. Let the line be wispy at the ends to give it a sharper look.

# NEEDLE OUTLINES

BETTER!

GOOD

POOR

**Figure 5-22 Needle Symbol Outlines**
Examples of dashing, spiking, and zigzag outlines.

**Zigzag Outline**  Similar to the spiking outline, the zigzag outline is drawn continuously in a back-and-forth pattern. Unlike the spiking outline, it is drawn with sharp points on the inside as well as the outside of the outline.

## Needle Detail (Figure 5-23)

**Dash, Spiking, and Zigzag Detail**  Repeat the outline pattern on the interior of the symbol.

## Radial Symbol

With the **radial symbol**, lines start at the center dot and run sharply to the outline of the symbol, like spokes radiating from the center of a wheel (Figure 5-24). The lines do not

# NEEDLE DETAIL

**Figure 5-23 Needle Symbol Detail**
Examples of dashing, spiking, and zigzag detail.

have to meet the outline but, rather, go over or under it slightly. Because the radial lines create a form, this symbol can be created without an outline (Figure 5-25).

Use an H or HB lead to get bold lines, since the interior lines, rather than the outline, define the symbol. Using a 2H in combination with the H or HB can create variation among lines.

This detail can be enhanced at the end of the design process when using a 2B lead to add weight to the center of the symbol (Figure 5-26). Adding more weight to the center gives a sense of height to the middle of the symbol.

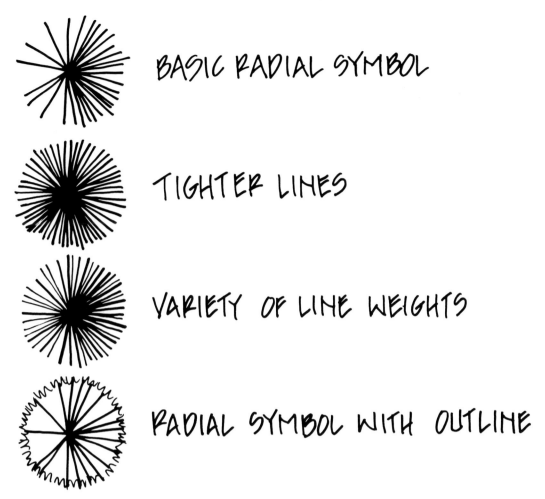

BASIC RADIAL SYMBOL

TIGHTER LINES

VARIETY OF LINE WEIGHTS

RADIAL SYMBOL WITH OUTLINE

**Figure 5-24 Radial Symbol**
Heavy radial detail, with or without an outline, can be used to represent needle plants.

---

**Tip Box:** Elevating Center of Radial Symbol

Coming back over a radial detail with a 2B lead in the center portion of the symbol will increase the line weight and create a good sense of height.

---

## Branched

The **branched symbol** is typically used to represent deciduous plants but can also be used for any plant with strong, or unique, branching habits (Figure 5-27). Deciduous plants drop their leaves in the winter and grow new foliage in the spring. Deciduous plants are mostly broadleaf, but there are also deciduous plants that have needlelike foliage, most notably dawn redwoods, bald cypress, and larch (Figure 5-28). Branching symbols are often used for specimen plants because they are detailed symbols that attract attention (see the section "Specimen and Foundation Symbols").

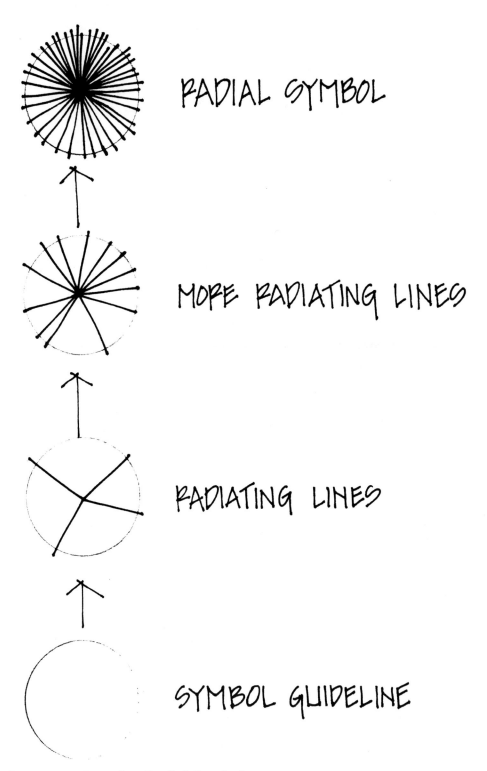

RADIAL SYMBOL

MORE RADIATING LINES

RADIATING LINES

SYMBOL GUIDELINE

**Figure 5-25 Drawing Radial Symbol**
Use a guideline to draw radial lines from the center dot out to the guideline. Lines do not have to end exactly on the guideline but can extend slightly over or under it.

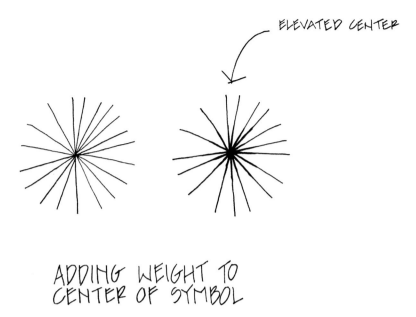

ELEVATED CENTER

ADDING WEIGHT TO
CENTER OF SYMBOL

**Figure 5-26 Drawing Radial Symbol**
Adding line weight to the center of the radial symbol can give a sense of height.

**Figure 5-27 Branching Structure**
Plants that are deciduous exhibit their branching form when they drop their leaves in the winter.

***Figure 5-28*** **Deciduous, Needlelike Foliage**
Some plants, such as the bald cypress, have needlelike foliage yet are deciduous.

### Drawing Branched Symbols

Begin with a guideline. Start three or five branches at the center dot and draw them out to the guideline (Figure 5-29). This will be the primary branching structure.

From the primary branches, draw smaller branches coming off and ending near the guideline of the symbol. Move around the entire symbol, drawing branches coming off of branches and always ending near or beyond the guideline. Avoid ending branches throughout the middle of the symbol. This often results in a "snowflake" symbol (Figure 5-30).

When most of the branches are drawn, come back to the primary branches and add weight to them by thickening the lines. Keep lines loose and informal to look like natural branching. Allow the thickness of the primary branches to taper off toward the outline.

### Branched Outline

This symbol may or may not be drawn with an outline (Figure 5-31). If an outline is used, any of the outlines in the prior sections can be drawn.

### Branched Detail

When branching is completed, foliage detail can be added right over the top of the branches. Add looping foliage around the symbol. Just a few leaves can be a nice accent to the symbol.

## Miscellaneous Symbols

There are numerous objects that will need to be illustrated on the plan drawing that can be difficult to draw, such as fences, arbors, and lattice panels (Figure 5-32). Use the following guidelines when illustrating something you don't find in this book.

## DRAWING BRANCHED SYMBOL

**Figure 5-29 Drawing Branching Symbol**
Steps to draw branching symbol (a) start with three or five primary branches, (b) add secondary branches extending to the guideline, and (c) beef up primary branches.

NO

YES!

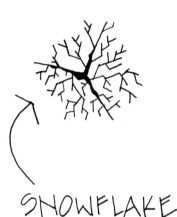
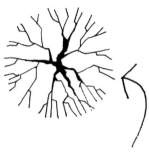

SNOWFLAKE

ALL BRANCHES
GO TO OUTLINE

**Figure 5-30 Extend All Branches to Guideline**
All branches should extend out to the guideline.

 BRANCHED SYMBOL

 BRANCHED WITH OUTLINE

 BRANCHED WITH FOLIAGE

**Figure 5-31 Branching Symbol Variations**
Branching symbols can be drawn with or without an outline and foliage.

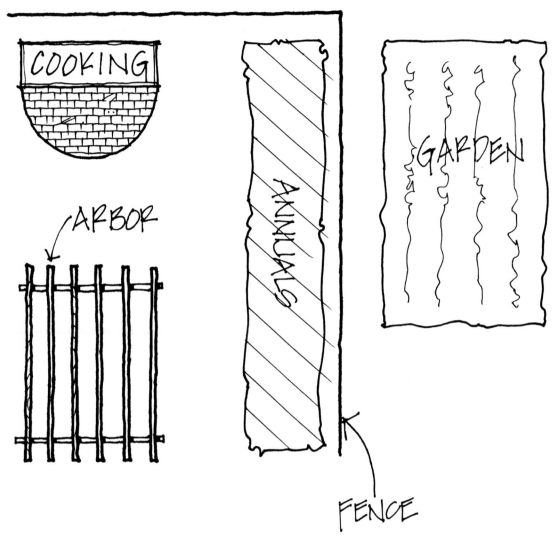

***Figure 5-32* Miscellaneous Symbols**
For unclassified symbols, draw from a bird's eye.

## Bird's-Eye View

Keep in mind that, no matter what you are illustrating, the plan drawing is a view from directly overhead. Therefore, nothing should be drawn with any three-dimensional quality. Picture what it would look like if you were standing on a ladder and looking down on it. For example, a fence will look like a line and nothing more.

## Simple Label

Never hesitate to add a short label to describe the symbol. The most important point of a plan drawing is to communicate clearly. Therefore, when in doubt, label it. For example, how would you know that the thick line along the right side of the property is a proposed fence? A simple label could be included: 3' picket fence.

# Existing Trees

Existing trees that will remain in the landscape should be located on the plan drawing. How they are drawn can vary. Giving them symbols makes sense in order to blend with the symbols of the proposed plants. However, there are exceptions and variations to this rule.

## Center Dot Designation

As mentioned earlier in this chapter, some designers use a center dot different from symbol of new plants to identify existing trees that remain integral to the design, such as a small circle instead of a dot.

## Simplify Symbol

Using a generic symbol will identify the plant without drawing undue attention to it (Figure 5-33a). The design should show off the proposed, not the existing, plantings. However, this is up to the discretion of the designer. There will be cases that an outstanding specimen plant already existing on the property will be designed around and featured; therefore, it would be advisable to use an appropriate symbol instead of a generic one.

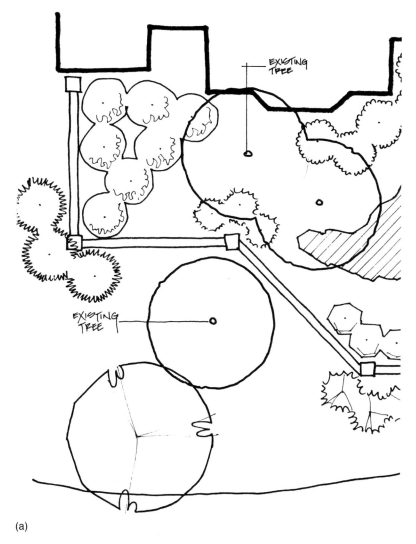

(a)

***Figure 5-33* Existing Tree Symbols**
(a) one approach is to symplify the symbol.

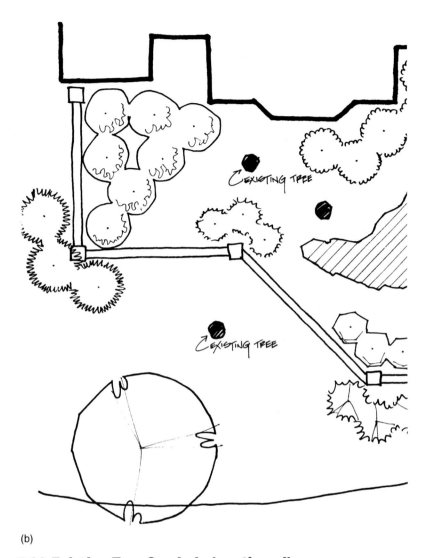

(b)

***Figure 5-33* Existing Tree Symbols (continued)**
(b) another is to omit the symbol and level the trunk only.

## No Symbol

In some cases, there may be so many existing plants—in particular, trees—that to include them in the drawing would only confuse the plan (Figure 5-33b). Remember, a clear plan is the most important quality. In cases such as these, do not draw any symbol but simply indicate the trunks of the existing plants. Often, these should be enlarged, similar to the diameter of the trunks, so they are easy to read.

## Simple Label

It is advisable to include a label on several of the existing symbols, if not all of them, to indicate what they are. A simple label that states "Existing Tree" can be satisfactory. This is particularly true when only the trunks are located with no symbol, since they look like a large dot. The label can be more specific to the species of the existing plant, such as "Existing Oak." An alternative to labeling it on the plan is to include it in the plant list.

### Legend

An option to the simple label is a short legend somewhere on the plan. Using the same symbol, place a small footnote at the bottom of the plan that indicates an existing tree. Therefore, you can use the same generic symbol that anyone would recognize as an existing plant. If you wish to be more specific about the species, the open center dot can be described in the legend or specific symbols.

# The Role of Symbols in the Design

## Specimen and Foundation Symbols

The degree of detail in which the symbol is drawn is reflective of its use in the landscape design. **Specimen plants** are used in a design as an accent to draw your eye to specific parts of the landscape (Figure 5-34).

A specimen plant has some outstanding quality that makes it a plant that can stand alone. Plants that are used primarily for mass planting are not considered specimen plants. Some specimens may have attractive foliage, such as the *dissectum* varieties of Japanese maples that are deep red and feathery (Figure 5-35). Others may have a unique form, such as the upright, weeping form of the mulberry (Figure 5-36). Still other plants have a combination of qualities that make them outstanding specimens, such as the Natchez Crape-myrtle, which has a nice multi-trunk form, excellent cinnamon-brown bark, and a wonderful show of flowers throughout the summer months (Figure 5-37). Because the role of specimens in the design is to attract attention, the symbol should attract attention as well. Therefore, it is drawn with greater detail to reflect its outstanding quality.

Inversely, **foundation plants** add little excitement in order to balance the specimen plantings as well as provide connection throughout the design (Figure 5-38). They are not intended to draw attention. These symbols are drawn with a simple outline and minor detail to reflect that role.

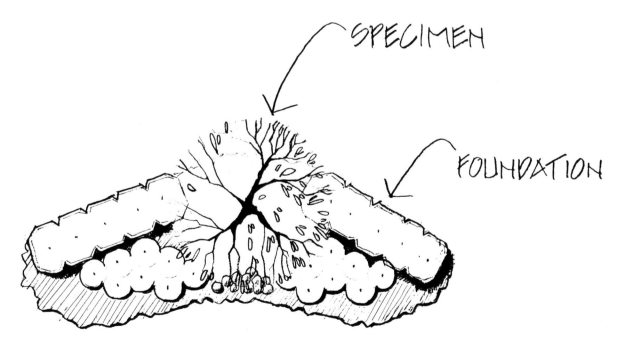

***Figure 5-34* Specimen and Foundation Plants**
Specimen plants attract attention, while foundation plants provide balance and connection. The symbols should reflect these qualities.

***Figure 5-35*** **Specimen Plant**
Japanese maple has attractive foliage.

***Figure 5-36*** **Specimen Plant**
Weeping mulberry has unique form.

*Figure 5-37* **Specimen Plant**
Natchez Crapemyrtle has attractive bark.

*Figure 5-38* **Foundation Plants**
Planted in mass to add balance to specimens.

# Complexity

Do not get caught up in trying to find a different symbol for every plant on a design. Beginning students often become frustrated when they run out of options. This is not the intent. In fact, too many symbols could make the design look chaotic.

The objective is to make the plan drawing read well by making the symbols for different plant materials separate themselves. By using only a few basic symbol types, a plan drawing can be created by changing the complexity of the symbol as well as the scale. Thus, the plan still effectively shows where plants are repeated and what plant characteristics are used throughout the design. A basic symbol can be used in a variety of ways to denote different plants that have similar characteristics (Figure 5-39).

> ### *Tip Box:*   Vary Symbols with Complexity
>
> Not every plant needs a unique symbol. Instead, focus on separating symbols with various degrees of complexity.

# Overhead Canopies

In order to avoid confusing the detail of plantings underneath the canopy of a large tree, keep the overhead symbol simple. It should be limited to an outline with very little detail or just a few radiating lines (Figure 5-40).

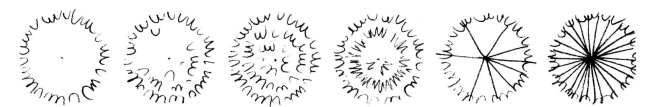

**Figure 5-39 Symbol Variation**
A symbol type, such as the spiking outline, can have varying degrees of complexity to represent different plant material. This provides good continuity throughout the design, in addition to avoiding the frustrating search for new symbols.

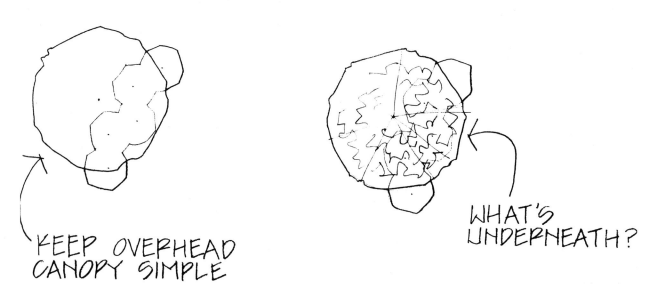

**Figure 5-40 Overhead Canopy**
Keep the symbol of an overhead canopy simple, so that it does not confuse the details underneath.

# Texture

Another quality that could be reflected in symbols is texture. One way **texture** can be measured is the size of the leaf (Figure 5-41). Larger leaves are coarse and smaller leaves are fine. Plants with larger leaves can be drawn with larger loops, compared with plants with smaller leaves (Figure 5-42).

**Figure 5-41 Plant Texture**
The fatsia (right) has large leaves, which give it a coarse quality, in contrast to the yaupon holly (left), which has smaller leaves.

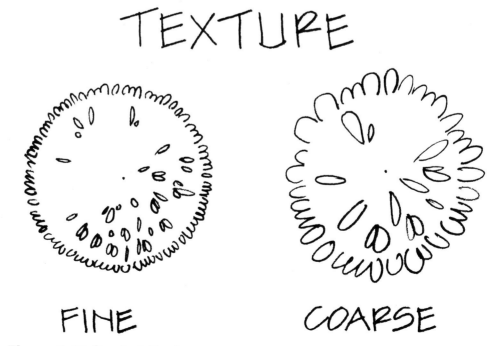

**Figure 5-42 Symbol Texture**
Symbols can be drawn with various degrees of texture to illustrate the contrast between plants.

# Form

Form is difficult to capture in the two-dimensional plan, such as ornamental grass and weeping trees but there are some techniques that can reflect it (Figure 5-43). Ornamental grass is drawn

ORNAMENTAL
GRASS

(a)

PALM

(b)

***Figure 5-43* Plant Forms**
(a) Ornamental grass and (b) palms have a unique form that can be difficult to capture with a two-dimensional symbol.

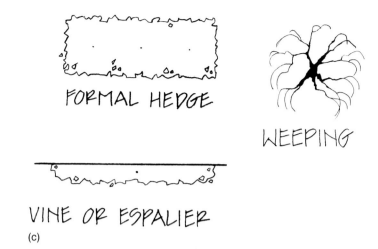

FORMAL HEDGE

WEEPING

VINE OR ESPALIER

(c)

***Figure 5-43*** **Plant Forms (continued)**
(c) Other unique symbols include weeping trees, formal hedges, vines, and espalier.

***Figure 5-44*** **Mass Planting**
Several shrubs are planted closely in order to grow together to create a large form.

with a feathery, deeply incised outline. Palms are drawn with foliage that reflects the palm leaves. Weeping trees can be illustrated with a branched symbol that curves at the end of the branches.

Other forms include formal hedges, vines, and espalier plants. **Formal hedges** are sheared into geometric shapes, quite often rectangular. **Espalier plants** are trees and shrubs trained to grow flat, either against a wall or on a rack. Vines may be planted to grow up a wall or to grow up and over an arbor.

## Mass Plantings

Small- to medium-sized plants are often planted in groups (Figure 5-44). The plants are spaced so that they will grow into each other and form a large **mass**. This is a unique way to create larger forms with several plants.

# MASSING

POOR                                    GOOD

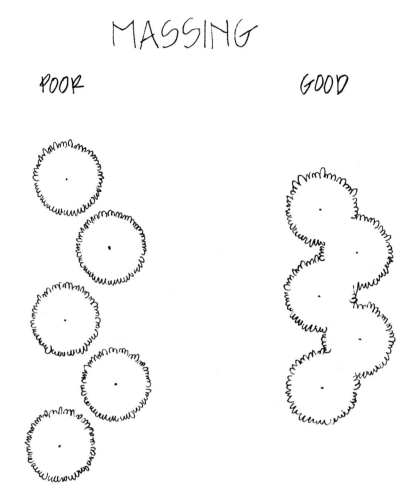

***Figure 5-45* Overlapping Massed Symbols**
Symbols in mass plantings should overlap.

Symbols of mass plantings should merge together to reflect plants growing together in a larger form (Figure 5-45). Each individual symbol slightly overlaps the plant symbols next to it. The outline of the mass planting is drawn around the outside of the mass instead of each symbol. The darker outline emphasizes the mass form, while the interior guidelines that may or may not be present indicate individual plants that build the mass. Center dots are placed to indicate the individual plants, especially when they may be in the interior of the mass. To further emphasize unity, some designers like to use a line and connect the center dots (Figure 5-46).

Because several symbols are used in overlapping fashion, a simple rather than complex symbol works best to avoid causing confusion between symbols. Overlapping complex symbols become hard to distinguish from one other (Figure 5-47).

When massing small plants, such as liriope or daylilies, that are only 1′ to 2′ in diameter, individual circles may be avoided and only an outline around the mass used (Figure 5-48). The interior portion is drawn with some detail to identify the mass and separate it from others. The number of plants used in that mass can be designated in the label (Figure 5-49).

**Figure 5-46 Connecting Dots of Massed Symbols**
Some designers like to connect the center dots of symbols that are grouped in mass to further emphasize unity.

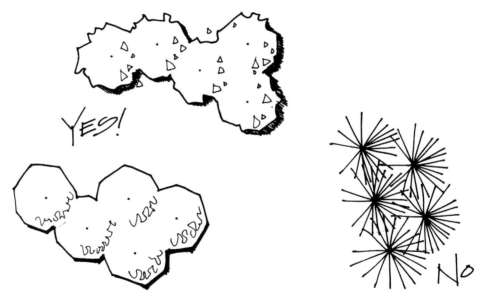

**Figure 5-47 Simplify Massed Symbols**
Symbols should be simple. Complex symbols can become confusing.

# Adding Shadows to Symbols

**Shadows** are placed on symbols to create a sense of depth and scale. With shadows added to symbols and objects, the plan reads easier by hinting at scale because a large plant casts a longer shadow. Just as important, shadows add to the aesthetics by creating depth in a drawing that would otherwise look flat.

---

---

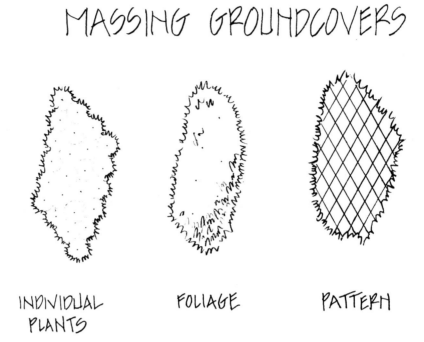

**Figure 5-48 Massing Outline for Smaller Symbols**
When massing small plant material, an outline around the mass can be used with simple detail instead of drawing individual circles.

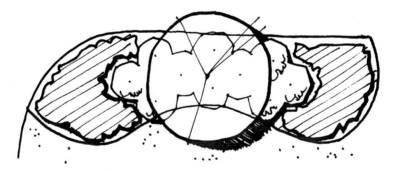

**Figure 5-49 Indicating Number of Massed Symbols**
The mass of junipers on the outside is outlined with a pattern.

## Anatomy of Shadows

Before learning the techniques of drawing shadows, let's look at how light falls on an object. The shape of a tree or shrub canopy is basically a sphere. Observe how light falls on a round object (Figure 5-50). Notice how the darker portion of the sphere is crescent-shaped and wraps partially around the center. The **highlight** is a point where the light is most intense. Notice that the highlight is located slightly away from the edge of the sphere

(a)

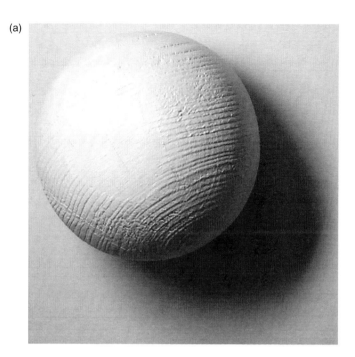

LIGHT SOURCE

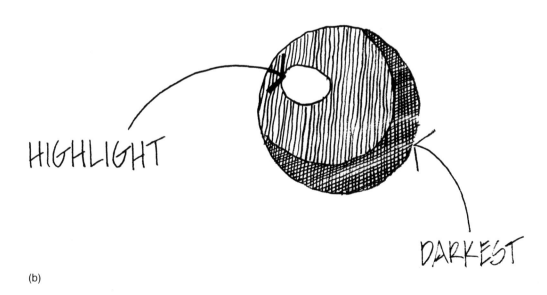

HIGHLIGHT

DARKEST

(b)

**Figure 5-50 Anatomy of Shadows**
(a) As light falls on a spherical object, which represents a plant canopy, (b) it creates recognizable areas: highlight, gray, and dark.

and not directly in the middle. If the highlight were located in the middle, then the shadow would fall directly under the object and wouldn't be seen.

### Symbol Details with Shadow Weight

The highlight on the symbol can be drawn with little or no detail, as if light were *washing out* the texture (Figure 5-51). The shadow portion of the symbol can be drawn with more

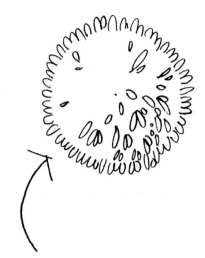

DETAIL HAS SHADOW WEIGHT

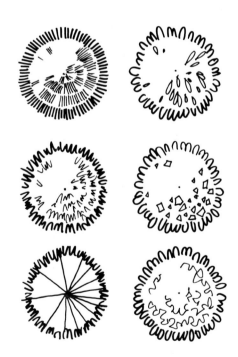

SYMBOL DETAIL WITH SHADOW WEIGHT

***Figure 5-51* Symbol Detail with Shadow Weight**
Detail can be drawn to appear as if light is falling across the symbol. The shadow side of the symbol has more detail, while the highlight has less detail.

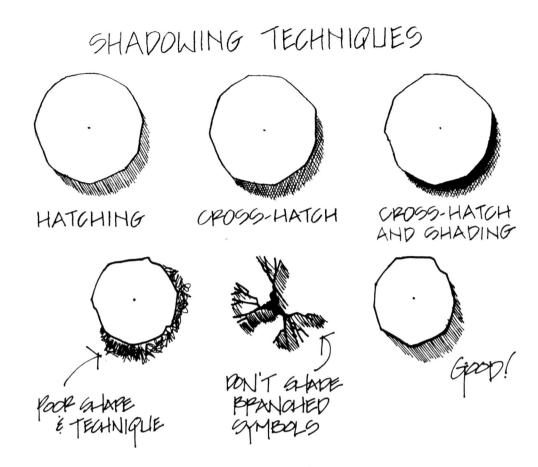

*SHADOWING TECHNIQUES*

HATCHING  CROSS-HATCH  CROSS-HATCH AND SHADING

POOR SHAPE & TECHNIQUE  DON'T SHADE BRANCHED SYMBOLS  GOOD!

***Figure 5-52*** **Shadowing Techniques**
Hatching, cross-hatching, and cross-hatching and shading.

detail in order to give it more weight and darker value. Drawing detail this way gives the canopy a rounded appearance.

# Drawing Shadows (Figure 5-52)

### Draw Shadow Outline with 4H Lead

Because most plants are rounded, the easiest way to get an accurate shadow is to use the same-size circle on the template, place it over the symbol, then slide it toward the direction of the shadow and draw the outline (Figure 5-53).

### Fill in Shadow

There are a couple techniques to fill in the shadow:

**Hatching:** Draw a series of parallel lines running in the direction of the shadow. The direction of the lines falling away from the tree appear as a loose shadow.

**Cross-hatching:** Begin by hatching the shadow; then draw another series of tight lines going across in another direction. This texture carries more weight than hatching and deemphasizing the direction of hatch lines.

### Shading for Additional Shadow Effect

Shading with an H lead along the symbol edge can further develop the shadow (Figure 5-54). Continue using smooth strokes that blend with the rest of the shadow. A 2B lead can then be

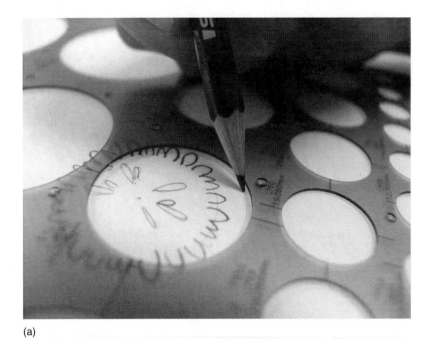

(a)

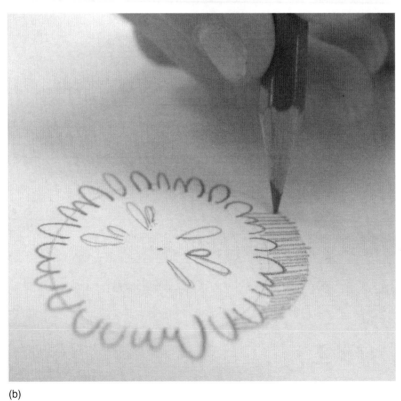

(b)

### *Figure 5-53* Shadow Outline

(a) Use a 4H lead to draw the outline of the shadow. Use the same-size circle by sliding the circle template to the shadow side. (b) Then fill in the shadow by hatching or cross-hatching.

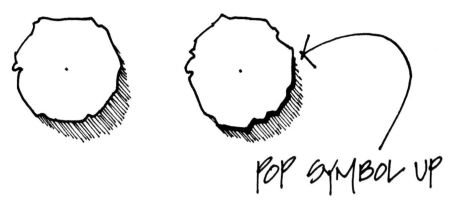

**Figure 5-54 Shadow Lift**
Give symbol more visual lift by darkening shadow with 2B lead.

used to darken the symbol outline within the shadow. You should notice how that extra weight along the edge gives the symbol additional lift.

# Shadowing Guidelines

## Limit Shadows to the Ground Plane

When a shadow falls on the ground, it mirrors the outline of the object. However, when the shadow of a tree falls across small shrubs, it takes on a different outline because of the odd-shaped terrain. If the shadow is drawn flat across underlying shrubs, it makes them appear flat on the ground. Draw shadows only on the ground plane or at least slightly shorter when they fall on objects (Figure 5-55).

**Figure 5-55 Shadows on Ground Plane**
Limit shadows to the ground plane to avoid a flat look to the objects below.

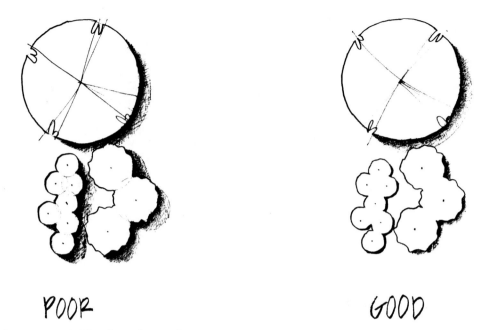

POOR                                    GOOD

***Figure 5-56* Shadow Length**
The length of the shadow on the ground suggests the height of the objects.

## Longer Shadow for Larger Plant

The taller a plant, the longer the shadow it will cast. If all the shadows were the same length for different-size plants, they would appear flat. Shadows for tall trees will take time to develop, but for small shrubs a quick line across the shadow side is all that is needed (Figure 5-56).

## Outline of Shadow Reflects Plant's Form

A conical tree, such as a Christmas tree, will cast a much different shadow on the ground than a rounded tree (Figure 5-57). Reflecting the shapes accurately can give an interesting touch to the drawing.

## Shadows Are the Last Detail Drawn

Shadows are prone to smudging, especially when soft lead is used. Drawing them too early could create excessive smudging.

## All Shadows Fall in the Same Direction

In reality, shadows fall in an east-west direction, depending on the time of day, and always slightly to the south. However, shadows do not have to fall in an east-west direction in a plan drawing. The shadows are not meant to be an indication of direction but, rather, an artistic touch. They should be drawn consistently throughout the design (Figure 5-58).

Ideally, shadows will fall somewhere below the object and not above it or to the side. Shadows below the symbol appear more balanced.

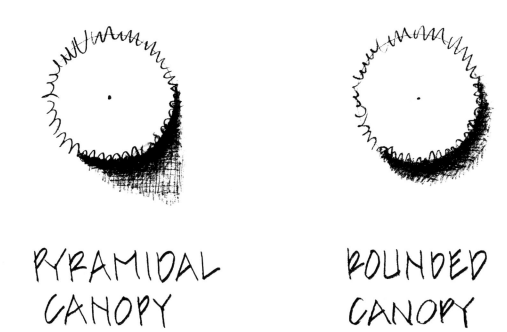

PYRAMIDAL CANOPY          ROUNDED CANOPY

***Figure 5-57* Shadow Shape**
The shape of the shadow can indicate the form of the object.

POOR

← WRONG DIRECTION

GOOD

***Figure 5-58* Shadow Direction**
All shadows should fall in the same direction.

# Summary

Symbols represent the placement and size of plants. More than that, they also communicate characteristics of the plants and make it easier to locate plant material on the plan drawing. Symbols are drawn to represent a characteristic of the plant, such as broadleaf, needle, branching, texture, or form, or to reflect the plant's role in the design, such as foundation, specimen, or mass plantings. Symbols are drawn to a scale that quite often reflect the mature diameter of the plant, although large trees are drawn less than the mature width because of the time it takes to reach that size. Some designers prefer to scale symbols less than the mature width to reflect the design in five to seven years. When all symbols are completed, shadows can be added to symbols to create depth and visual interest in an otherwise flat drawing. For further examples, see the figures in the appendix at the end of the chapter.

# Key Words

**Bananas:**   detail for broadleaf symbols that looks like banana bunches.

**Branched symbol:**   typically used to represent deciduous plants but can also be used for any plant with strong, or unique, branching habits.

**Broadleaf:**   plant that has a flat, wide leaf.

**Cross-hatching:**   begin by hatching the shadow; then draw another series of tight lines going across in another direction.

**Dot:**   located in the center of the symbol, it shows the approximate size and placement of plant material; some designers differentiate dots, depending on whether the symbol represents a plant to be installed or removed or an existing plant.

**Espalier plants:**   trees or shrubs trained to grow flat, either against a wall or on a rack.

**Formal hedges:**   foundation plants sheared into geometric shapes, quite often rectangular.

**Foundation plants:**   add little excitement in order to balance the specimen plantings as well as provide connection throughout the design; not intended to draw attention.

**Generic symbol:**   represents any type of plant, generally used for foundation plants.

**Hatching:**   series of parallel lines running in the direction of the shadow.

**Highlight:**   point on a sphere where the light is most intense.

**Mass:**   plants are spaced so that they will grow into each other and form a large group.

**Radial symbol:**   needle symbol; lines start at the center dot and run sharply to the guideline radiating from the center of a wheel.

**Scale:**   diameter of the plant symbol illustrates the width of the canopy.

**Shadows:**   placed on symbols to create a sense of depth and scale.

**Specimen plants:**   used in a design as accents to draw your eye to specific parts of the landscape; it has some outstanding quality as a stand-alone plant.

**Static:**   detail for broadleaf symbols; scribbly lines that conform to the shape of the circle.

**Texture:**   can be measured as the size of the leaf.

**Triangles and squares:**   detail for broadleaf symbols; variety of triangles and squares.

# Appendix: Generic Symbols

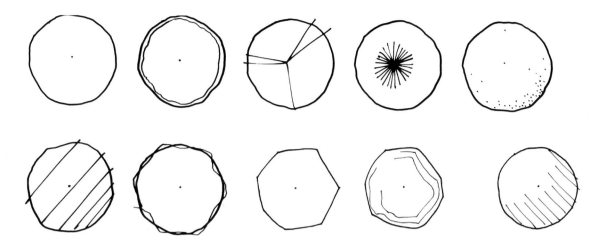

# Broadleaf Symbols (Looping Outline)

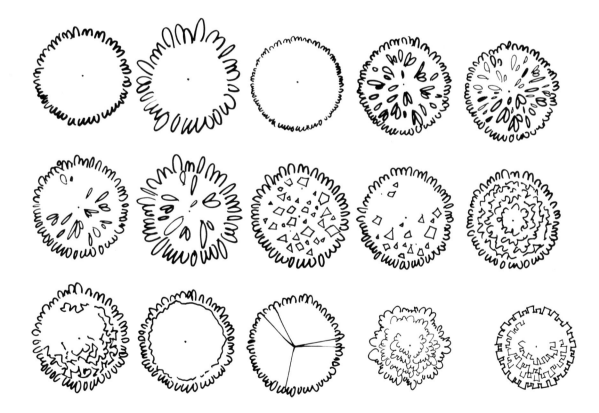

# Broadleaf Symbols (Static and Umbrella)

# Needle Symbols

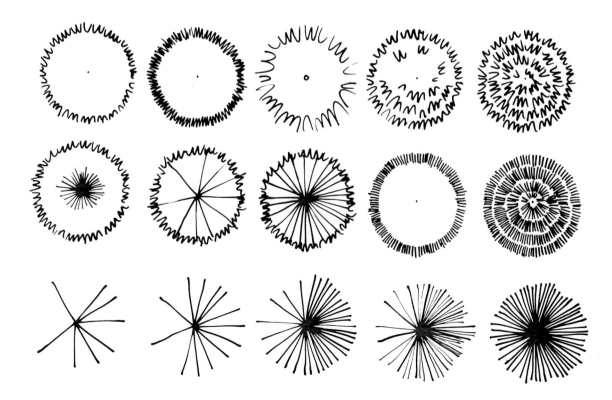

# Branching Symbols

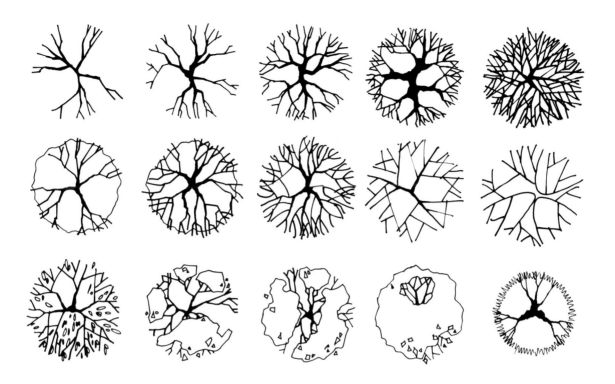

# Palms, Grass, Weeping, and Formal Symbols

# 6 Ground Plane

### Objectives

- Learn the components that make up the ground plane
- Learn the textures that represent the ground plane
- Learn techniques for drawing textures

The plan drawing consists of many components that are located on the **ground plane**, such as driveways, sidewalks, decks, beds, and turf. Textures help define these areas.

**Texture** is simply an organization of lines, much like a pattern. Textures may be made up of dots, circles, dashes, lines, or combinations of these. Much as symbols reflect and differentiate trees and shrubs, textures help to characterize ground plane components. They may be literal drawings of the material or abstract patterns to define an area (Figure 6-1).

## Textures Representing the Ground Plane

Texture might be a true reflection of the material, such as individual bricks in a paved walkway. In this case, the texture tells the observer that the walkway will be built with rectangular pavers, and it may indicate the pattern in which the pavers are installed. The downside is that literal drawing can be very time-consuming for large areas.

Texture may also be a bit more abstract, simply representing the character of the material. This would be evident in an area of groundcover where the lines of texture are

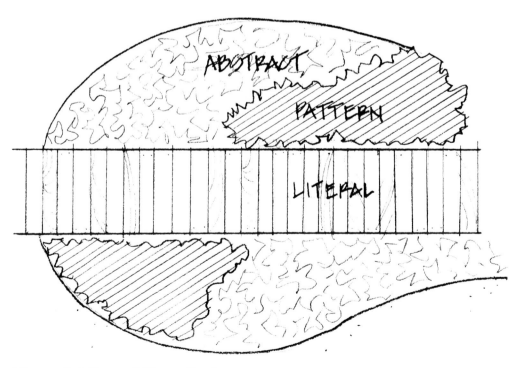

***Figure 6-1* Ground Plane Textures**
Textural drawing is used three ways: *literal* texture of a flagstone path, *abstract* texture of **groundcover**, and a *pattern* to designate areas of pine straw.

loose and random, representing the foliage, rather than a literal drawing of the individual leaves.

Texture may simply be a structured pattern that helps differentiate certain areas from others. A pattern of diagonal lines does not reflect the character of pine straw mulch, but it will be an easy pattern to identify pine straw areas across the design.

## Fewer Labels

With many lines on a drawing, it can be difficult and time-consuming to look for labels to determine which areas are lawns, beds, and driveways (Figure 6-2). Once a texture for a

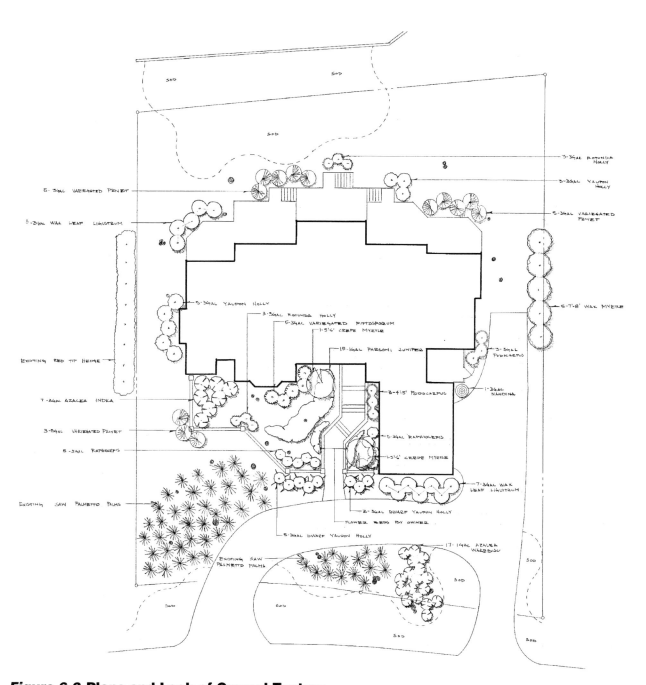

***Figure 6-2* Plans and Lack of Ground Texture**
Without textural development, it can be difficult to tell if areas designate mulch, groundcover, or turf. *(Drawn by Doug Hihn)*

material is established, the plan drawing reads quickly and easily. In some cases, there are fewer labels on the ground plane.

## Visual Interest

Texture is intended to add detail, graphically enhancing the defining lines in the plan drawing. Without any texture development, plan drawings appear like line drawings out of a coloring book. Even with symbol development, the ground plane appears flat and uninteresting. Developing the ground plane with textures adds depth and presentation quality.

# Textural Drawing Techniques

## Guidelines

Many of the textures represented in this chapter follow a few guidelines for effective presentation and efficient technique.

### Lighter Line Weight

Texture is drawn with lighter lines, generally with a 2H lead (Figure 6-3). The purpose of texture is in supporting the defining outlines. The lines in texture should not be noticed as much as the value it creates. When texture is drawn with lines as heavy as the defining

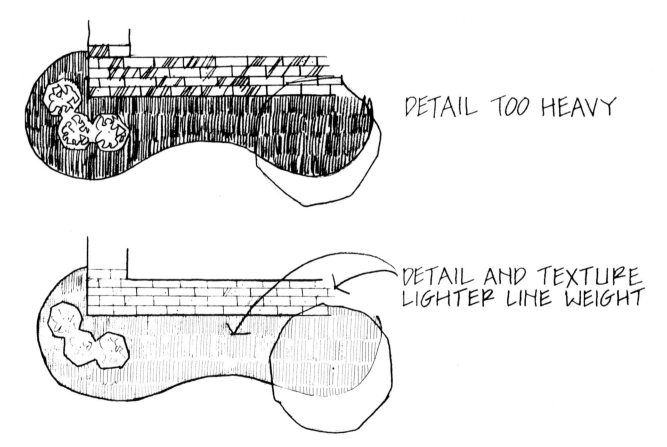

*Figure 6-3* **Detail Lighter Line Weight**
Texture and detail should be drawn with lighter line weight to support, rather than compete with, the defining outlines.

outlines, there is little contrast and less interest. Texture can become dominant and muddle the details.

## Define the Perimeter

Many of the textures will look less cluttered and take less time by drawing them in the following manner (Figure 6-4):

*Heavy perimeter:* More of the texture is drawn around the outside of the area. This helps to more effectively support and define the outline. For instance, more dots around the perimeter of an area creates darker value.

*Light center:* As the texture moves toward the center, it becomes less frequently drawn and lighter in weight. This creates a more interesting pattern with a wider range of value and line weights. In the stippling example, fewer dots are placed near the center of the area.

## Stippling

**Stippling** creates tonal value on the ground plane using a series of dots. It is a great way to create an interesting texture. As dots are placed closer together, the value becomes darker (Figure 6-5).

Stippling is done most effectively with a marker. The marker tip lays down a dark, consistent dot very quickly. If stippling with a pencil, use an HB lead. Twisting the pencil with each dot helps create a solid dot.

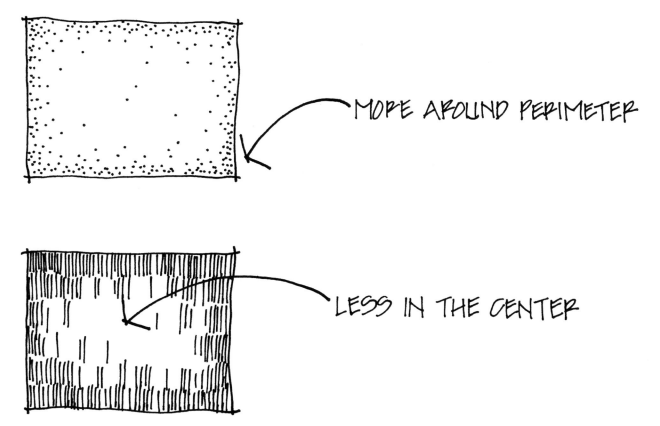

*Figure 6-4* **Define Perimeter**
More texture around outside of area and less in center can be more effective and take less drawing time.

***Figure 6-5* Stippling**
Dots are used to create tones. As the dots are placed closer together, the tones appear darker.

### Common Stippling Flaws

The following are common stippling flaws (Figure 6-6):

*No transition:* Dots are kept tight against the edge, with little movement toward the middle.

**Slashing:** When stippling is done too quickly, the dots turn into slashes because the marker is not lifted high enough between dots. This is very common with pencil stippling because it is more difficult to get a dark dot.

**"Chicken pox":** Stippling is even across the area, giving no movement or support for defining lines.

## Hatching and Cross-Hatching

**Hatching** creates tonal variation using short lines drawn in the same direction. The closer together the lines are drawn, the darker the value appears. **Cross-hatching** is similar to hatching, with short lines drawn in one direction but with another set of lines drawn in another direction over the first set (Figure 6-7). Both techniques offer a unique texture. Either one, or a combination of the two, can be used to get a wide range of values in an area.

It is important to be consistent with hatching lines (Figure 6-8). They should be drawn at the same angle to create a rhythm.

## Pattern

The term **pattern** is in reference to a structured, or formal, arrangement of lines (Figure 6-9). Examples are crossing patterns or diagonal lines. A straightedge is often used to get crisp, straight lines. A pattern is a formal result, compared with the loose, freehand approach of hatching and cross-hatching. It is good to use in large areas because it can provide long, straight lines.

---

***Tip Box:*  Parallel Glide Pattern**
The parallel glider is a tool that can be used to draw parallel lines quickly.

---

# STIPPLING FLAWS

NO TRANSITION

(a)

SLASHING

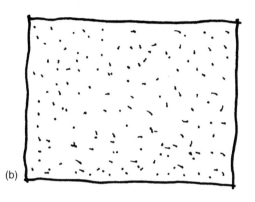

(b)

"CHICKEN POX"

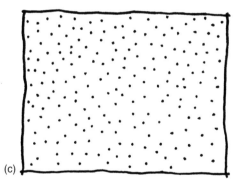

(c)

***Figure 6-6* Stippling Flaws**
(a) No transition—stippling does not move gradually to the center and lacks a range of value. (b) Slashing—when the marker or pencil is not lifted high enough between dots and looks sloppy. (c) "Chicken pox"—little interest because there is little range of value.

## Shading

**Shading** with pencil creates a smooth, wide range of values when done properly. However, it should be limited to creating shadows from objects rather than texture on the ground plane (Figure 6-10a). It takes a long period of time to properly develop a large area and any

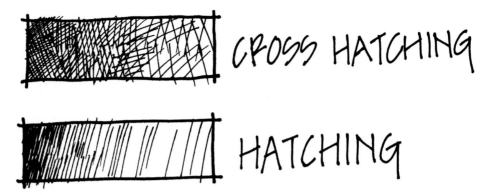

**Figure 6-7 Hatching and Cross-Hatching Texture**
*Hatching* uses lines in one direction to create tonal variation. *Cross-hatching* uses lines running in two directions.

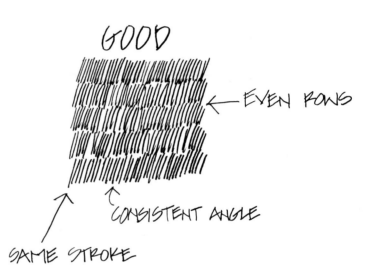

**Figure 6-8 Texture Rhythm**
Establish a rhythm by keeping lines consistent in direction and angle.

effort short of that comes out looking sloppy. Small areas work well. Hold the pencil so that it is nearly flat and use multiple soft strokes (Figure 6-10b).

---

> ### Tip Box:   Limit Shading to Symbol Shadows
> Because shading reproduces poorly, limit shading to shadows from symbols.

---

# Scale

When possible, draw textures to the correct scale, or at least keep them within the reasonable scale of the drawing (Figure 6-11). It may not be prudent to draw brick **pavers** to the actual 8″ × 4″ dimensions at a 1/8″ scale, but textures blown too far out of proportion distort the perception of the plan. For instance, individual bricks drawn to the same scale as the garage are too large.

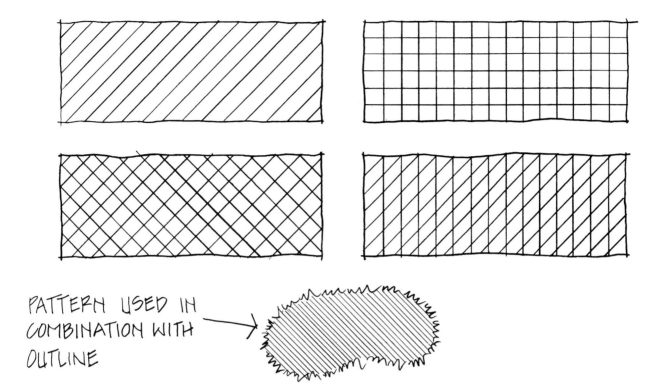

PATTERN USED IN COMBINATION WITH OUTLINE

### *Figure 6-9* **Patterns**
A formal, structured organization of lines is good for large areas.

(a)

SHADING

(b)

### *Figure 6-10* **Shading**
(a) Shading creates a superb range of value when done correctly. However, it should be avoided over large areas because it takes so much time and reproduces poorly. (b) Hold the pencil nearly flat on the paper and use several soft strokes.

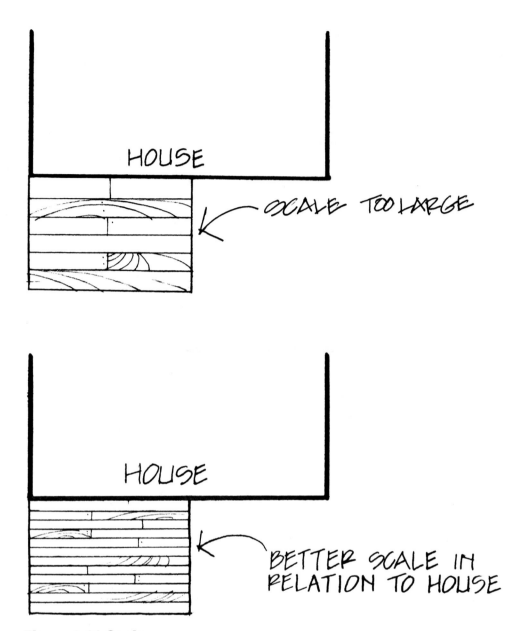

*Figure 6-11* **Scale**
Texture should be kept to a reasonable scale within its surroundings.

## Sampling

Large areas may be time-consuming to fill with texture, especially with detail-oriented textured bricks. With any texture, draw it around the perimeter and in the corners of the area gradually, tapering off toward the center. Not only does this reduce drawing time but it also creates visual interest with a broader range of value within the area (Figure 6-12).

## Contrast Ground Plane and Symbols

The overall value of the ground plane should be opposite of the symbols in order to create contrast (Figure 6-13). This can be achieved by having a dark-textured ground plane with lighter, open symbols or vice versa.

Lacking this contrast creates a design that lacks visual interest and can even make details difficult to read.

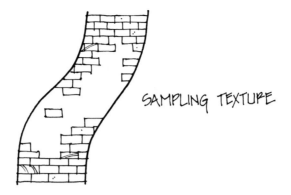

### *Figure 6-12* **Sampling Texture**

For large areas, drawing small samples of the texture throughout can still communicate the intended material without having to fill in the entire area.

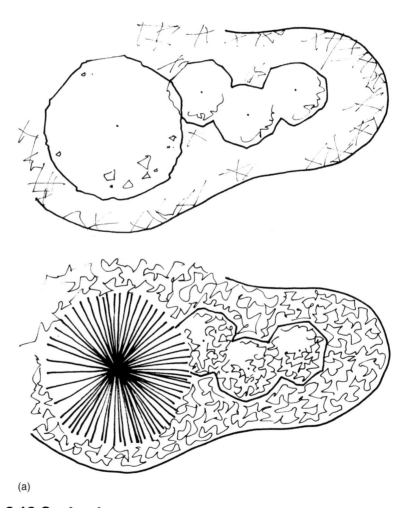

(a)

### *Figure 6-13* **Contrast**

Creating contrast between the ground plane and the symbols to improve readability. (a) Lacks contrast.

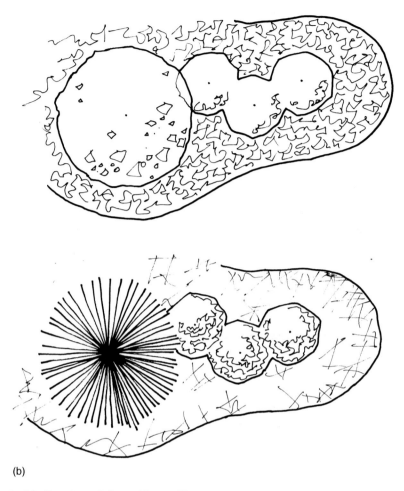

(b)

***Figure 6-13*** **Contrast (continued)**
Creating contrast between the ground plane and the symbols to improve readability. (b) good contrast.

# Ground Plane Components

## Plant Material

### Turf

Areas of **turf** (Figure 6-14a) are typically designated by stipples (Figure 6-14b).

*Edges:* Keep most of the stipples around the edges and in the corners. This supports the outline that defines the area.

*Center:* Place fewer dots as you move toward the center to get a gradual change in value. In some cases, create a natural movement over large areas, like waves blowing across a wheat field, by stippling flowing bands across the middle (Figure 6-14c).

(a)

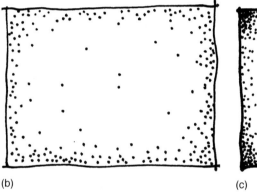

(b)

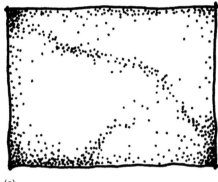

(c)

**Figure 6-14 Turf**
(a) Turfgrass in lawn area. (b) Stippling is commonly used to designate turf. (c) Stripples flowing across an area can create interest.

---

***Tip Box:*** **Simplify Stippling**

Stippling is often overdone and time-consuming. Stippling can be effective with fewer dots and a label for the area (Figure 6-15).

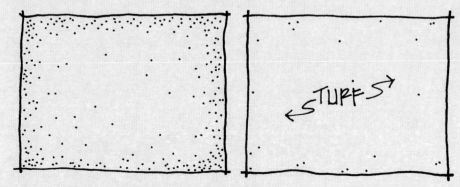

**Figure 6-15 Ground Plane Labels**
Along with texture, labels on the ground plane help clarify areas.

## Groundcover

Plants used for groundcover are low-growing and often have a spreading growth habit. They can be either broadleaf or grassy (Figure 6-16). Groundcovers generally cover a large

(a)

(b)

(c)

**Figure 6-16**
**Groundcover**
(a) Low-growing plant material used to cover small to large areas. It can be either (b) grassy or (c) broadleaf.

# GROUNDCOVER

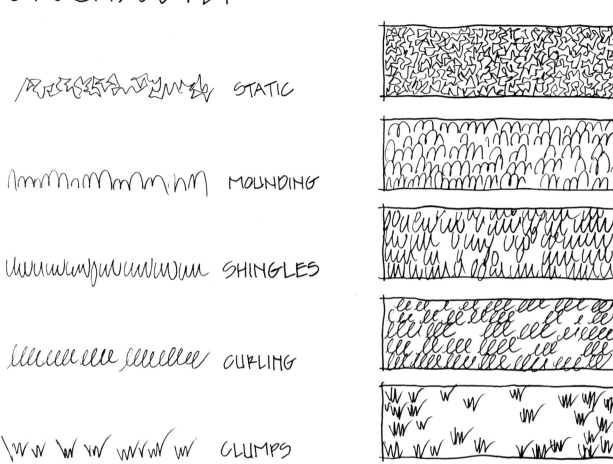

STATIC

MOUNDING

SHINGLES

CURLING

CLUMPS

**Figure 6-17 Groundcover**
Draw groundcover textures loosely, representing the foliage characteristics.

area. There are several textures that present a loose foliage and can be drawn quickly (Figure 6-17). Patterns can also be used to designate the area as groundcover.

## Hardscapes

Materials that are non-living are considered **hardscapes**. Examples include concrete, bricks, pavers, flagstone, wood, and mulch.

### Concrete and Exposed Aggregate

**Concrete** and **exposed aggregate** are well represented by stipples due to the grainy texture of sand and gravel (Figure 6-18). The stipples are of a coarser texture, using a variety of dots, circles, and triangles (Figure 6-19).

### Mulches

**Mulches** are used throughout planting beds to reduce weeds and moisture loss. Mulches are is used between trees and shrubs where turf is not used (Figure 6-20).

Mulches come in several different qualities and types (Figure 6-21). Organic mulches are made from various species of wood: pine, cypress, cedar, eucalyptus, and various hardwoods. These mulches can be cut into different grades: double-cut (fine shred), shredded,

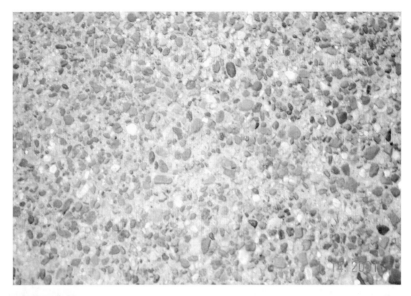

***Figure 6-18* Exposed Aggregate**
Pea gravel embedded into concrete.

mini-nuggets, and course nuggets. Pine straw (pine needles) is utilized in the South. Rock (gravel) can be utilized as inorganic mulch.

Textures used for mulch are fairly nondescript, representing the coarse, dark qualities that contrast with other ground planes, such as turf and concrete (Figure 6-22).

## Bricks and Pavers

**Bricks** and pavers come in various shapes and colors (Figure 6-23). They are used in various patterns to create different looks. Drawing paved areas with a running bond (staggered

# CONCRETE AND EXPOSED AGGREGATE

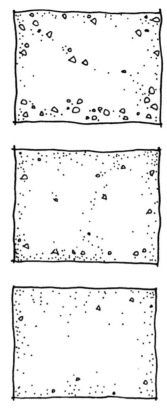

***Figure 6-19* Concrete and Exposed Aggregate**
Stipple with dots and small circles for a coarser texture. The more circles, the coarser the texture.

***Figure 6-20* Mulch**
Used in planting beds to reduce weeds, moisture loss, and mowing.

(a)

(b)

(c)

(d)

***Figure 6-21*** **Mulches**
(a) Cypress chips; (b) shredded cypress; (c) pine straw; (d) coarse nuggets.

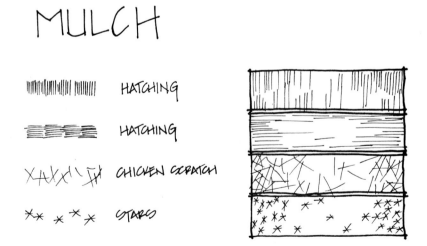

***Figure 6-22*** **Mulch Texture**
Hatching, cross-hatching and other examples to represent mulch materials.

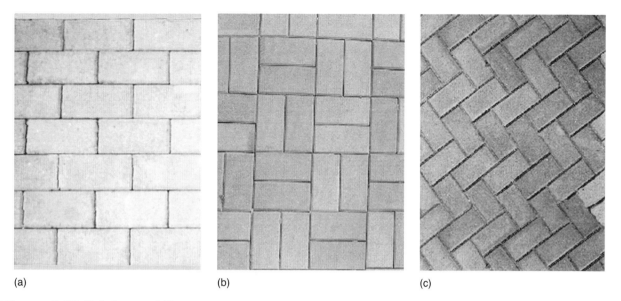

(a) (b) (c)

***Figure 6-23* Bricks and Pavers**
Used in various colors, shapes, and patterns, such as (a) running bond, (b) basketweave, and (c) herringbone.

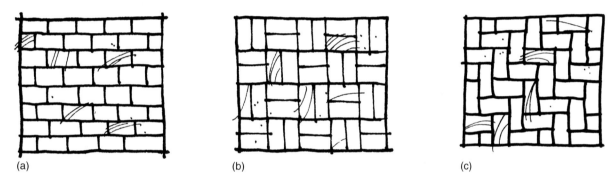

(a) (b) (c)

***Figure 6-24* Bricks and Pavers Texture**
Running bond texture.

brick pattern) is the easiest (Figure 6-24). Other patterns, such as herringbone and basketweave, can be drawn, although they tend to be time-consuming and more difficult to draw than running bond.

## Stone

**Flagstone** is sheetlike stone that comes in various colors and sizes (Figure 6-25). It is a material that is often used as an informal walkway, providing nice texture and informality. Some stone walkways utilize **cut stone** that is rectangular and appears more fitted and formal. **Cobblestone** patterns are less common but are a rounded version of the informal flagstone walkway.

Texture should reflect the shape of the stone used (Figure 6-26).

## Wood

Decking is the most common feature that illustrates **wood** texture on the ground plane (Figure 6-27). Use a straightedge to draw individual boards the length of the deck. Then draw end lines within each board. Be sure to stagger the ends like brickwork.

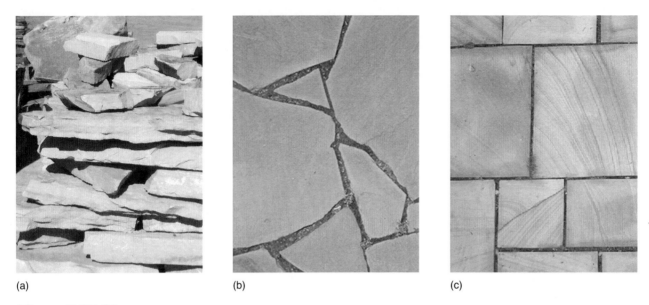

(a)                    (b)                    (c)

### *Figure 6-25* Stone

(a) Flagstone stack; (b) flagstone; (c) cut stone. Like bricks and pavers, stone comes in various colors, shapes, and patterns, such as informal flagstone and cut stone.

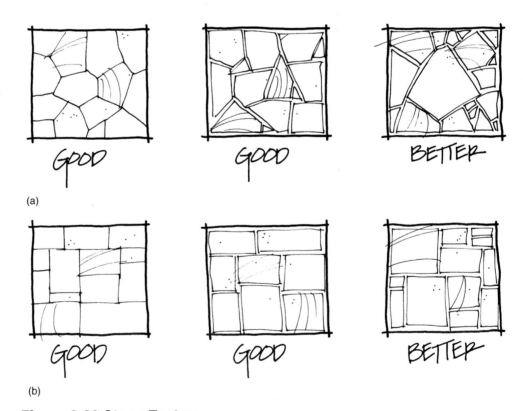

(a)

(b)

### *Figure 6-26* Stone Texture

Examples of (a) flagstone, (b) cut stone texture.

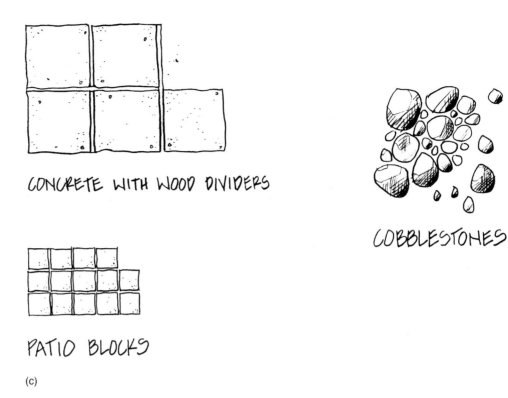

CONCRETE WITH WOOD DIVIDERS

COBBLESTONES

PATIO BLOCKS

(c)

*Figure 6-26* **Stone Texture (continued)**
Example of (c) other textures.

*Figure 6-27* **Wood**
Commonly used as decks in the landscape.

Rather than draw detail on every board, sample several areas throughout the deck to give it a textural impression. At the end of several boards, randomly locate the nail heads. Then, using a lighter line weight (2H), add a curving detail of grain to several boards on the deck (Figure 6-28).

## Water

**Water features** are used as focal points because of their fluid movement, soothing sound, and naturalizing effects (Figure 6-30). They can easily be drawn with rippling texture that

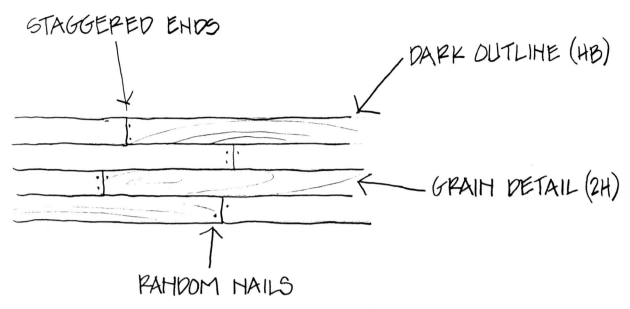

**Figure 6-28** Wood Texture
Draw the board with staggered ends and sample several boards with a light grain.

reflects water movement (Figure 6-31). As if a pebble were thrown in the middle, start with a small circle; then draw large circles around it (Figure 6-32). Some circles may not be complete, as if light reflection were obscuring the line. If there are objects located in the water, such as rocks, show a few ripples emanating from them as well.

Simple wave *patterns* can also be used (Figure 6-33).

## Boulders

**Boulders** are often used with water features as a naturalizing effect (Figure 6-35). They are drawn with a variety of hatching and cross-hatching textures (Figure 6-36).

Draw irregular circles for the outline. Then select a few angular areas on the rock to hatch. Cross-hatch those areas that are on the shadow side.

---

### *Tip Box:*   Lettering Guideline to Draw Boards and Bricks

To get consistent width for wood and paver textures, use the Ames lettering guide (Figure 6-29).

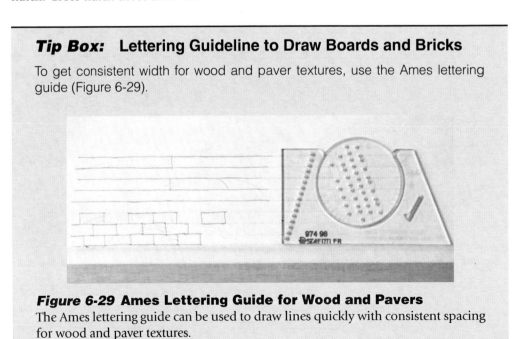

**Figure 6-29 Ames Lettering Guide for Wood and Pavers**
The Ames lettering guide can be used to draw lines quickly with consistent spacing for wood and paver textures.

---

***Figure 6-30* Water Feature**
Water is an effective focal point in a landscape.

***Figure 6-31* Water Ripples**
The texture can simply be a wavy pattern or appear like ripples moving out from the center as if a pebble were thrown.

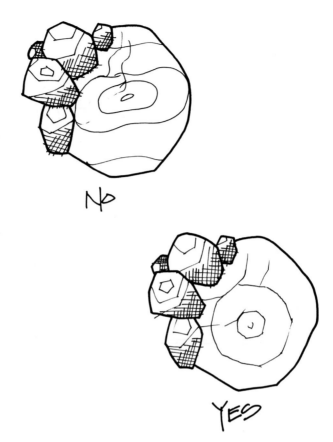

*Figure 6-32* **Water Texture**

*Figure 6-33* **Wave Texture**
This is a simple pattern to illustrate water texture.

***Tip Box:*** **Circle Template for Ripples**

Use a circle template to get light guidelines to freehand draw concentric ripples for water texture (Figure 6-34).

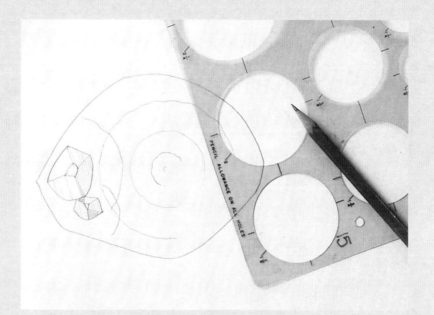

***Figure 6-34*** **Circle Template for Water Ripples**

The circle template can be used to draw light concentric guidelines (using a 4H lead) to develop ripples for a water texture. An H lead can be used to draw the guidelines to lend a wary, natural look to the ripples.

***Figure 6-35*** **Boulders**

Rocks can be used as a naturalizing effect in the landscape. Use a combination of hatching and cross-hatching textures to capture the rough surface quality.

BOULDERS

***Figure 6-36***
**Boulder**
**Textures**

# Summary

Just as symbols represent plants and make the drawing more presentable and easier to read, textures help define, represent, and locate areas on the ground plane. Texture brings more detail to the plan and makes it more visually appealing. The ground plane areas covered in this chapter are turf, groundcover, concrete, pavers, stone, wood, mulchces, water, and rocks. There are several drawing techniques used to create texture, such as stippling, hatching, cross-hatching, and patterns. In order to support the symbols and not create confusion, the ground plane should contrast with the value of the symbols. For instance, when darker textures are developed on the ground plane, then open, lighter symbols should be used for contrast. The opposite, lighter ground with darker symbols, is also true. Examples of ground plane textures are in the appendix at the end of the chapter.

# Key Words

**Boulders:**   often used with water features as a naturalizing effect.

**Bricks:**   used to pave sidewalks, patios, and driveways; come in various shapes and colors; used in various patterns.

**"Chicken pox":**   stippling is even across the area, giving no movement or support for defining lines.

**Cobblestone:**   large, rounded stones.

**Concrete:**   represented by stipples using a variety of dots, circles, and triangles due to the grainy texture of sand and gravel.

**Cut stone:**   flagstone that is shaped into rectangles and appears more fitted and formal.

**Exposed aggregate:**   see *concrete*.

**Flagstone:**   sheetlike stone that comes in various colors and sizes.

**Ground plane:**   components that are located on the ground, such as driveways, sidewalks, decks, planting beds, and turf.

**Groundcover:**   plants are low-growing and often have a spreading growth habit; they can be either broadleaf or grassy.

**Hardscapes:**   materials that are non-living.

**Mulches:**   used throughout planting beds to reduce weeds and moisture loss.

**Pattern:**   structured, or formal, arrangement of lines.

**Pavers:**   see *bricks*.

**Shading:**   creates a smooth, wide range of values when done with short strokes of the pencil held on its side.

**Slashing:**   when stippling is done too quickly, the dots turn into slashes because the marker is not lifted high enough between dots.

**Stippling:**   technique that uses dots to create a texture.

**Turf:**   typically designated by stipples.

**Water features:**   used as focal points because of their fluid movement, soothing sound, and naturalizing effects.

**Wood:**   commonly used to illustrate decks on the ground plane.

# Appendix: Sample Designs—Texture Development

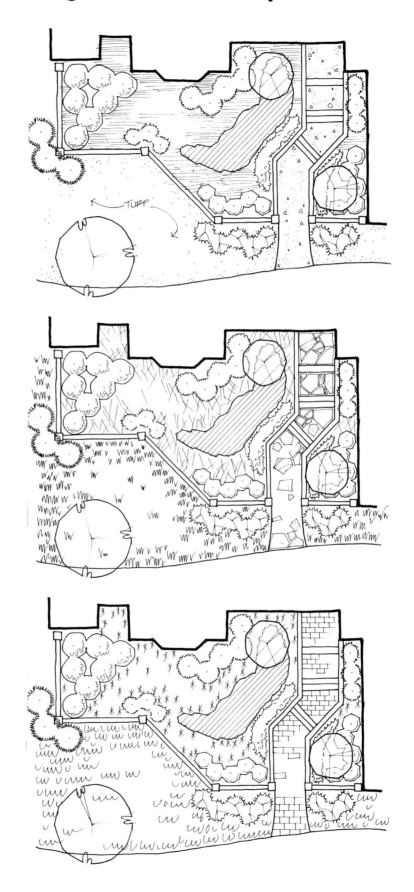

TURF

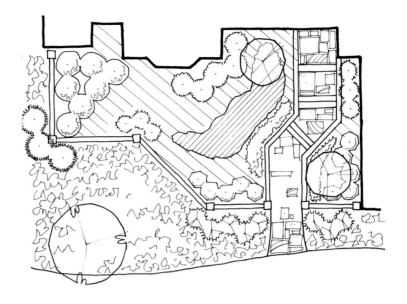

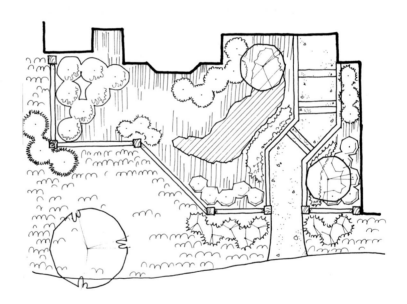

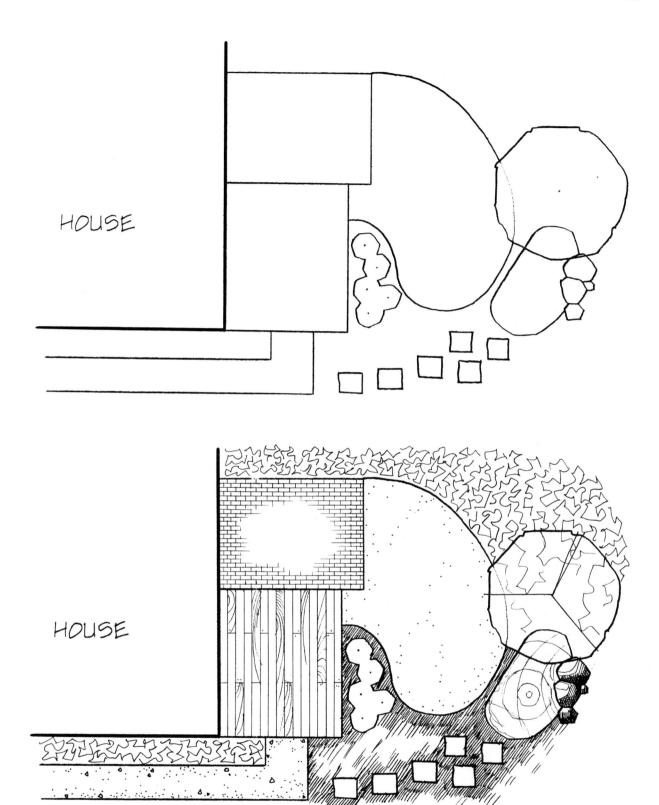

HOUSE

HOUSE

# 7 The Plan Drawing

## Objectives

- Learn how to lay out the plan drawing
- Learn how to draw the border and title block
- Know the vital information included on the plan
- Understand various approaches to labeling symbols and the ground plane
- Know what information is included in the plant list
- Learn how to create a plant list

Having gained a thorough knowledge of drafting tools, drawing, lettering, and symbol development from the previous chapters, it is now time to bring the entire plan drawing together into the final composition.

# Plan Drawing Elements

## Paper

**Vellum** or **mylar** is typically used for plan drawing. (See the section on paper in Chapter 2.) For many projects, a scale of 1/8″ = 1′ or 1″ = 10′ will be an adequate size for drawing detail without being too large. Use whatever scale is appropriate.

## Border

A **border** around the perimeter of the paper can be used to define the drawing space, although some designers prefer the open informality without a border.

The border is drawn 1/2″ to 1″ off the edge of the paper (Figure 7-1). The thickness of the line should be about 1/8″. A round tip marker is ideal for drawing the border. The border can be drawn as a single line around the perimeter of the paper. Carefully draw all four sides with the same line thickness for good balance (Figure 7-2).

### Drawing the Border

**Use T-square or Parallel Rule as a Straightedge**   By using the T-square or parallel rule, you will be able to draw a continuous line along the length of the paper without having to stop. If the T-square does not reach and needs to set on the opposite side to finish the line, then be careful to avoid blotting and inconsistencies. Square the paper to the T-square.

**Pencil in the Border with 4H Lead**   Use the T-square to draw the border with light lines. This will help locate where the lines cross at each corner, as well as provide a guideline to follow. Locating where the borders cross will help you draw sharp corners.

*Wooden T-squares* have a 1/2″ strip of Plexiglas on both sides, which is used as a straight edge. Use the width of the Plexiglas to act as a guide to draw the borders 1/2″ from the edge of the paper by lining up the edge of the paper with the lip of the wooden strip, so that the straight edge of the Plexiglas is 1/2″ from the edge of the paper (Figure 7-3).

*Steel T-squares* will require guide marks to be placed 1/2″ off the edge of the paper because there are no 1/2″ Plexiglas strips to follow.

**Use a Marker to Draw the Border**   A round tip marker provides a good line width about 1/8″ thick.

½" TO 1" FROM PAPER EDGE

BINDING STRIP

**Figure 7-1 Borders**
Borders frame the design. A 3″ to 4″ space is left at the top when the design will be bound with other plan drawings of the same project.

**Figure 7-2 Borders**
Example of border drawn on 24″ × 36″ vellum.

---

**Tip Box:** **Dry-Erase Markers on Vellum**

**Dry-erase markers** will fade from vellum when erased. They are more forgiving than permanent markers.

---

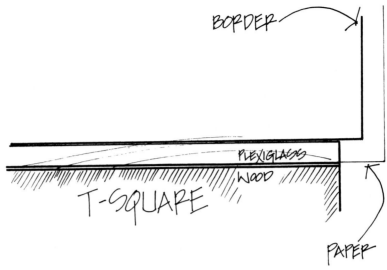

**Figure 7-3 Drawing Border**
Use the 1/2″ strip of Plexiglas on the T-square as a guide.

**Hold the T-square Firmly in Place**   If you put too much pressure against the straightedge with the marker, it will move and cause your line to run off course. While drawing the line, hold the head of the T-square firmly against the table edge with the non-drawing hand.

Place the marker at the beginning point (where the guidelines intersect) and draw a line with an easy, slow pace. Allow the ink from the marker to bleed onto the paper and create a dark line. Going too fast will make the line thinner and lighter. *If your speed with the marker varies, then so will the line consistency.*

# Binding

Oftentimes, projects will have several plan drawings that are bound together at the top (Figure 7-4). One plan may show the planting layout, while the other plan drawing may show topography, dimensions, or construction details.

If this type of plan is to be bound with other plans, leave the border on the left side or the top (the short side, depending on the orientation of the plan drawing) for the binding to be put in place.

# Border Tape

**Border tape** is black tape (approximately 1/8″ wide) used to lay down the border (Figure 7-5). Border tape provides a great line quality with excellent consistency. It is also forgiving because it can be moved around and cut at the exact length for perfect corners.

# Predrawn Border

Paper can be bought with the border and title block already drawn on the paper. Custom-ordered title blocks that include the company name and logo can also be purchased. Paper with a **predrawn border** costs extra, but it saves time (Figure 7-6).

***Figure 7-4* Binding Strip**
Several plan drawings of the same project may be bound together.

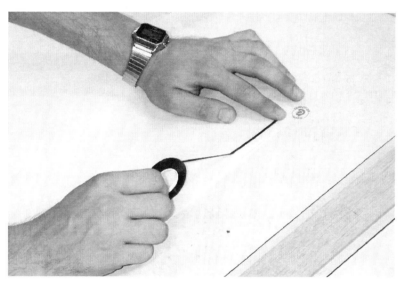

***Figure 7-5* Border Tape**
Black tape (1/8″ wide) can be used to lay down a border.

# Plan Drawing Layout

## The Title Block

The title block contains vital information pertaining to the design. It should be placed, according to the orientation of the drawing, in the following locations (Figures 7-7a and 7-7b):

*Horizontal drawing*: bottom or right side of paper

*Vertical drawing:* bottom of paper

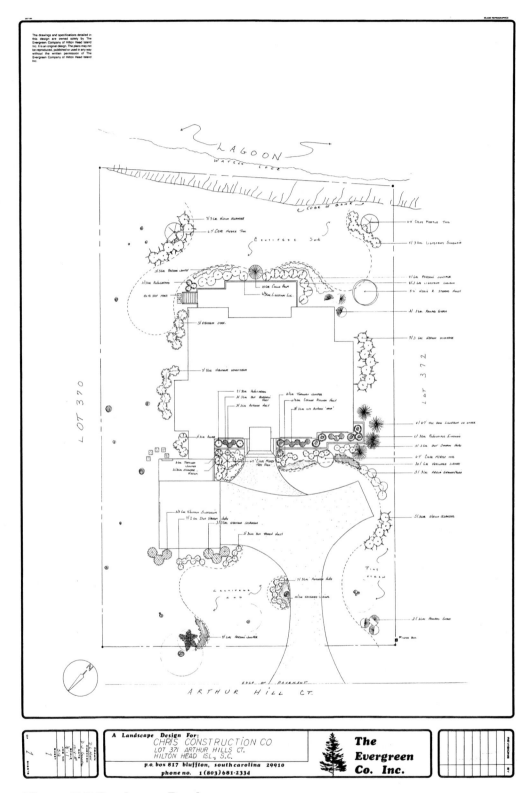

### Figure 7-6 Predrawn Border

Paper can be specially ordered with the border and title block already drawn on the paper. *(Plan drawing provided by Doug Hihn)*

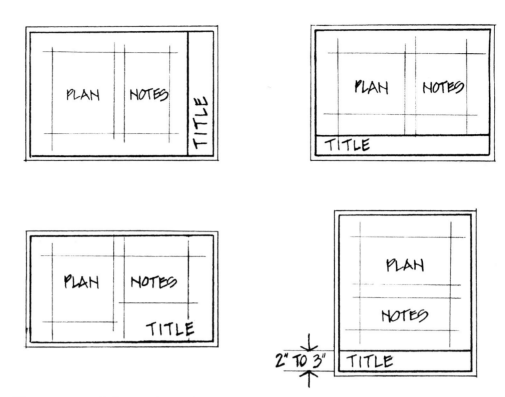

**Figure 7-7a Orientation of Title Block**
Various ways to orient drawing and title block.

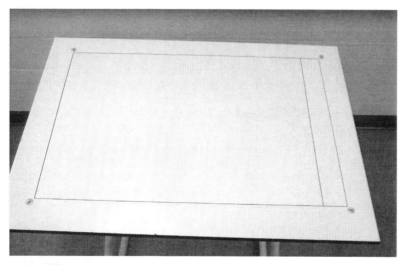

**Figure 7-7b Title Block and Border**
Completed border and title block on 24″ × 36″ vellum.

The title block is drawn 2″ to 3″ high. It can be integrated with the border and drawn as wide as the paper, or it can be drawn freestanding apart from the border.

The following information should be included in the title block (Figures 7-8a and 7-8b):

*Client's name and address:* written in the largest font. The client's name identifies the project and should be the easiest to read. The name, or project, should be written in 1/2″ letters, while the address is written in 1/4″ letters.

*Figure 7-8a* **Title Block**
Typical title block organization in a predrawn format. *(Provided by Doug Hihn)*

> MASTER PLAN
> PAGE 1/1
> AUGUST 6, 2001
> 1/8"-1'
>
> HEATHER GRANT
> 124 W MARKET SUMMERVILLE SC
>
> N↑
> pelican designs

*Figure 7-8b* **Title Block**
Example of information in a hand-drawn title block. Client name is drawn in 1/2" letters, while other letters are 1/4".

*Designer:* name or logo of the individual or company that created the design

*Date:* To keep accurate records, the date when the design was finalized should be written in a small font with the designer's name or logo.

*Plan number:* the number given to plans that are bundled together in a project. The plan number reads "2 of 5," meaning this is the second plan in a bundle of five.

*Type of plan:* identifies the plan drawing as a concept, preliminary, master plan, or other

*Revisions:* indicate modifications and updates

*File number:* used according to the company's filing system

The following information, often represented by symbols, can be included inside the title block or on the plan drawing: the north arrow and scale.

The **north arrow** designates magnetic north on the plan drawing. The north arrow can be represented by many different symbols. It may be very decorative or a simple arrow (Figure 7-9).

Why is it important to know the north direction in the landscape? Because North America is located in the Northern Hemisphere, the sun always falls from the south. This means that the south side of objects will get full sun most of the day, and the north side of objects will receive shade. Thus, the south side of objects is warmer than the north side. This is why snow always melts off the south side of a hill first. This could have a great impact on the plant selection.

Scale is vital for understanding the size and proportion of the design (Figure 7-10). The scale can be shown graphically or it can be written. Many designers prefer to include both graphical and written scales. The **graphical scale** shows segments of different lengths, such as 1', 5', 10', and 20'. Any observer can look at the scale and get an idea of how long of a line would equal 5' or 10', without any understanding of architect scale or engineer scale.

The **written scale** is expressed as 1/8" = 1' or 1" = 20'. This gives any observer an idea of scale but does not visually help the person with the scale. The written scale helps designers know what scale to use or when information is being transferred from one plan to another.

When writing the scale, architect scale is written as what fraction (or whole) of an inch equals *1 foot,*—for example, 1/8" = 1'. Engineer scale is written to express *one inch* represents *how many feet*—for example, 1" = 10'.

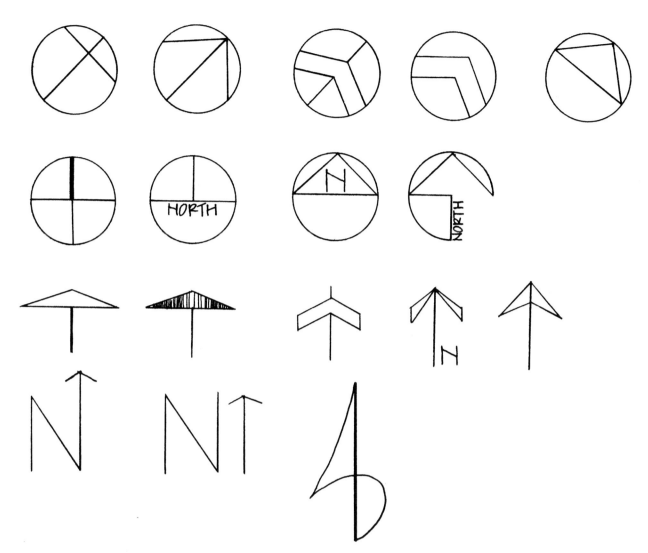

**Figure 7-9 North Arrow**
Examples of north arrow symbols.

Why should the plan drawing be to scale? When drawn to scale, the plants and materials can be accurately located on the property. Also, square footage can be calculated to estimate sod and mulch requirements.

# The Site Plan

A **site plan** is a drawing of the property lines and floor plan, sometimes referred to as the footprint, of the house (Figure 7-11). Some people refer to this as a **plat, plot plan**, or **mortgage survey**. Clients should have a copy of a site plan of their residence along with their closing papers, or it can be found at the mortgage company or the city surveyor. If you do not obtain a site plan, you will have to make measurements and locate property lines yourself.

## Centering the Site Plan

Determine at what scale the plan drawing will fit within the borders. A 1/8″ scale (1/8″ = 1′) or a 10 scale (1″ = 10′) will be used on a 24″ × 36″ plan drawing for most residential properties and will vary on the size of commercial properties.

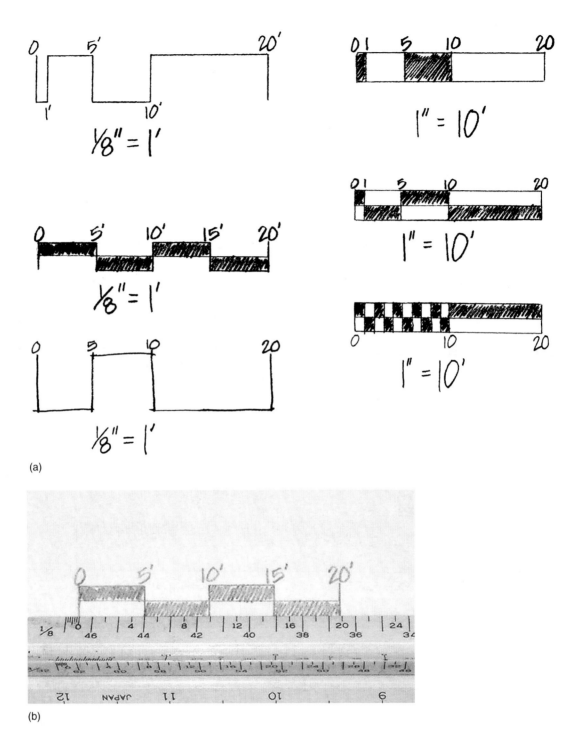

**Figure 7-10** **Scale**

(a) Examples of various ways to represent scale graphically. (b) The graphical scale should have increments equal to the scale, in this case an architect scale ($1/8'' = 1'$).

Considerable time can be wasted if the entire site plan is drawn to scale and then it does not fit on the paper. On the other hand, if the scale is too small, the details will be difficult to understand and look unbalanced with all the unused space.

**Do a Quick Scale Test**     Choose a scale and draw the longest line to be included in the plan drawing and see if it fits. This will most likely be the property line. If it is too large, then try a smaller scale and retest.

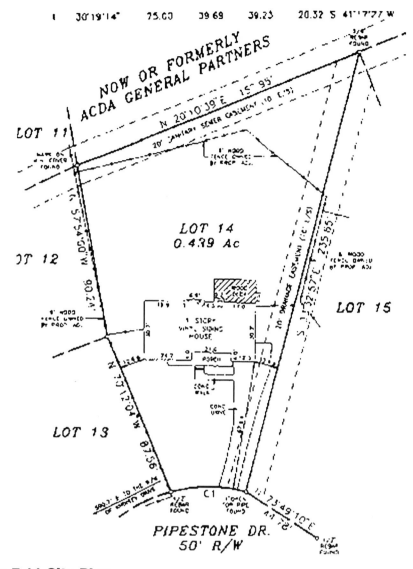

### *Figure 7-11* Site Plan

Site plans are a survey of the property that includes property lines, footprint of the house, easements, **right-of-way**, and other information. Residents should have a copy of a site plan of their property.

**Create a Site Plan Template** The site plan can be drawn on *tracing paper,* so mistakes and line quality is not a concern, then later transferred to vellum (Figure 7-12). Locate the property lines, house, and driveway, as well as any other object located on the site. Also be sure to include setbacks, easements, and right-of-way information for reference.

**Enlarge the Plat for Easy Template** One quick way to get a site plan accurately to scale is to enlarge the size of the site plan (Figure 7-14). Every time the site plan is doubled in size, the scale decreases by half. For example, if the site plan is at a 40 scale (1″ = 40′), then having it doubled will create a site plan at a 20 scale (1″ = 20′).

There can be a little math required to move between scales or to avoid working in an odd scale. For instance, if a plat is in a 30 scale, meaning 1″ = 30′, then it would be in a scale of 1″ = 15′ when enlarged. If doubled again, it would then be 1″ = 7.5′. These aren't very common scales. Also, surveyors draw plats with an engineer scale. If the designer wants to use an architect's scale, how would the plan be enlarged to convert it from an

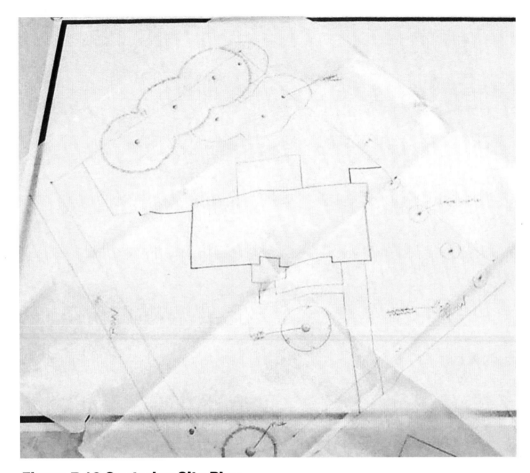

***Figure 7-12* Centering Site Plan**
Draw the site plan to scale on tracing paper; then transfer to vellum.

engineer's scale? Some simple math can be applied to arrive at a multiplication factor (see the following table).

| Existing Scale | Convert to 1/8" Scale | Convert to 1/4" Scale | Convert to 10 Scale | Convert to 20 Scale |
|---|---|---|---|---|
| 10 scale | 1.25× | 2.5× | | |
| 20 scale | 2.5× | 5× | 2× | |
| 30 scale | 3.75× | 7.5× | 3× | 1.5× |
| 40 scale | 5× | 10× | 4× | 2× |
| 50 scale | 6.25× | 12.5× | 5× | 2.5× |
| 60 scale | 7.5× | 15× | 6× | 3× |

Divide the number of feet in an inch of the larger scale by the number of feet in an inch of the small scale you want to convert the plat into—for instance, going from a 30 scale to a 10 scale. Thirty scale is smaller. There are 30' in an inch. Divide 30' by 10' (of the 10 scale) to come up with a factor of 3. This means that, if you enlarge the 30 scale plat 3 times (or 300%), then you would convert it to a 10 scale.

What if the 30 scale plat needs to be converted to 1/8" architect's scale? We've already established there are 30' in an inch for the 30 scale, but how many feet are there in an inch for the 1/8" scale? The answer is 8; therefore, divide 30 by 8 to come up with a factor of 2.5. Enlarge the 30 scale plat 2.5 times to convert it to a 1/8" scale.

## *Tip Box:* Include the Right-of-Way

A site plan is a document of the residential property only. It may not include the right-of-way, which is the land from the front property line to the curb (Figure 7-13). The right-of-way can include 10′ to 15′ of the resident's front yard.

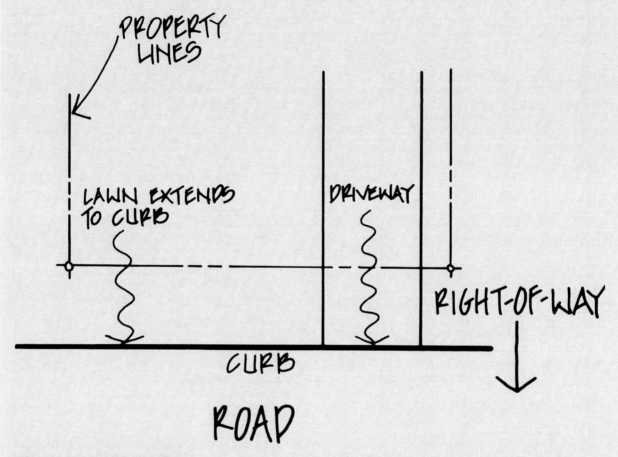

**Figure 7-13 Right-of-Way**
When working from a site plan, do not forget the right-of-way. The site plan shows the property lines, but not the ground between the front property line and the curb, which may be an extension of the front lawn.

## *Tip Box:* Have Printer Increase Size of Site Plan

The site plan is often given to clients on an 8 1/2″ × 11″ piece of paper. A printer can increase the size of the site plan and keep the measurements within scale. Every time the site plan is doubled in size, the scale is reduced by half. If the original scale is 1″ = 40′, then having the site plan doubled will create a document to the scale of 1″ = 20′.

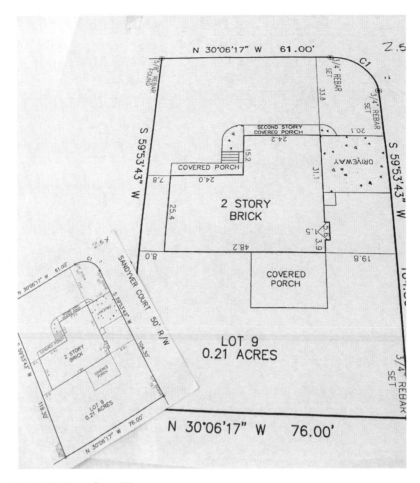

***Figure 7-14*** **Enlarging Plan**
An easy way to enlarge plan to scale is to have printer do it. Every time plan is doubled, scale decreases by half.

**Centering the Template Under Paper**    Slide the template under the vellum (or mylar) and move it around until it is centered in the drawing space. The site plan should be balanced with empty space, title block, and plant list. It is very distracting to see a plan drawing crowded against one side of the paper because it is not balanced.

---

### *Tip Box:*   Center Site Plan with Plant List

If a plant list is to be included on the plan drawing, be sure to make room for it. The plan drawing will be unbalanced if the site plan is centered in the middle of the drawing space and the plant list is squeezed in between it and the border.

---

**Trace the Site Plan onto Paper**    Once the paper is centered, be sure both template and paper are secured to the drawing table; then trace the site plan.

     Once the site plan is on vellum, additional copies can be made if other plans are to be included in the project. If you do not have ready access to a printer, hold on to the tracing paper in case other plans are drawn.

# Labeling

Once your plan drawing is complete with line weights, symbols, and textures, it needs to be **labeled.** All material is labeled for identification.

## Ground Plane

Areas on the ground plane are represented by texture and should be adequately labeled as well (Figure 7-15). Most areas can be labeled directly, such as turf, mulch, and driveway. These areas can be detailed further in the **plant list** under the same heading to indicate amount and variety. (See the section "Plant List" later in the chapter).

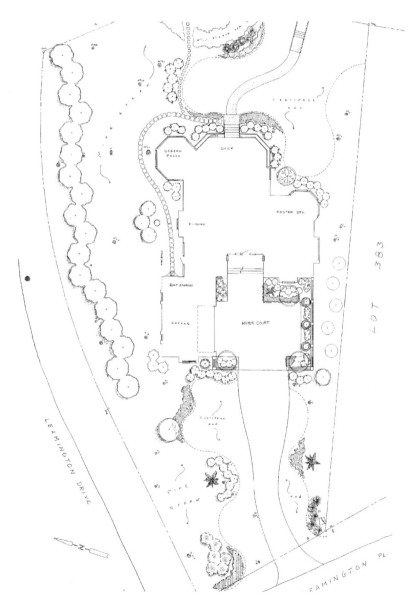

***Figure 7-15* Labeling Ground Plane**
Simple labels and arrows help identify various ground plane areas, such as turf, mulch, and hardscapes. *(Drawn by Doug Hihn)*

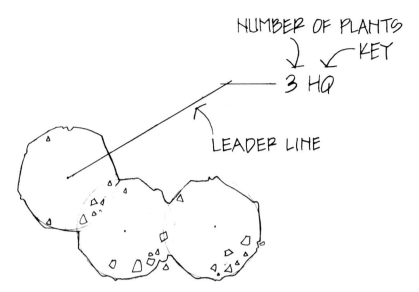

**Figure 7-16 Labeling Symbols**
A leader line points to the center of symbol. The number indicates how many plants are in group; the key refers back to a plant list.

## Symbols

Symbols are typically labeled with a **leader line**, a plant name or **key**, and the number of plants in the group (Figure 7-16). Symbol masses are labeled as a group. This reduces the number of labels that appear on the design, making it less crowded.

## Leader Lines

A leader line is a lightweight line that extends from a symbol to a plant name or key. Most designers prefer that the leader line connect to the center dot of the symbol. A 2H lead will create a thin, light line that will show on a copy.

Be consistent with leader line angles (Figure 7-17). When the leader lines are shooting off across the design in different directions, they are very distracting. At the end of the leader line will be a plant label or key. The leader line should point to the center of the plant symbol (Figure 7-18).

---

**Tip Box:   Creating Consistent Leader Lines**

Keep your leader lines consistent by drawing them with a triangle on a T-square (Figure 7-19).

---

## Label Placement

There are two approaches to the location of the label in proximity to the symbol. Regardless of how it is done, the overall rule is to make sure labels are clear and easy to read.

### Outside the Design

Some designers prefer to place all the labels around the outside of the design (Figure 7-20). This approach avoids any labels within the boundary of the property lines.

*Advantage:* Labels can be neatly justified along the left and right sides.

*Disadvantage:* Long leader lines can get far enough away from the symbols to be difficult to follow.

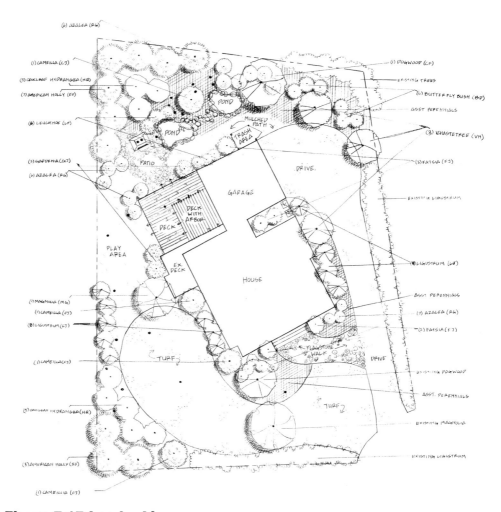

***Figure 7-17* Leader Lines**
Be consistent with leader line angles, so that the drawing does not appear chaotic, like this drawing.

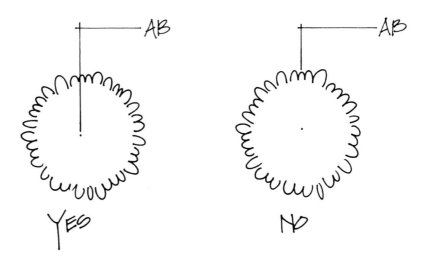

***Figure 7-18* Leader Line**
The leader line should print to the center dot.

***Figure 7-19* Leader Lines**
Using a triangle in conjunction with a T-square can keep leader lines consistent.

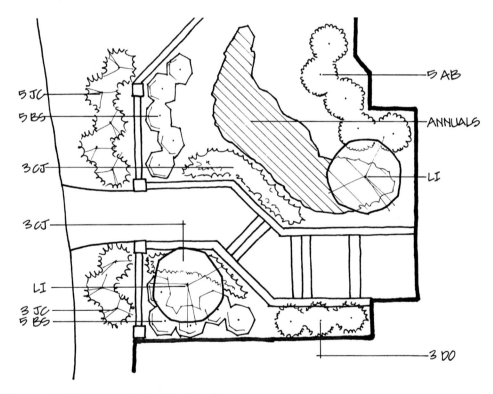

***Figure 7-20* Label Outside Design**
Some designers prefer to place all labels outside the design.

## Inside the Design

This approach places labels near the symbol (Figure 7-21). Labels can be placed within the design and not necessarily outside of it.

*Advantage:* It is easy to find the label.

*Disadvantage:* It can get crowded within the details of the drawing.

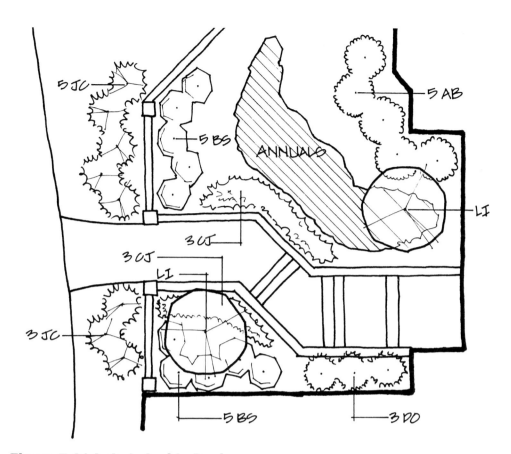

***Figure 7-21* Labels Inside Design**
Some designers prefer to place labels inside the design.

# Building the Plant List

Ideally, the plant list should be alphabetized to locate information easily.

## Hand-Drawing the Plant List

If lettering quality is good, this approach will look good on the plan. However, the major drawback to this approach is that changes are difficult to make. A lot of planning will have to go into alphabetizing the list.

## Printing the Plant List

A more efficient approach is to computer-generate the plant list on a spreadsheet. Any changes can be made easily without having to redraw the list. Also, the list can be automatically alphabetized, which makes keying out the plants easier when there are a lot of plants on the list. The plant list can be printed on bond paper and taped or glued for a print.

Another effective option is to print the list onto an adhesive film, referred to as **sticky back,** that can be easily attached. The low-tack adhesive makes it easy to peel it off and attach a revised plant list. Sticky backs, however, are more expensive than bond paper.

# Plant Label

The plant label will often indicate the name and number of plants in a group.

### Number of Plants

The first thing that appears in the plant label is the number of plants in the group being labeled. This way, the number of plants in a group can be quickly identified without having to count the symbols. If there is only one plant, no number is used in the label.

### Plant Name or Key

Following the number of plants is the plant identity. There are two general methods of labeling: *direct labeling* and *plant keys*.

**Direct Labeling**   Direct labeling uses the entire name of the plant. This is the easiest approach for an observer to read the design because the name of the plant is located right along with the symbol. This way, one does not have to trace a key back to a plant list and sort through information to find the plant name. Some designers include additional information along with the number and name, such as the planting size (see the section "Plant List.").

The downside to this approach is the amount of time it takes to label the plan drawing because each plant name is written in its entirety.

**Plant Keys**   A plant key uses letters to indicate the plant information found in a plant list (Figure 7-22). Plant keys are designed in the following ways: two-letter key, four-letter key, or alphabet labeling.

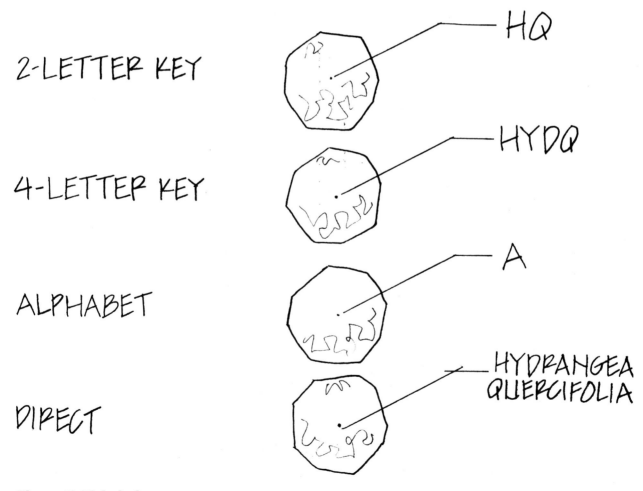

*Figure 7-22* **Labels**
Various ways to label symbols: alphabet, two-letter key, four-letter key, and direct labeling.

The **two-letter key** is based on the first letter of the *genus* name and the first letter of the *species* name. Both letters are written in uppercase. You can use additional letters to differentiate between keys of different plants that appear the same or cultivars of a species.

**Two-Letter Keys**

CP—*Cornus florida*

BS—*Buxus sempervirens*

**Cultivars of a Species**

IV—*Ilex vomitoria*

IVP—*Ilex vomitoria* 'Pendula'

IVN—*Ilex vomitoria* 'Nana'

**Different Species**

ICR—*Ilex crenata*

ICO—*Ilex cornuta*

The **four-letter key** is based on the first three letters of the *genus* name and the first letter of the *species* name. All four letters are written in uppercase. This approach has the flexibility to avoid identical keys while always maintaining four letters.

ILEC—*Ilex cornuta*

In order to avoid identical keys, you can use the first two instead of one letter from the species name and only two letters from the genus name.

ILEC—*Ilex cornuta*

ILCO—*Ilex convexa*

If a cultivar of a species is being used, put the first letter of the cultivar at the end of the key and use only the first two letters of the genus to maintain a four-letter key.

ILCB—*Ilex cornuta* 'Burfordii'

If the cultivar name has two words, you can use the first letter of each word and only the first letter of the genus.

ICDB—*Ilex cornuta* 'Dwarf Burford'

In **alphabet labeling**, the symbols are lettered starting with *A* and continuing through the alphabet, doubling the letters if the end of the alphabet is reached such as *AA, BB, CC,* and so on.

# Legends

Some designers will use a **legend** when appropriate (Figure 7-23). This way, the symbols can be organized in a separate block (legend) and labeled. The observer can find the symbols in the design and refer back to the legend for identification, thereby avoiding labeling all the symbols in the design.

# Plant List

Sometimes referred to as a **planting schedule**, the plant list organizes the plant keys and other information (Figure 7-24). This creates a concise list of all plants and materials that can be used by the designer to create estimates or bids. Plant lists contain columns of the following information:

*Key:* includes all the keys from the plan drawing. Ideally, the list should be alphabetized according to the keys to make it easier to locate the plant on the list

*Botanical name:* genus, species, and cultivar (if necessary)

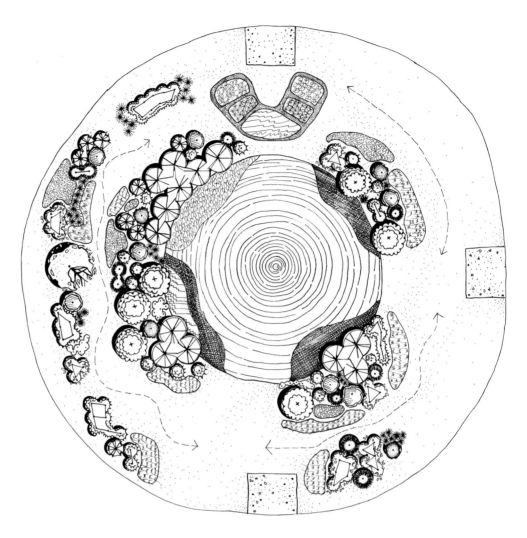

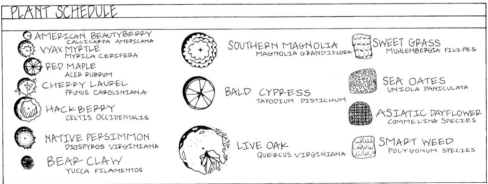

***Figure 7-23* Legend**
Organize and label symbols in a legend for identification in the plan, instead of labeling each symbol. *(Drawn by Courtney Smith)*

*Common name:* common name as compared with the scientific name of the plant

*Quantity:* total number of each plant used in the design

*Size:* indicates the container size of plants sold at nurseries. It may also be used to specify the height and width of the canopy or the caliper (diameter of trunk), especially if the plant is balled and burlapped. The smaller the plant size, the less the material will cost. However, smaller plants take longer to grow into the intended design.

| KEY | BOTANICAL NAME | COMMON NAME | QTY | SIZE | NOTES |
|-----|----------------|-------------|-----|------|-------|
| AJ | *Acer japonicum* | Fullmoon Maple | 5 | 3 gal | |
| AP | *Acer palmatum* | Japanese Maple | 1 | 3 gal | 1" caliper |
| AT | *Asimina triloba* | Pawpaw | 3 | BB | |
| AUJ | *Aucuba japonica* | Japanese Aucuba | 10 | 3 gal | |
| AJL | *Aucuba japonica* 'Longifolia' | Longleaf Aucuba | 8 | 1 gal | |
| BG | *Berberis x gladwynensis* 'William Penn' | William Penn Barberry | 22 | 1 gal | |
| BD | *Buddleia davidii* ' Black Knight' | Black Knight Butterfly Bush | 11 | 3 gal | can subst. Purple |
| CS | *Cortaderia selloiana* | Pampasgrass | 3 | 3 gal | |
| GA | *Gardenia augusta* | Gardenia | 3 | 3 gal | |
| VM | *Vinca minor* | Periwinkle | 70 | 4" pots | 6" OC spacing |

**Figure 7-24 Plant List**
Information that is included in a plant list: key, botanical name, common name, quantity, size, (sometimes spacing) and notes.

*Spacing:* distance between plants that are used in mass. This is typical for areas of groundcover where individual plants are often placed 4" apart. Some designers omit this column and include spacing notations in the "Notes" column.

*Notes:* additional comments, if necessary. This might include things such as flower color, substitutions, espalier, multi-trunk tree, or plant spacing (if "Spacing" column is not used).

# Plant List Location

The plant list is organized into a formal box and located on the plan drawing. Be sure to think ahead of plant list size and proportion when centering the site plan. If you center the plan without making room for the plant list, you will have to crowd it into a small space.

The plant list is contained by a border similar to the border around the plan drawing, but generally with narrower lines. Ideally, the border conforms to the exact length of the list, although some extra space allows for additional information.

## *Tip Box:* Sticky Back Plant List

The plant list is printed on adhesive film that can be attached to the plan (Figure 7-25). This plant list can be easily replaced with a revised plant list.

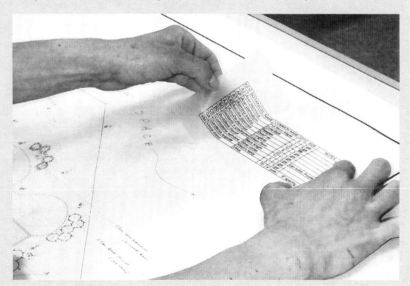

**Figure 7-25 Sticky Back Plant List**
Plant list is created on spreadsheet and printed on a low-adhesive paper that can be placed on plan and easily removed for revisions.

# Sketches and Details

Additional drawings may be included on the plan drawing, such as section drawing, three-dimensional sketches, and construction details. These drawings can give clients a quick idea of the proposed design. Many people find it difficult to visualize the three-dimensional aspect from the bird's-eye view of the two-dimensional plan drawing. Construction details provide instructions on planting and hardscape construction and can serve as a legally binding document for installation by a contractor. Section drawing will be covered in Chapter 9.

# Summary

This chapter covered the elements that make up the plan drawing. The plan drawing is the culmination of the design, including symbols, textures, and labels, which will be presented to the client. The basic layout of the final drawing includes a title block that contains vital information pertaining to the project, such as client name and address, designer, scale, north arrow, date, and type of plan—it may also include revision number and page number. A border is drawn around the perimeter of the paper to help define the plan, although some designers prefer to work without a border. Once the site plan is drawn on separate paper, it can be slid under the drawing and placed in balance with the title block, plant list, and space of the plan. The balance is important to the presentation of the plan. All areas on the ground plane and the symbols should be labeled, either with the entire name of the material or with a key that refers back to a plant list. The plant list is an organized list of all the material in the design. It should include the name (botanical and common), quantity, size, and additional notes for each plant. Notes can include things such as color, detail, spacing, or other specifications.

# Key Words

**Alphabet labeling:**   identifying symbols with labels starting with *A* and continuing through the alphabet, doubling the letters if the end of the alphabet is reached, such as *AA, BB, CC,* and so on.

**Border:**   drawn around the perimeter of the paper to define the drawing space; some designers prefer the open informality without a border.

**Border tape:**   black tape, approximately 1/8″ wide, used to lay down the border.

**Direct labeling:**   labels the plant with the entire name instead of a key.

**Dry-erase markers:**   can be used to draw the border because they will erase from vellum without tearing the paper.

**Four-letter key:**   identifies a symbol based on the first three letters of the genus name and the first letter in the species name.

**Graphical scale:**   shows segments of different lengths, such as 1′, 5′, 10′, and 20′.

**Key:**   refers back to a plant list to identify symbols.

**Labeled:**   identifying material on the plan drawing.

**Leader line:**   lightweight line that extends from a symbol to a plant name or key.

**Legend:**   symbols organized in a separate block and labeled; the observer can refer back to the legend for identification.

**Mortgage survey:**   see *site plan.*

**Mylar:**   drafting film that can be used for the final drawing.

**North arrow:**   designates magnetic north on the plan drawing.

**Plant list:**   organization of plant keys and other information; the plant list is used by the designer to create estimates or bids.

**Planting schedule:**   see *plant list*.

**Plat:**   see *site plan*.

**Plot plan:**   see *site plan*.

**Predrawn border:**   border and title block already drawn on the paper.

**Right-of-way:**   land from the front property line to the curb, which may include 10′ to 15′ of the resident's front yard.

**Site plan:**   drawing of the property lines and footprint of the house.

**Sticky back:**   adhesive used to attach the plant list to the plan, making it easy to revise and replace the list.

**Two-letter key:**   identifies a symbol based on the first letter of the genus name and the first letter in the species name.

**Vellum:**   high-quality paper used for the final drawing.

**Written scale:**   does not visually help the person with the scale, as the graphical scale does; examples are 1/8″ = 1′ and 1″ = 20′.

# Design Example

Example of labeling symbols and ground plane *(Drawn by Sandy Plance)*

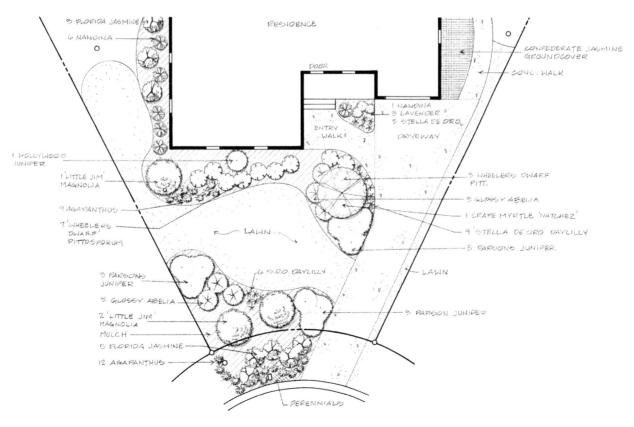

# 8 Color

## Objectives

- Understand the basic approach to color development
- Learn basic coloring techniques for pencils and markers

Plan drawings can be greatly enhanced for presentation by color rendering. If color is to be used, symbols and the ground plane can be kept very simple because color enhancement will define them.

Color on a print of the plan drawing. Never attempt to color the original drawing. Bond paper works fine for coloring. There are several very effective means of color rendering. For the beginning student, only two coloring media will be covered in this chapter: *pencils* and *markers* (Figure 8-1).

# Pencils

Beginning students feel more comfortable starting color development with color pencils. **Color pencils** are similar to drawing pencils but contain a wax-based material instead of lead.

(a)

(b)

**Figure 8-1 Pencils and Markers**
Typical sets of color pencils and professional markers. (a) Professional markers come in a wide range of colors, usually with a chisel tip at one end and a fine point at the other. (b) Color pencils also come in a wide range of colors, often the same colors as markers. They have a soft, wax-based medium.

For the beginning student, starting with a set of 24 pencils will provide an acceptable range of colors. These sets are available at arts and crafts stores or on the Internet at similar sites. **Sanford Prismacolor** and **Design Spectracolor** are very popular brands because of their ease of application.

In addition to the set, individual pencils can be purchased. Consider purchasing additional variations of green because this will be the range of color you will be using the most.

---

### Tip Box:   Additional Greens

Purchase additional variations of green because it will be the color used the most.

---

# Technique

With pencils, achieving a smooth value is key to appealing color. Holding the pencil in a **flattened position** uses the side of the pencil. This approach applies a color smoothly without lines (Figure 8-2). When the pencil is held in an **upright position**, it provides more "bite" between the pencil and the paper. This technique is used to get darker values near the perimeter of the area or object. However, it will dull the tip very quickly and, if overused, a waxy appearance will develop (Figure 8-3).

***Figure 8-2* Flattened Position**
Hold the pencil flat to the paper to get a smooth, even value.

***Figure 8-3* Upright Position**
Hold the pencil upright to get darker values.

# General Color Development

## Surface

Imperfections on the drawing surface can ruin color. Be sure that the surface is smooth and clear of debris, such as eraser bits. When shading with pencil, any bumps or bits underneath the paper will show up as dark spots (Figure 8-4).

---

### *Tip Box:*   Foam Board Surface

A 1/4″ foam board is an inexpensive, versatile surface. It can be cut into smaller sections and used to color on any table or your lap. The surface is exceptionally smooth. However, foam board will puncture and dent, so limit its uses to shading. If it becomes damaged, it can be easily replaced.

---

## Value

**Value** of color is the degree of darkness or lightness. **Shade** of color is a darker value, while **tint** is a lighter value of a color (Figure 8-5).

*Do not* approach the color development of a plan drawing as if it were a coloring book. See the color inserts. When areas and symbols are filled in with an even value of one color, the plan drawing appears flat and uninteresting. Instead, developing a *range* of value enhances the depth and creates more visual interest.

***Figure 8-4* Surface**

The quality of the surface will readily show through the shading of pencil. On the left, the surface is perfectly smooth, but on the right the same surface has bits of debris that show through.

***Figure 8-5* Value**

Value is the range of darkness to lightness of a color.

---

> ***Tip Box:*** **Broaden the Range Value**
>
> An even value of one color looks much like a coloring book. Developing a range of value creates visual interest.

---

## Define Perimeter

For symbols and areas, a general approach that is appealing is to develop darker value near the outline to help define the object or area (Figure 8-6). Using a black line to outline the symbol will further improve the defining quality.

## Rhythm

Continue to use a **rhythmic stroke** for coloring, as done for hatching. With shading, there is generally a hint of the direction. In fact, this can lend a loose, abstract quality (Figure 8-7). Be consistent!

# Color Development of the Ground Plane

## Wash

Start by evenly "washing" the entire area, holding the pencil in a flattened position. **Washing** refers to a light, even value across the entire area. This will give it a base to build a range of values on top.

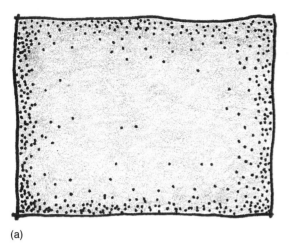

(a)

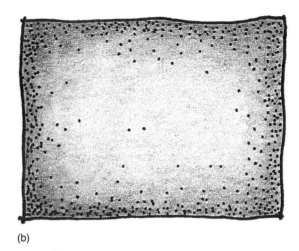

(b)

***Figure 8-6* Ground Plane with Pencils**
(a) This is referred to as "wash," a light, even base. (b) The perimeter has been darkened with the same color, creating a wide range of value as well as further defining the area with much more interest.

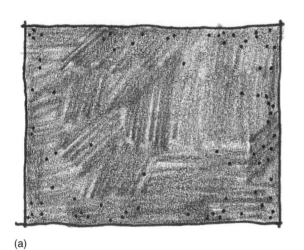

(a)

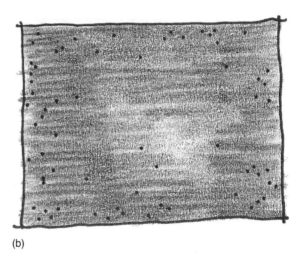

(b)

***Figure 8-7* Rhythm**
(a) Avoid coloring in too many directions. (b) Maintain rhythmic, consistent strokes with color pencils.

## Darken Perimeter

Once the wash is complete, create darker value near the outline by going back over the wash. Adding more pressure with the pencil and using an upright position near the line will help develop a darker value that blends smoothly into the wash.

## Moving Lines

In some large areas, a quick, slashing line can be struck across the area to lend motion and interest. A **moving line** acts as an accent but should be used with caution so as not to be overdone (Figure 8-8).

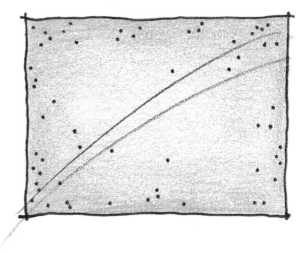

### *Figure 8-8* Moving Lines

Lines can be used to break up large areas for interest.

---

### *Tip Box:* Color Sticks

Using pencil can be time-consuming on large areas. Consider using **color sticks.** These are essentially the wax-based material in the pencils formed into 1/4″-thick square sticks. These are not **pastels,** which are a *chalky* medium (Figure 8-9).

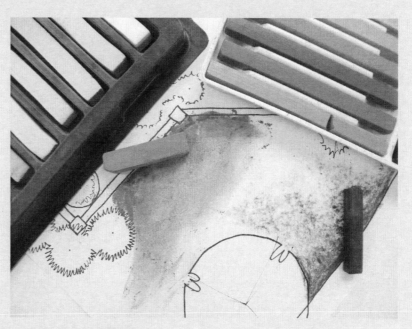

### *Figure 8-9* Color Sticks

These are 1/4″-thick sticks of the wax-based material in color pencils. They are excellent for coloring large areas.

Sticks can be used on their side to fill in the area with broad strokes. It is important that the drawing surface be smooth. With this approach, irregularities will show up in the color.

## Color Development of Symbols

### Color

Obviously, green colors will be used to develop symbols. Having several green colors on hand will give some variation between designs. However, be careful not to use too many greens in one design because it will appear too busy. In a design, stick with only a few greens.

Colors other than green can be used for accent effects. Ranges of blue, red, violet, and yellow can be used, especially when relating to a flowering color or a fall color.

### Wash

Start by lightly washing the entire symbol. If you are using several colors for the symbol, start with the lightest color (Figure 8-10a).

### Shading

Start on the shadow side of the symbol and, with the pencil in a flattened position, develop darker value in a crescent pattern that wraps around the highlight (see light anatomy, page 110). Keep the value smooth and blend it evenly into the wash. To get the darkest value around the perimeter of the symbol, use the pencil in an upright position (Figure 8-10b).

### Outline

When completely finished, outline the symbol with a black pencil. Use thicker outlines for canopies that are farther from the ground plane to lift them higher off the ground and closer to the observer (Figure 8-10c).

### Shadows

To develop shadows, use a black pencil to lightly darken the ground plane. Avoid blotting out the ground plane with a solid black shadow.

# Markers

Most beginning students find markers very difficult to use. However, once they grasp the techniques, they can create excellent color drawings.

Professional **markers** have a chisel tip for wide and narrow lines. Initially, the lines are wet but, because they are alcohol-based, they dry quickly. Be aware that some professional markers use xylene as a carrier rather than alcohol, which can smear lines of a photocopy. Chartpak markers are the most popular xylene-based markers. It is always safest for the beginning student to start with alcohol markers.

As with color pencils, a set of 24 markers is good for starters. In comparison with pencils, markers are very expensive. In some cases, beginning students prefer to start by purchasing individual markers in a range of green (although many other colors will be used).

## Gray Markers

Gray markers generally come in a set of 12. They range in color from very light to black. Gray markers are used quite often to develop concrete and shadows.

The variations of gray markers include the following:

**French gray markers** are slightly yellowish red.

**Warm gray markers** are reddish.

**Cool gray markers** are bluish.

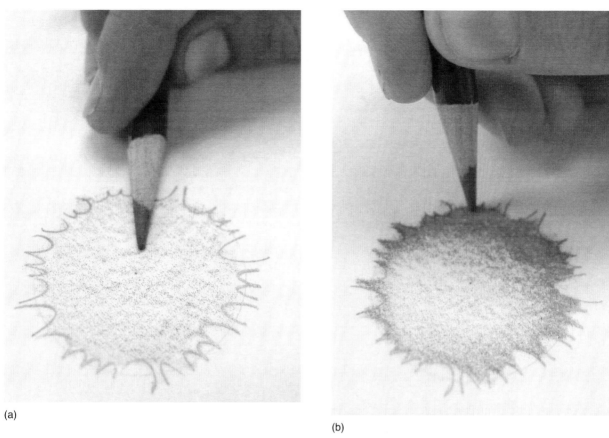

(a)

(b)

(c)

## *Figure 8-10* Symbol Color with Pencil

(a) Washing the symbol starts with an even value across the entire symbol. (b) Creating darker values on the shaded portion of the symbol (crescent shape). (c) Outlining the symbol with black pencil for definition.

*Figure 8-11* **Bleeding and Layering**
Applying a wash of marker while it is still wet will bleed and blend the stripes together. Once the wash dries, another layer of the same marker will create a much darker value. The area on the left was completely dried before the marker was reapplied, as opposed to the area on the right that was reapplied while the wash was still wet.

# Bleeding

Markers have a tendency to **bleed.** As a stroke is made, color can creep away from the original line. The degree of bleeding depends on the type of marker and paper being used. Bleeding is useful when blending lines together. While the line is still wet, the line drawn right next to it will bleed into it and blend (Figure 8-11).

If the line is allowed to dry before another is drawn next to it, the lines will not blend together but tend to layer and look more like two separate lines. However, layering can be a good technique to develop darker value.

## Blender

A **blender** is a transparent marker that contains no dye. It is used to help blend two colors by bleeding them together with the alcohol carrier of the blender.

## Layering

While the wash is wet, going back over it with the same marker will help blending, since it is bleeding together. Once the wash has dried, **layering** back over it with the same marker will create much darker value, which can be helpful in defining the perimeter.

## Scratch Paper

Markers have a tendency to bleed through the drawing, so have **scratch paper** underneath to avoid staining the desk (Figure 8-12).

# Color Development of the Ground Plane

## Wash

Wash the area with a selected color. Start on one side and make steady, even strokes that allow the marker to bleed into the paper. If the stroke is too quick, it will show uneven, light color (Figure 8-13a).

Do not allow the lines to dry before applying the next stroke. Each stroke should be made while still wet to allow them to blend together and minimize striping. Striping also occurs when markers get old or lose their charge and do not effectively bleed into the paper.

## Define Perimeter

Layering the same marker once the area has dried can darken the value around the outline. Go around the perimeter in short strokes to increase the value. By feathering the end of the stroke, you can blend the perimeter nicely (Figure 8-13b).

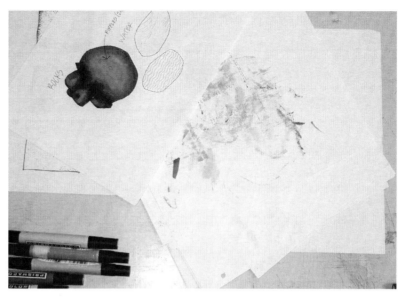

***Figure 8-12* Scratch Paper**
Use scratch paper under the plan being colored with marker, so that it does not bleed through onto the desk.

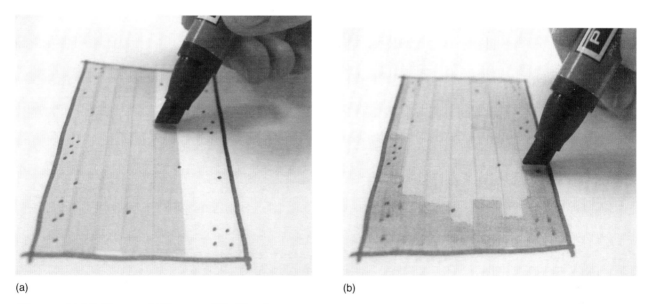

(a)  (b)

***Figure 8-13* Ground Plane with Markers**
(a) Begin by washing area with light color. (b) Define perimeter with short strokes that blend with wash.

## Additional Development

The ground plane can also be further developed with other colors. By abstractly developing the area, you can use random strokes that are not blended with wash layer. This can create an interesting pattern.

# Color Development of Symbols

## Color

As mentioned in the section on color pencils, the number of greens should be limited. Choose a green color to develop the symbol. Not all symbols have to be colored with green. Other colors can be used to add some variation. This is especially appropriate for specimen plants. Using color can also highlight foliage or flowering color of a particular plant.

## Wash

Evenly wash the symbol (Figure 8-14a). Be careful to start the lines just inside of the symbol outline to allow for bleeding. Also, be sure to work continuously while the lines are wet, so that bleeding can help blend the lines together.

Once the wash is complete, go back over the symbol to create a darker value and develop a crescent shadow (Figure 8-14b). After the symbol has dried, layering the shadow side of the symbol will increase the darker values.

## Shadows

To develop shadows, the easiest approach is to use a gray marker (Figure 8-14c). This will lend a darker value to the ground plane colors. Black markers blot out the ground plane.

## Outline

Outline the symbol with a black marker to define it (Figure 8-14d). Wait until the colors have dried before outlining with black, or else the black marker will bleed into the symbol. Use a thicker outline to lift the symbol higher in the air.

## Highlights

**Pencil Highlights**   For **pencil highlights,** use color pencils over markers (Figure 8-15). Once a symbol has been colored with markers, use pencils for detail. This works great for radial needle symbols. However, avoid using markers over pencils because they will not cover the waxy line of the pencil.

**Stippling Highlights**   Another unique approach is to **stipple** the symbol for texture. Once the wash is complete, use one or two colors of green and stipple the crescent shape of the shadow instead of shading (Figure 8-16).

# Overhead Symbols with Color

When coloring a symbol with other symbols or detail underneath, poor technique can make a mess. It's always best to keep your color development simple to avoid confusion.

## Color Only Overhead Symbol

One approach is to color only the overhead symbol and let the detail below read from the lines only (see color plate). Some color can be added, but too much, especially for the beginner, can become a problem.

## Color Only Underneath Detail

The opposite approach is also effective—that is, do not color the overhead symbol but, instead, the plan detail underneath (see color plate). To be effective, this technique should be different from the techniques covered in this chapter. In order to lift the overhead canopy so that it reads clearly, color the underneath detail with a washed-out, or flat, technique. Color without any range of detail and lighter than the coloring outside the overhead symbol. This causes the overhead symbol to lift off the ground plane because the detail underneath contrasts with the detail outside the overhead canopy and seems as if the viewer is looking *through* the overhead canopy to see it.

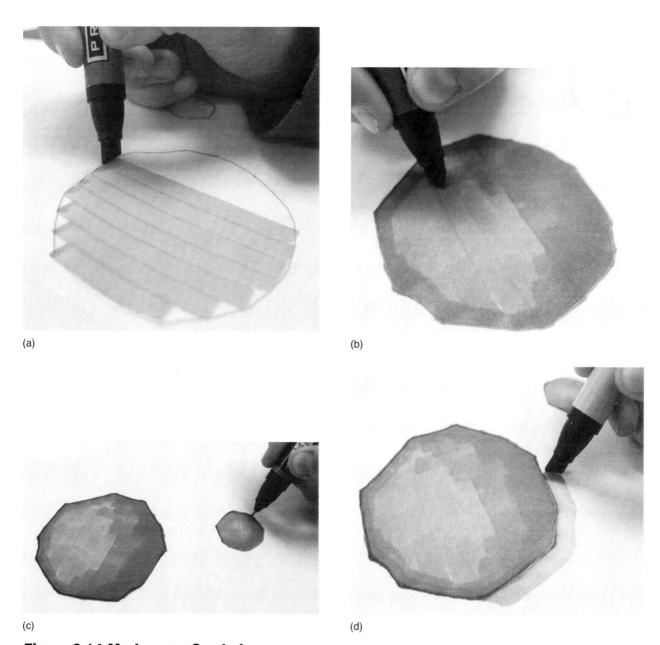

(a)

(b)

(c)

(d)

### *Figure 8-14* **Markers on Symbols**

(a) Start with a wash of the entire symbol. (b) Layer the shaded portions of the symbol. (c) Outline the symbol with black once all the colors have dried to avoid bleeding into the symbol. (d) Shadows can be applied with a gray marker using the chisel tip to get a good, quick shape.

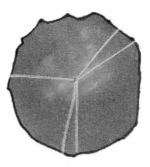

***Figure 8-15*** **Pencil Highlights**
Pencil can be used over marker for an accent.

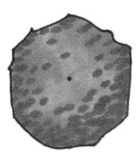

***Figure 8-16*** **Stippling Highlights**
Use a marker to stipple over wash for a different texture.

# Summary

Color rendering the plan drawing can make a more visually captivating presentation. Color on a copy of the plan drawing, never on the original. For beginning students, color pencils and sticks are the easiest tools to use, as well as the most economical. Starting with a set of 24 color pencils will be adequate; however, consider purchasing additional varieties of green. Color markers are another option for the beginning student. They are more difficult to use as well as much more expensive. It does take a lot of practice to learn how to blend effectively. Markers and pencils can be combined to create interesting effects. With either technique, broadening the range of value (lightness or darkness of a color) will improve it.

# Key Words

**Bleed:** a marker can creep away from the original line; this is useful when blending lines together.

**Blender:** transparent marker that contains no dye; it is used to help blend two colors by bleeding them together with the alcohol carrier of the blender.

**Color pencils:** similar to drawing pencils but contain a wax-based material instead of lead.

**Color sticks:** waxy, 1/4"-thick square sticks.

**Cool gray markers:** bluish color.

**Design Spectracolor:** brand of color pencils and markers.

**Flattened position:** holding the pencil in a flattened position uses the side of the pencil and applies a color smoothly without lines.

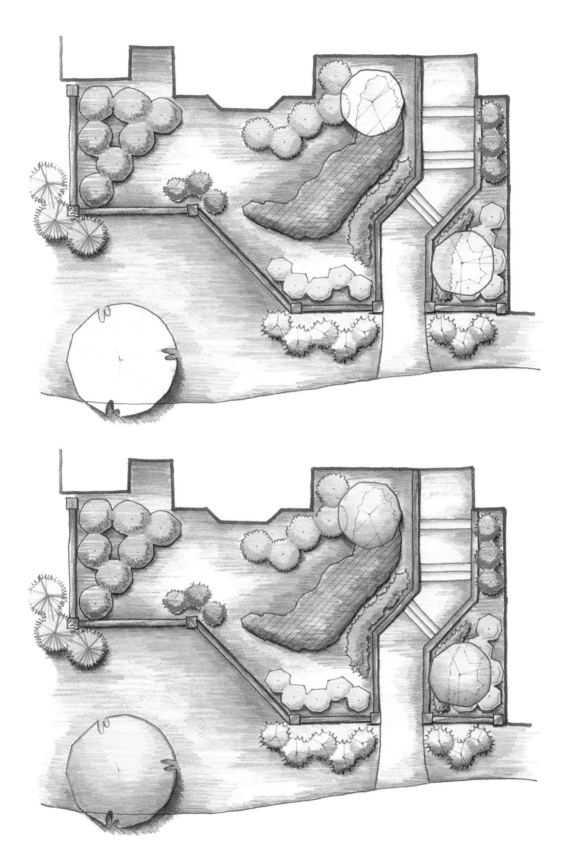

**PENCIL**
**Color on overhead symbols. Leave overhead symbols blank and just wash detail underneath (top) or color overhead symbols only (bottom)**

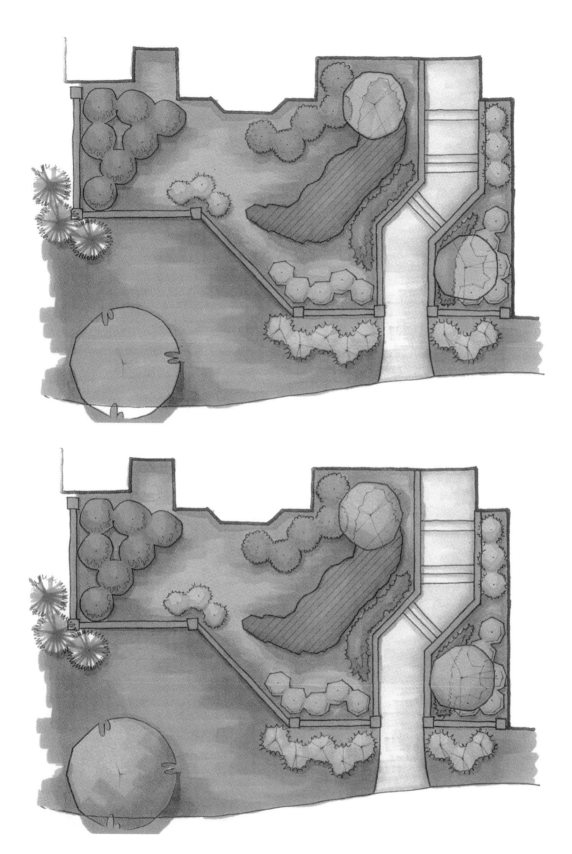

**MARKER**
**Color on overhead symbols. Leave overhead symbols blank and just wash detail underneath (top) or color overhead symbols only (bottom)**

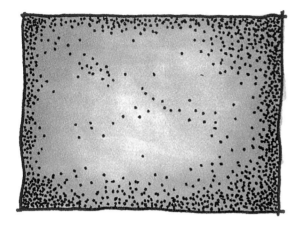

**Turf Texture with Marker**

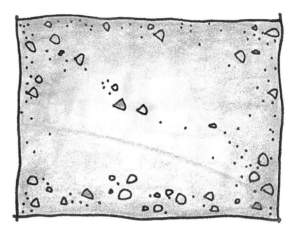

**Concrete Texture with Marker and Color Pencil**

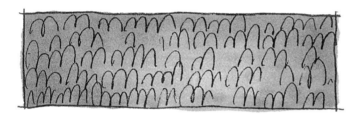

**Groundcover Texture with Marker**

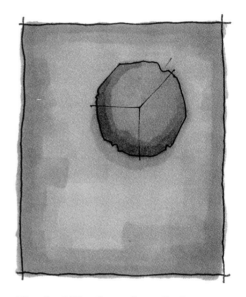

**Alcohol Marker: One Color (Layered)**

**Mulch Texture with Marker**

**Alcohol Marker: One Color (Layered)**

**Xylene Marker: One Color (Layered)**

**Alcohol Marker: One Color (Layered)**

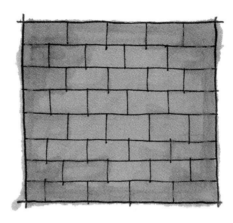

**Xylene Marker: One Color (Layered)**

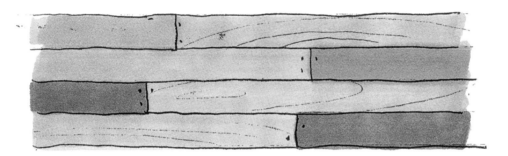

**Wood Texture with Marker**

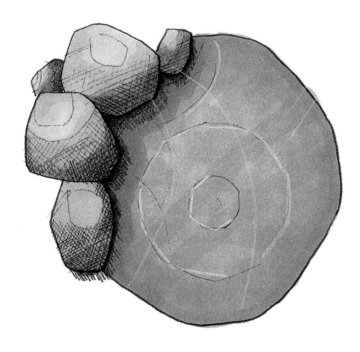

**Xylene Marker: One Color (Layered)**

**Water Texture with Marker and Color Pencil**

**Pencil: One Color**

**Pencil: Three Colors**

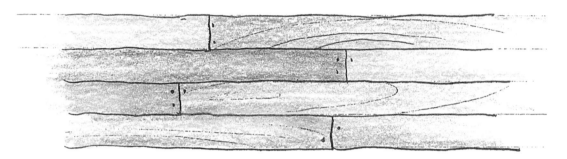

**Wood Texture with Color Pencil**

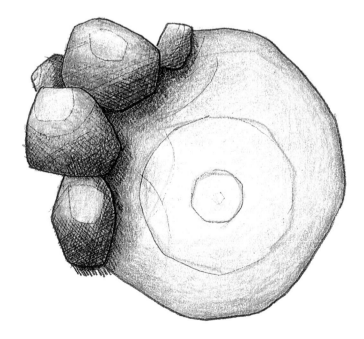

**Pencil: Three Colors**

**Water Texture with Color Pencil**

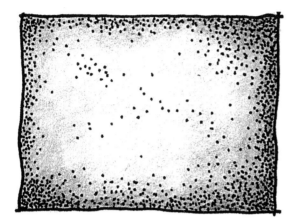

**Turf Texture with Color Pencil**

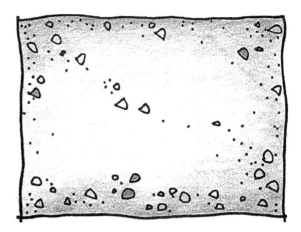

**Concrete Texture with Color Pencil**

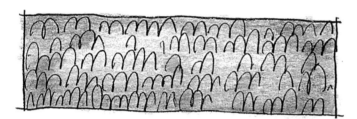

**Groundcover Texture with Color Pencil**

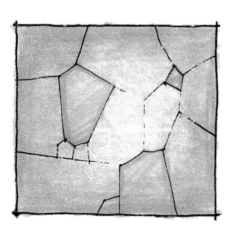

**Mulch Texture with Color Pencil**

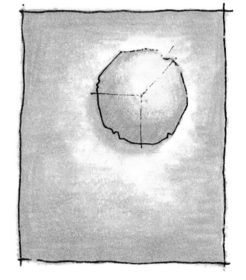

**Pencil: One Color**

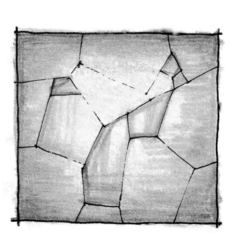

**Pencil: One Color**

**Pencil: Three Colors**

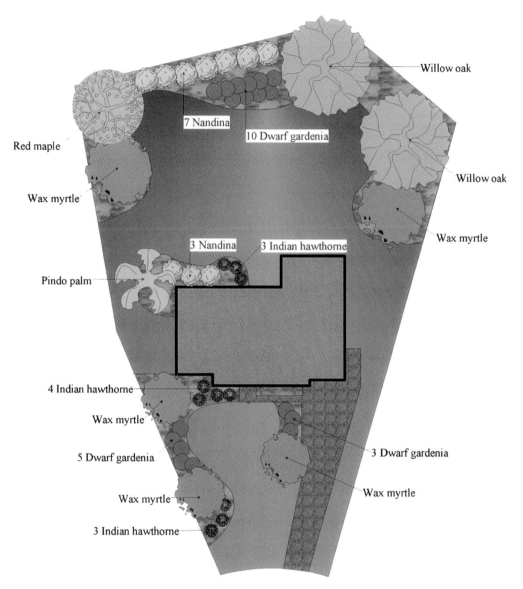

Willow oak

7 Nandina

10 Dwarf gardenia

Red maple

Willow oak

Wax myrtle

Wax myrtle

3 Nandina    3 Indian hawthorne

Pindo palm

4 Indian hawthorne

Wax myrtle

5 Dwarf gardenia

3 Dwarf gardenia

Wax myrtle

Wax myrtle

3 Indian hawthorne

**Plan Color Rendered with Software**

**Plan Colored with Pencil with Good Range of Value
and Defined Perimeters**

**Plan Colored with Pencil that Lacks Range of Value**

**Symbols Colored with Color Pencil**

**Symbols Colored with Marker**

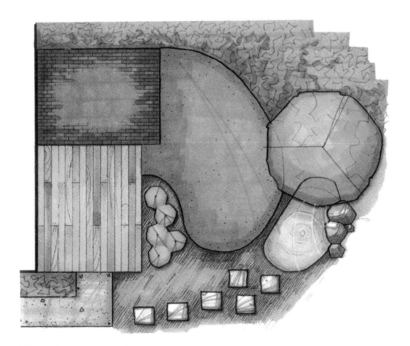

**Plan Colored with Marker**

**French gray markers:**   slightly yellowish red color.

**Layering:**   going back over color with the same marker to help blend together.

**Markers:**   have a chisel tip for wide and narrow lines; initially, the lines are wet but, because they are alcohol-based, they dry quickly.

**Moving line:**   technique that can be used in large areas; a quick, slashing line can be struck across the area to lend motion and interest.

**Pastels:**   chalky medium.

**Pencil highlights:**   using color pencils over markers.

**Rhythmic stroke:**   hint of the direction to shading.

**Sanford Prismacolor:**   brand of color pencils and markers.

**Scratch paper:**   markers will bleed through the drawing, so have scratch paper underneath to avoid staining the desk.

**Shade:**   darker value of a color.

**Stipple:**   place dots with a marker over the symbol to develop texture.

**Tint:**   lighter value of a color.

**Upright position:**   provides more "bite" between pencil and paper.

**Value of color:**   degree of darkness or lightness.

**Warm gray markers:**   reddish color.

**Washing:**   light, even value across the entire area.

# 9 Section Drawing

## Objectives

- Understand the purpose of section drawing
- Know how to locate a section drawing on the plan drawing
- Learn to draw the elements of a section drawing
- Learn to draw trees, shrubs, grass, and human figures in section drawings

The plan drawing is useful for organizing space on the ground plane. However, its lack of vertical dimensions limits the visualization of the finished product. Someone viewing the plan drawing, who has little knowledge of plant material, will have difficulty picturing the design.

Section drawings present a realistic view of the design by presenting a picture of it—horizontally *and* vertically. This allows anyone to see elements of the design that are difficult to perceive in the plan drawing.

## Vertical Elements

**Section drawings** illustrate how the **vertical dimensions** create balance and flow, much like the horizontal dimensions in the plan drawing (Figure 9-1). Certain objects do not read well on the plan drawing, such as retaining walls and fences.

### Form

Trees and shrubs are unique in their **form** and texture. Form can be described as the outline, or mass, of plants and objects. **Section-elevations** illustrate the variations of each plant with the canopy outlines, branching, and foliage.

### Spatial Relationships

How is space experienced? Section drawings show areas of enclosure, circulation, and resting.

### Views

Section drawings show how views are directed toward focal points or how favorable views are created and framed. A section drawing also illustrates how unsightly areas are screened from view.

### Topography

Section drawings show existing grade or grade changes.

## Locating a Section Drawing on the Plan Drawing

A section drawing is created from a plan drawing as if the plan were sliced open with a knife and viewed along that cut line from the side (see Figure 9-1). The section drawing is indicated on the plan drawing by the cut line (Figure 9-2). To indicate the direction in which the section is being viewed, arrows are drawn at each end of the cut line.

When there is more than one section drawing, the cut line is identified with letters on both ends. For example, the first section may be identified as section A-A. Some drawings can simply be labeled if they are easily recognizable.

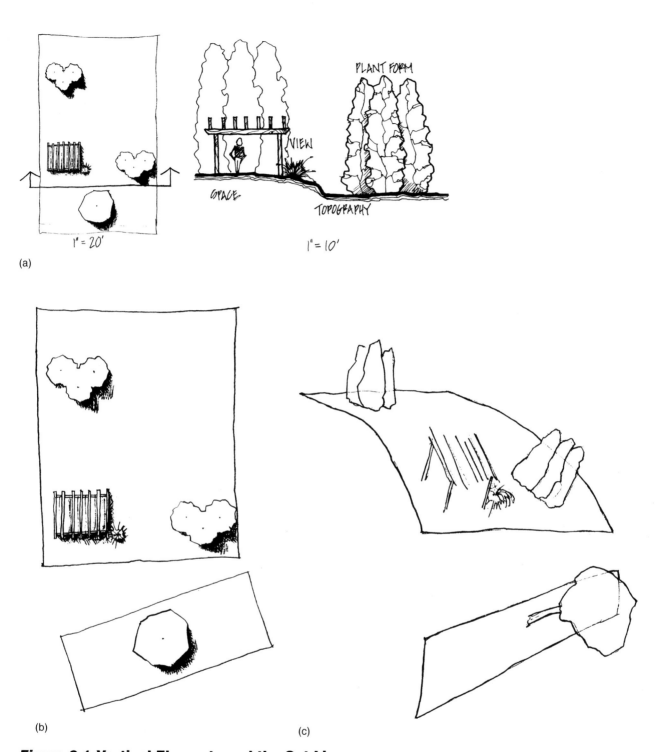

PLANT FORM

VIEW

GRADE

TOPOGRAPHY

1" = 20'

1" = 10'

(a)

(b)                    (c)

## *Figure 9-1* **Vertical Elements and the Cut Line**

(a) The section drawing shows the columnar form of trees and the weeping form of the ornamental grass, the steep grade change, and the wood construction of the arbor. (b and c) The **cut line** acts as if the plan were cut along that line and then viewed from the side.

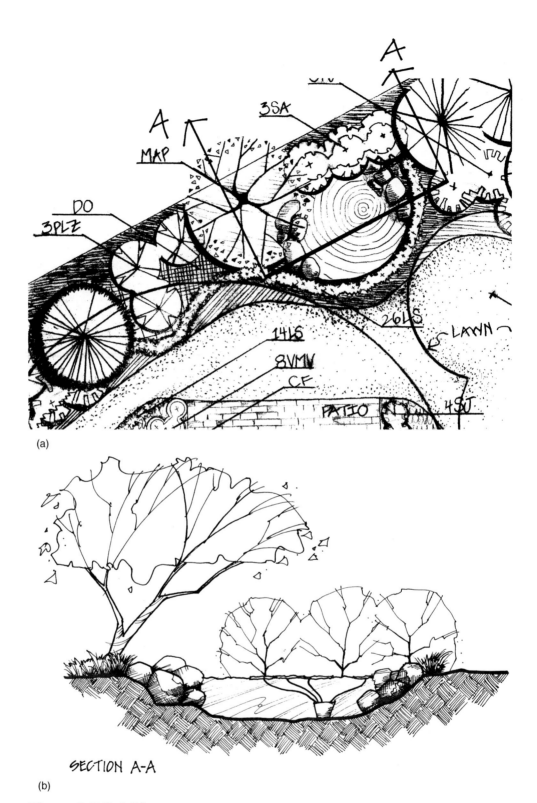

(a)

(b)

SECTION A-A

**_Figure 9-2_ Cut Line**
(a) The arrows on the cut line show the direction of view. The cut line runs through the pond, (b) so the section view illustrates the ground line running under the water. *(Plan drawing by Courtney Smith)*

A true section drawing shows only what is located on the cut line and nothing beyond it (Figure 9-3). Section drawings are used to illustrate architecture and construction details, but not necessarily landscapes.

# Section-Elevation

In a section-elevation, objects beyond the cut line are included to add a sense of depth (Figure 9-4). The number of objects to include is determined by the illustrator. Including too many items will clutter up the drawing.

## Elements of the Section-Elevation

### Ground Line

The **ground line** indicates the ground surface. It is drawn with the heaviest line weight in the drawing to create balance with a solid base. The ground line should be drawn with a 1/8″ to 1/4″ round tip or chisel point marker (Figure 9-5). The ground below should be hatched or supported with thinner lines to help ground the drawing as well as indicate the solidity of material beneath it.

### Scale

Draw all the objects to scale to give an accurate representation of the design (see Figures 9-1 and 9-6). This does not necessarily have to be the same scale as the plan drawing. Most drawings are going to be in the neighborhood of 1″ = 10′; however, the amount of the design and material will dictate the appropriate scale. The designer needs to adjust it appropriately. In sections that illustrate construction details, the scale may be much larger (1″ = 1′). A quick way to establish scale is use the plan as a reference in the same (Figure 9-7).

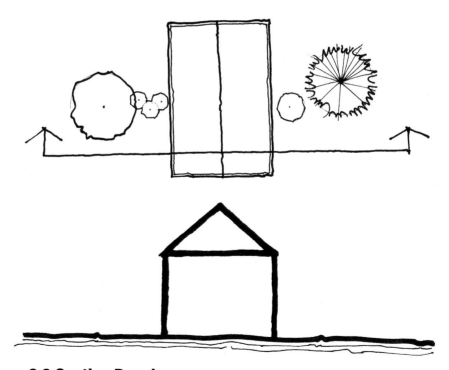

***Figure 9-3* Section Drawing**
A true section drawing shows only what occurs directly on the cut line. It is typically used to show construction details.

### Figure 9-4 Section-Elevation

A section-elevation drawing shows objects that occur beyond the cut line. It is typically used to illustrate landscape designs.

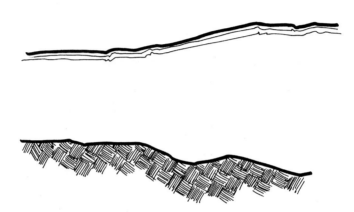

### Figure 9-5 Ground Line

The ground line indicates the ground surface, whether soil, turf, or concrete. It is illustrated as the heaviest line in the drawing.

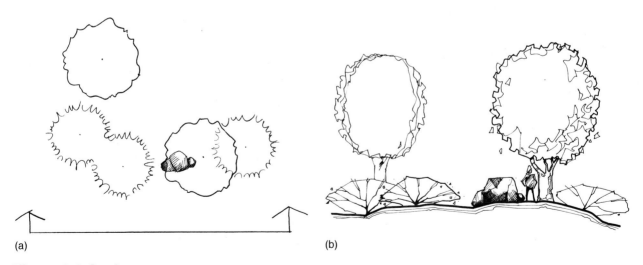

(a)                                                           (b)

### Figure 9-6 Scale

All the objects are drawn to the same scale, regardless of how far away they appear. (a) The plan illustrates the cut line for the section-elevation. (b) In this drawing, the tree in the back is the same as the one in the front. It is drawn to the same scale, but lighter line weight and lack of detail cause it to appear farther back in the section-elevation.

### *Tip Box:* Quick Section-Elevation

An easy way to draw a quick section-elevation with accurate property scale is to lay paper over the plan and draw it directly from the symbols.

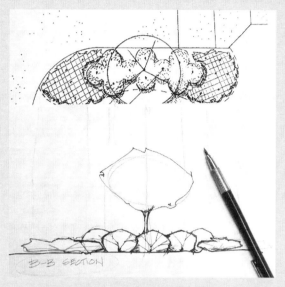

**Figure 9-7 Quick Section-Elevation**

### *Tip Box:* Quick Perspectives (Figure 9-8)

Perspective drawings are much more difficult to draw than section-elevations. A perspective involves vanishing points and depth of field, which require a lot of time to set up and draw adequately. One way to draw a quick perspective is to trace the house from a picture, then add landscaping. Digital pictures work well because they can be printed at larger sizes to give sufficient detail.

**Figure 9-8 Quick Perspective**
Trace over a picture to get a quick perspective sketch.

## Drawing Vertical Elements

In the section-elevation, all vertical elements are drawn to the same scale, regardless of how far away from the cut line they appear. To get a feeling of depth, the objects can be illustrated with line weight and detail (see Figures 9-6 and 9-9).

**Close Objects**     Objects appear closer by drawing them with heavier line weight and more detail. This will make objects "come forward" in the section drawing. Use ink or HB lead. Detail is added to objects as well, such as additional foliage to trees or additional texture to rocks, tree trunks, and buildings.

**Midrange and Distant Objects**     Objects appear farther away by drawing them with lighter line weight and little to no detail. This causes objects to "recede." Use a 2H lead and only general outlines.

## Plants

You do not have to create a realistic drawing of plants but, rather, capture the form and texture of the plant (Figure 9-10 through Figure 9-15). It is important to represent an accurate depiction of the plants. For example, some trees have a strong central leader, such as sweetgums, as opposed to trees that do not, such as linden trees. Reflecting the branching patterns as well as the shape of the canopies gives a more accurate portrait of the design.

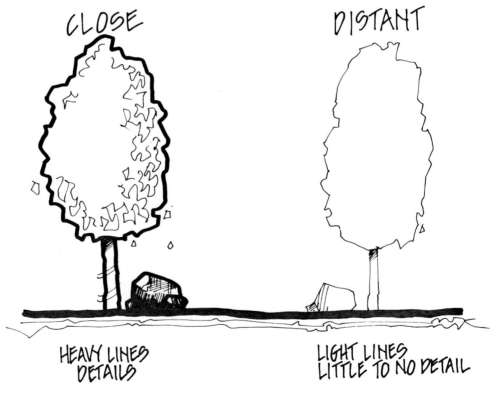

**Figure 9-9 Drawing Depth**
Objects appear closer by drawing them with heavier line weight and more detail. Conversely, objects appear farther away by drawing them with lighter line weight and less detail.

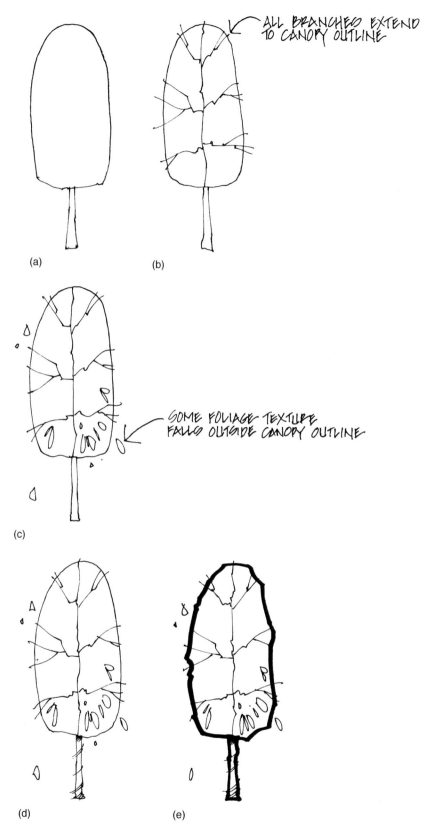

ALL BRANCHES EXTEND
TO CANOPY OUTLINE

(a)

(b)

SOME FOLIAGE TEXTURE
FALLS OUTSIDE CANOPY OUTLINE

(c)

(d)

(e)

***Figure 9-10*** **Drawing Trees**

(a) Begin with a simple outline. (b) Every branch should extend to the canopy outline. (c) Foliage texture can be added, with some foliage outside of the canopy to simulate movement. (d) Trunk detail is added. (e) Heavy outline defines the object and brings it forward.

(a)

***Figure 9-11* Trees**
(a) Outlines.

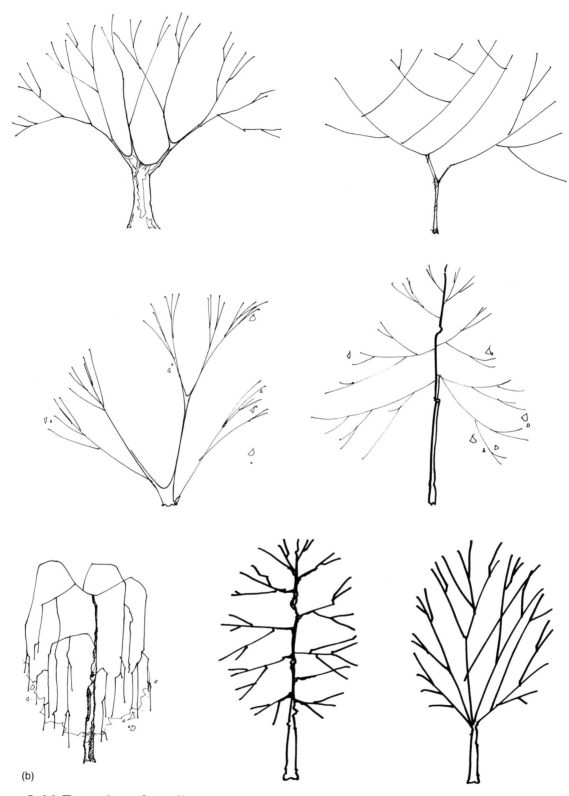

**(b)**

***Figure 9-11*** **Trees (continued)**
(b) Branched.

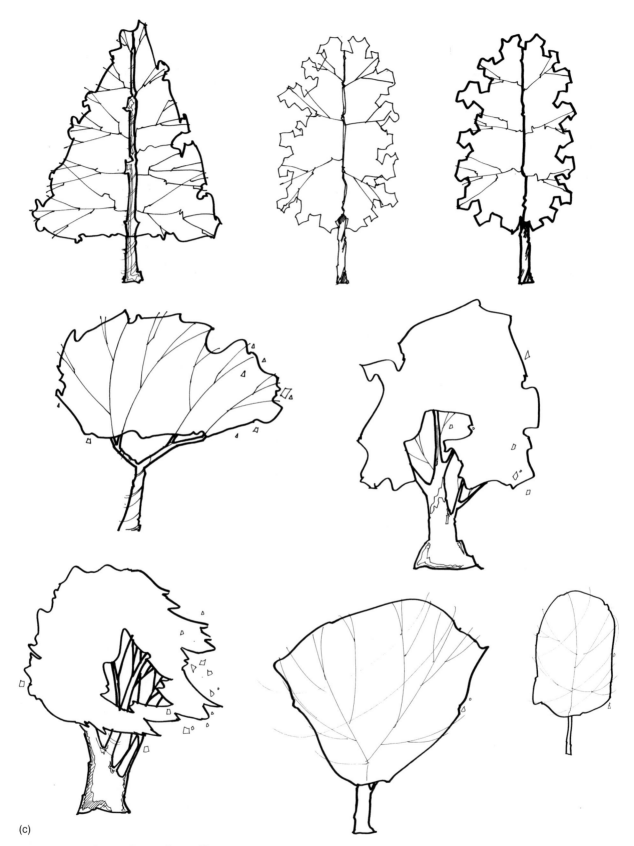

***Figure 9-11* Trees (continued)**
(c) Branched and outlined.

(c)

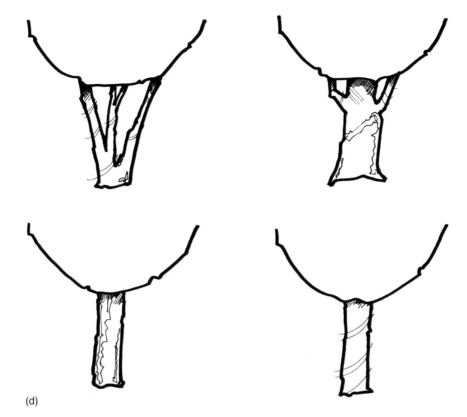

(d)

***Figure 9-11*** **Trees (continued)**
(d) Trunks.

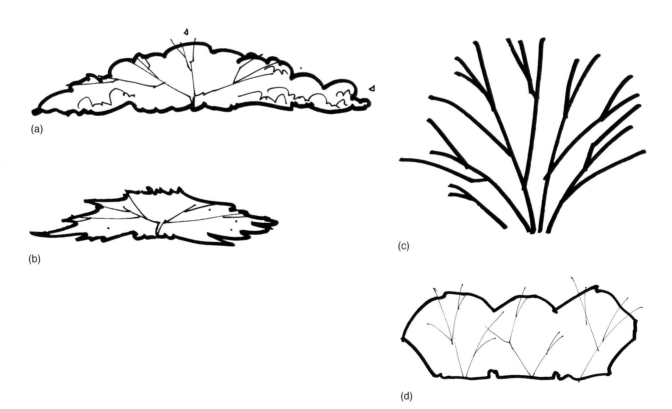

***Figure 9-12*** **Shrubs**

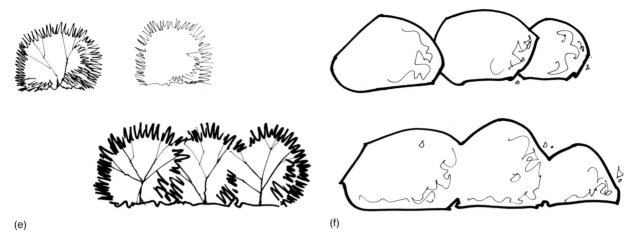

(e)

(f)

*Figure 9-12* **Shrubs (continued)**

(b)

(a)

(c)

*Figure 9-13* **Ornamental Grasses**

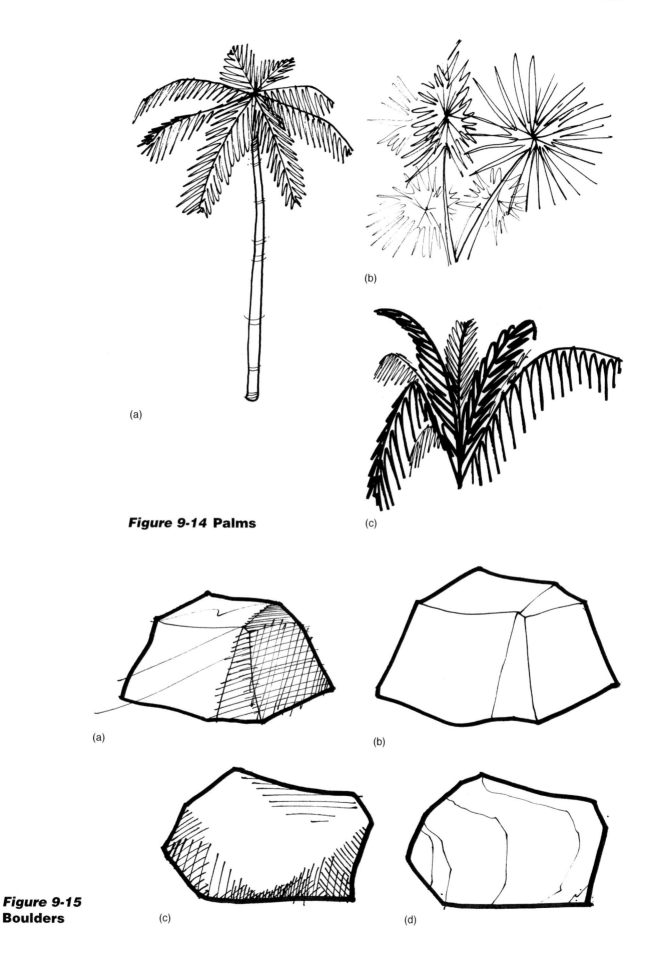

**Figure 9-14** Palms

(a)

(b)

(c)

**Figure 9-15**
**Boulders**

(a)

(b)

(c)

(d)

***Figure 9-16* Human Proportions**
The head is about one-eighth the entire body. The upper torso, in addition to the head, makes up about half the entire body, while the lower torso makes up the other half.

## People

Human figures provide a sense of scale. Although trees can vary from 10′ to 100′ tall, an average adult is typically about 5′ to 6′ tall. An observer can easily assimilate the size of the materials around the figures.

The most important feature is the correct proportion of head, torso, and legs (Figure 9-16). The amount of detail can vary from vague forms to facial features and clothing. The following general guidelines can be used:

### Head

*Size*: The head should be about 1/8 the entire body.

*Shape*: An oval shape appears more natural than a circle.

### Torso

*Size*: It should be slightly less than half the entire body, about three-eighths.

*Shape*: It varies from a square block to broad shoulders; with elbows located near the waist, the arms should extend halfway down the thighs.

### Legs

*Size*: They are half the entire body.

*Shape*: Legs taper slightly from waist to feet.

**Posing**    In the beginning, start by drawing figures that are facing forward, with hands on hips. Focus on the proportions and avoid details of clothing and facial features. After you become proficient with body proportions, try drawing figures in various positions. A natural appeal comes from figures assuming different postures and activities, such as talking or pointing. Observe pictures of people to get ideas of different poses.

# Summary

Plan drawings show the horizontal elements of the design, while section drawings illustrate the vertical elements of the design. Section drawings present views, topography, and forms that cannot otherwise be seen on the plan. They are created from a plan drawing as if the plan had been sliced, or sectioned, and viewed from the side. Sections are more accurately described as section-elevations because they illustrate objects that are beyond the cut line. All objects are drawn to scale without any changes in size like a perspective drawing. Instead, depth of the drawing is illustrated by drawing close objects with heavier line weight and more detail, while distant objects are drawn with lighter line weight and less detail. Human figures are generally included in section drawings to create a sense of scale. Because human figures are typically about 5 to 6 feet tall, elements around them can be viewed in comparison with the figure.

# Key Words

**Cut line:**   indicates where the section-elevation is located on the plan drawing and the direction in which it is viewed.

**Form:**   outline, or total mass, of plants and objects.

**Ground line:**   indicates the ground surface; it is drawn with the heaviest line weight in the drawing.

**Section drawings:**   show only what is located on the cut line and nothing beyond it; they are used to illustrate architecture and construction details and not necessarily landscapes.

**Section-elevations:**   unlike section drawings, include objects beyond the cut line.

**Vertical dimensions:**   much as the plan drawing illustrates the width of elements, section drawings show the height, or vertical, characteristics.

# 10 Computer Graphics

## Objectives
- Learn the uses of imaging and plan drawing software in landscape design
- Become familiar with basic techniques and tools of design software

## Brief History of Computer Graphics

Computer-aided design systems are referred to as CAD. **AutoCAD** is a software program that allows the user to draw lines, arcs, and circles. However, earlier versions of AutoCAD lacked a symbol library for landscape designers. Thus, **LANDCADD**, released in 1984, evolved from AutoCAD to include numerous symbols and applications that related to landscape design, irrigation, estimation, and construction details. Larger companies, such as landscape architecture, engineering, or commercial landscaping, commonly use Auto-CAD or LANDCADD. But for many landscape designers these software programs are very expensive and difficult to learn.

Since the mid-1980s, software programs that included imaging, plan drawing, and estimators have evolved into applications that are easier to learn and more applicable for many landscape designers.

In addition to AutoCAD and LANDCADD, which have been the main platform for computer-aided design, there are several other landscape design programs on the market. Each of these programs has advantages and disadvantages, whether dealing with the quality of the finished product, ease of learning, size of the image database, or cost. Although they vary in methodology and content, there are three basic components of landscape design software that will be discussed in this chapter: imaging, plan drawing, and estimator.

Only high-quality design software should be purchased. It is much better than the software that is sold at a local store for less than $50. Although inexpensive, these programs are limited in their applications, quality, and database of images. For a landscape designer, the professional-grade software offers a wide range of applications and high-quality prints, in addition to program and database upgrades.

This text does not intend to promote any of the products that are listed at the end of the chapter. They all have some outstanding qualities. But, regardless of which product is learned by the user, there are several common techniques used by each program. In this chapter, you will not learn how to use each program because the actual execution of the commands vary between products. Instead, you will get an idea of what the programs can do and what kind of finished products they create. If you decide to pursue design software, most products have very good tutorials that will walk you through the design process step-by-step.

Also, this chapter does not discuss the extent of what each program can do. What is described in this chapter is the basic approach to using design software.

## Advantages of Landscape Design Software

There are many advantages of using landscape design software.

## Design Tool

Some designers use software to help generate ideas; such as imaging software where plants can be inserted on a digital picture. In this way, a three-dimensional approach can be experimented with to get an accurate idea of the design.

## Efficiency

One reason many designers move to software is the efficiency of time. Once comfortable with software commands, a designer can quickly import a plat and lay out bedlines and symbols with a click of the mouse. In addition, changes can be made just as quickly by deleting and adding new symbols—no erasing, no redrawing.

## Presentation Tool

Before software, the only tools the designers had to develop a three-dimensional picture for the client was his or her ability to draw. Most clients cannot visualize a plan drawing because they are not familiar with reading plants and often do not know what material looks like. Here again, a picture of the site can be designed in a short amount of time and printed for the client to "see" the design.

## Cost

If there a disadvantage to design software, its cost. Good software can cost between $400 and $2,000, not to mention the cost of a computer, printer, and quality paper. Certainly, this investment would be recouped in time saved, but, compared with paper and pencil, it is a significant expenditure.

# Imaging Software

There are many graphic programs of professional caliber, such as Adobe Photoshop. Graphic programs allow the user to manipulate a photo by cutting and adjusting and coloring and cloning to improve or create a new image. The major difference between graphic programs and landscape design imaging programs is the database of plant images that will be added to the photo. Therefore, if a designer is familiar with many of the commands in Photoshop, he or she will adapt to a landscape imaging program with relative ease.

Landscape design **imaging** has been used to simulate landscape designs on an actual photo of the site. Older versions of imaging software often resulted in a photo with pictures of plants stuck on top like refrigerator magnets. Although this was helpful, it was not believable. Imaging software has advanced to the point that realistic photos of proposed designs can be easily created. As a result, a much more tangible product is created where clients see a picture of what they are purchasing instead of an artist's drawing. Rather than relying on descriptions and vague imagery to "paint" a picture of the design, a client sees what the actual plants and hardscape material look like. As a result, landscape designers can show their customers a more tangible product.

What are some of the reasons that have made imaging software for landscape design a viable product?

## Digital Images

**Digital images** of the site can be captured with a digital camera and immediately downloaded to a computer. Imaging software opens the picture and designing the site takes place. (Film can still be used; however, it requires development and scanning, which is time-consuming and costly.) These digital images can be printed or e-mailed to the client.

## More Realistic Objects

Because databases are extremely large, most plant material as well as various objects can be found. The objects are also much larger in detail (better resolution).

## Printers

High-quality color printers are affordable, and high-quality paper creates a photo of the design that is exceptional.

## Special Effects

Certain effects have helped blend objects into the site photo. Two of these special effects are shadows and perspective.

### Shadows

As objects are inserted on the image, they can be rendered with shading and shadows falling on the ground. This makes images blend into the photo and no longer appear like pictures pasted on top.

### Perspective

In the past when a sidewalk or wall was filled with a texture, it appeared flat and lacked depth. Presently, objects are filled with texture to an accurate depth. The texture gets smaller with less detail as it appears farther back in the image.

# The Imaging Process and Techniques

Because imaging is a simplified process that creates an image of the landscape design, the actual technique used depends on the product.

## Acquire an Image (Photo) of the Site

When using a digital camera, take as many photos as possible while on site. Whatever photos you do not need can simply be deleted from the camera at a later time. If you are using film, the prints can be scanned.

### Most Important Angle

The most important angle is from the road and capturing the front of the house and most of the side yard. Most clients are interested in the design of the front of the house.

### What Is a File Format?

**File formats** are various ways images are stored and read by the computer. When saving an image, you can select the file format. The following are suffixes that attach to the end of the file name, along with their commonly used formats.

**JPEG (Joint Photographic Experts Group)**  The JPEG format offers more colors and continuous tones. It is good for saving photo images of the site. The files are relatively small and easy to e-mail.

**GIF (Graphics Interchange Format)**  GIF is good for images that require sharp boundaries, such as lettering or line drawings. Like JPEG, GIF takes little memory.

**BMP (Bitmap)**  BMP is Microsoft Windows' native image format. This format will open in the Paint program, which is part of Windows. However, the files are very large.

**TIFF (Tag Image File Format)**   TIFF is the standard format for the computer-based publishing industry. It opens in various software programs. Like BMP, these files are very large.

### File Size

One advantage of a smaller file is that more images can be carried on a floppy disk and sent via e-mail much more easily. Only a few, if any, large images can be carried on a floppy disk.

# Open the Image of the Site

Open the design imaging program and then open the photo of the site you will be designing. Various tools can be used for this step of the process.

### Cropping

A **cropping** tool allows you to select a portion of the photo and delete the rest (Figure 10-1). For example, if there is too much sky, it can be chopped out of the image.

Cropping tools work by dragging a selection box over an area you want to keep. Left-click and drag the selection box and then release to select. Once the selection is completed, the area outside of the box is eliminated.

### Brightness/Contrast and Sharpness

If the photo appears too dark in areas, the **brightness/contrast** can be increased to show the details of shaded areas (Figure 10-2). Some software programs even have the capability to improve the **sharpness** and quality of the photo.

### Cloning

**Cloning** is a very useful tool that has endless applications. For example, it can be used to erase existing plants or other objects in the image (Figure 10-3).

(a)                                                                        (b)

***Figure 10-1* Cropping Tool**
(a) The *cropping tool* will cut out part of the image. The box around the house will crop the image like a cookie cutter. (b) The image after it has been cropped. *(Courtesy of Dorchester Habitat for Humanity: photos edited in Visual Impact Software)*

(a)                                                    (b)

***Figure 10-2*** **Brightness/Contrast**
(a) This image is too dark in areas. (b) The *brightness/contrast tool* is used to lighten the image. *(Photos edited in Visual Impact Software)*

Cloning operates by "painting" with textures from the image itself. Most cloning tools have two cursors: a *texture* box and an *apply* box. When the mouse is clicked and held, whatever appears in the texture box will be *painted onto the image* in the apply box.

Using this tool, one can place the texture box on the lawn and apply the turf texture over existing objects. This is very effective because it uses the textures as they actually appear in the image, rather than using a texture from the database that does not match.

## Viewing

The whole image of the site may be large and easy to work with when importing trees and shrubs. However, there may be detail work that requires zooming in on areas of the image. This can be accomplished in most programs by using the **zoom tool.**

One of the most convenient tools is the **zoom box** (see Figure 10-3). This is a done by dragging a selection box over an area. Whatever is inside the zoom box will increase in size. Unlike the cropping tool, the image is still intact and can be zoomed out to see the whole image again.

# Use the Image Database

Most programs will have an **image database** of objects and textures, often referred to as a **library** (Figure 10-4). The library organizes these objects into categories, such as trees, shrubs, grass, sidewalks, and driveways. Images can be viewed, then placed onto the photo.

The database contains a large number of objects that serve designers in all parts of the country. In comparison with the large number of items contained in the database, only a small number of the objects will need to be accessed. To avoid having to search through numerous images, a **customized library** can often be created with the most frequently used objects and textures.

Some programs give users the ability to add their own objects to the database. The user can download a picture of a plant or texture and use the image like any of the other objects in the library.

(a)

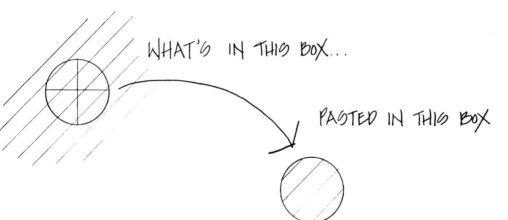

(b)

(c)                                                              (d)

### *Figure 10-3* Cloning Tool and Zoom Box

(a) The *cloning tool* will be used to erase the dog from the image. First, the *zoom box* is used to zoom in around the dog. (b and c) The *cloning tool* will copy the turf texture in the image and paste it over the dog. (d) Zooming back out to see the entire image, the dog has been completely erased. *(Photos edited in Visual Impact Software)*

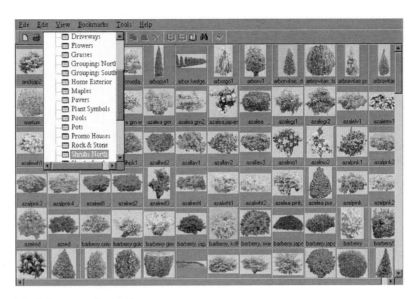

***Figure 10-4*** **Image Database**
A database of objects that is used to paste images of trees, shrubs, grass, and other items.
*(Photo edited in Visual Impact Software)*

# Move and Manipulate Objects

Objects can be moved and manipulated in a variety of ways.

## Grabbing

**Grabbing** an object refers to clicking and holding on an object in order to move it. When the left button is released, the object will be "dropped." Once placed, it can always be selected and moved again if needed.

## Sizing

Once an object is placed on the site, it can be changed in size and proportion (Figure 10-5). A sizing box appears with handles on the top and sides of the object. Grabbing one of the corner handles and moving it will proportionally change the size of the object. For example, grabbing the top handle and pulling up will make the object taller but not wider.

## Distorting

A **distort** tool can be used to change the proportion of the object (Figure 10-6). In this case, the sizing box handles move independently of each other. This function can be used to create odd-shaped objects or, most important, to create perspective on ground plane objects.

## Duplicating

Once an object is sized and placed on the design, a **duplication** tool can be used to quickly copy the object numerous times (Figure 10-7). In many cases, the object can be copied with each click. This is very useful when creating a mass of shrubs.

## Layering

As objects are placed on the image, they stack up, like **layers** one on top of another (Figure 10-7). The objects can be moved from back to front so that they appear either behind or in front of each other. Commands such as Send to the Front bring the selected object all the way to the front, while Send to the Back sends it all the way to the back.

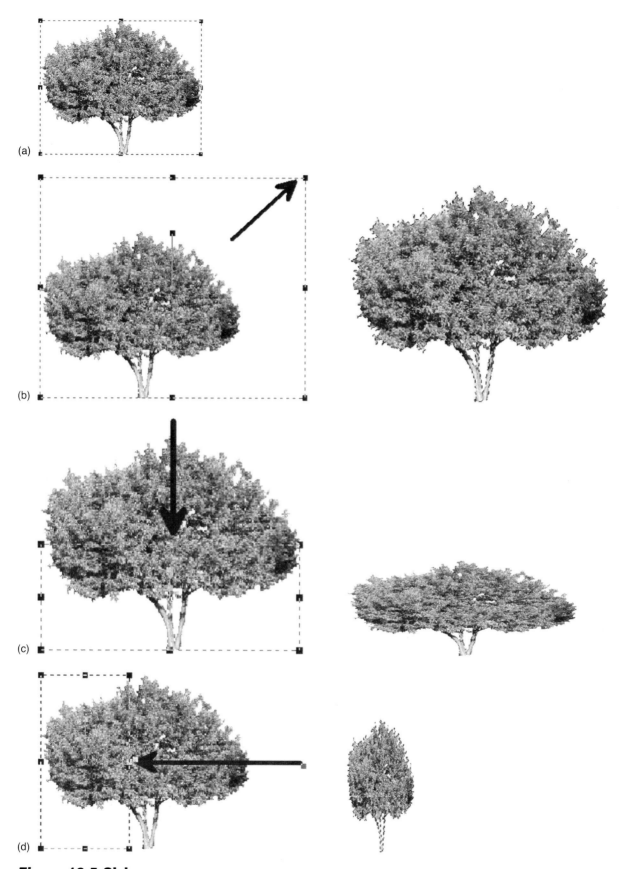

**Figure 10-5** Sizing

(a) Objects can be resized by grabbing and moving the handles on the box that appears around an object. (b) Objects can be made proportionately larger by pulling out the corner handle or proportionately smaller if the corner handle is pushed in. (c) Objects can be made shorter by pushing down the top handle or taller if the top handle is pulled up. (d) Objects can be made narrower by pushing in the side handle or wider if the side handle is pulled out. *(Photos edited in Visual Impact Software)*

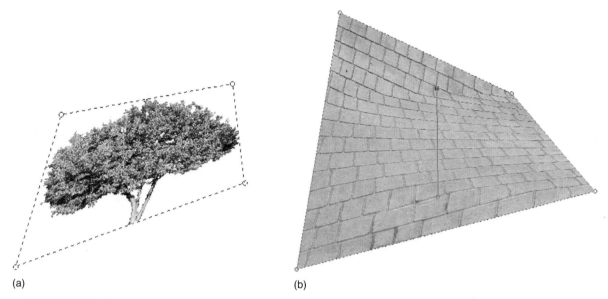

(a)                                      (b)

### *Figure 10-6* Distort

In this mode, all the sizing handles move independently of each other on any object, such as (a) a tree or (b) sidewalk. *(Photos edited in Visual Impact Software)*

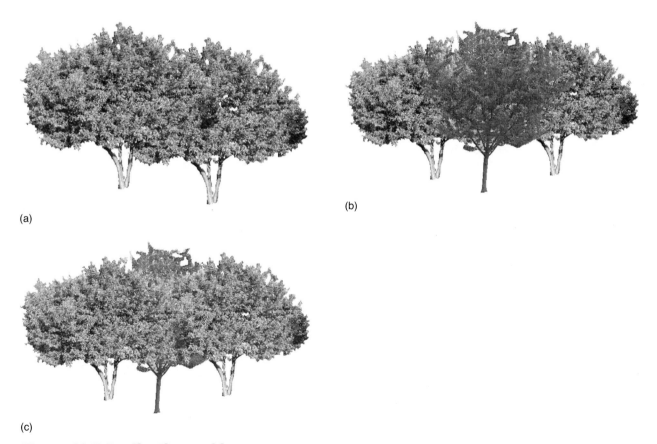

(a)

(b)

(c)

### *Figure 10-7* Duplicating and Layers

(a) The green tree has been duplicated to create two green trees. As objects are applied to the image of the site, they *layer* as if stacking them one on top of another and can be moved from front to back. (b) The tree in the center is in *front* of the other trees. (c) It can be moved *back,* or behind the other trees. *(Photos edited in Visual Impact Software)*

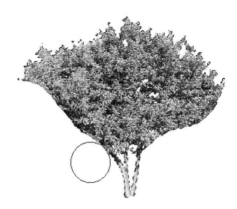

***Figure 10-8* Trim**

The *trimming tool* uses the cursor as an eraser to remove parts of an image. *(Photo edited in Visual Impact Software)*

## Trimming

Objects can be **trimmed** with a tool that acts as an eraser (Figure 10-8). Once the object to be trimmed is selected, the cursor can be used as an eraser. Clicking and holding the cursor will erase that portion of the image.

Trimming an object can be used to change the form of an object, such as trimming a tree so that it appears more vase-shaped or making shrubs appear more rounded. One favorite trick is to use the trimming tool to make an object, such as a tree, appear behind a house (Figure 10-9). This can be done by placing the tree at the corner of the house, then trimming away the tree along the edge of the house so that it appears as if the tree is behind the house.

## Shadows

As mentioned earlier in the chapter, one of the most effective tools for integrating objects into the site image is the use of shadows (Figure 10-10). Shadows lend a sense of depth and solidity to the object. The following is a quick technique for creating effective, realistic shadows.

**Duplicate the Object**   As light shines on an object, it creates a duplicate on the ground, which is skewed in proportion. This object will be turned into a shadow, then distorted to appear on the ground.

**Create the Shadow**   The duplicate of the object needs to be turned into a shadow. This can be accomplished in two steps. First, use a fill tool to fill the object with black color. The fill tool acts as if it is "filling" the selected object with a specific color.

**Create Transparency**   Turn the object, which is now solid black, into a semitransparent object. Without the transparency, the shadow will blot out any detail on the ground, which is not realistic. By using a **transparency tool,** the transparency of the object can be changed to any degree, such as 10% transparent (still very dark) to 90% transparent (nearly invisible). Set the transparency in the range of 60% to 70%.

**Place the Shadow**   Now that the shadow has been created, it needs to be placed in correct perspective. First, rotate the shadow-object on its side in the direction that the shadow will be falling. This can be accomplished with a sizing box. Second, rotate the shadow-object so that it "flattens" out and appears to be lying on the ground. This can be done by using the transforming tool, which distorts the shadow-object to the proper perspective. Once the proper perspective is achieved, move the shadow-object so that the bottoms of the objects meet.

To simulate the sun at a noon position in the sky, place the canopy of the shadow-object directly under the tree. Now the trim tool can be used to erase the trunk.

(a)

(b)

(c)

***Figure 10-9* Trimming**
(a) This tree can appear behind the house by (b) trimming away the tree so that (c) the house appears in front of the tree. *(Photos edited in Visual Impact Software)*

## Perspective

Object perspective is important to help create a realistic photo (Figure 10-11).

**Size**   To get an idea of the size of an object relative to where it is located in the landscape, use references found in the original photo. Generally, windows are 3′ wide and driveways are about 10′ to 12′ wide for single-car garages.

**Distance**   Objects that are closer to the observer are larger. To get some sense of perspective, when using the same tree up close and one closer to the house, size down the one farther away.

Objects farther away also have less detail than objects closer to the observer. When the object is farther away, use the **brightness contrast** tool to dull the image details.

# Creating the Ground Plane with Imaging

The ground plane consists of, but is not limited to, the following components: lawn, driveway, sidewalk, and mulch beds. Although there may be other elements that are created, these are the most common.

There are three main ways in which ground plane areas are created:

- Defining and filling an area with texture
- Ground plane objects

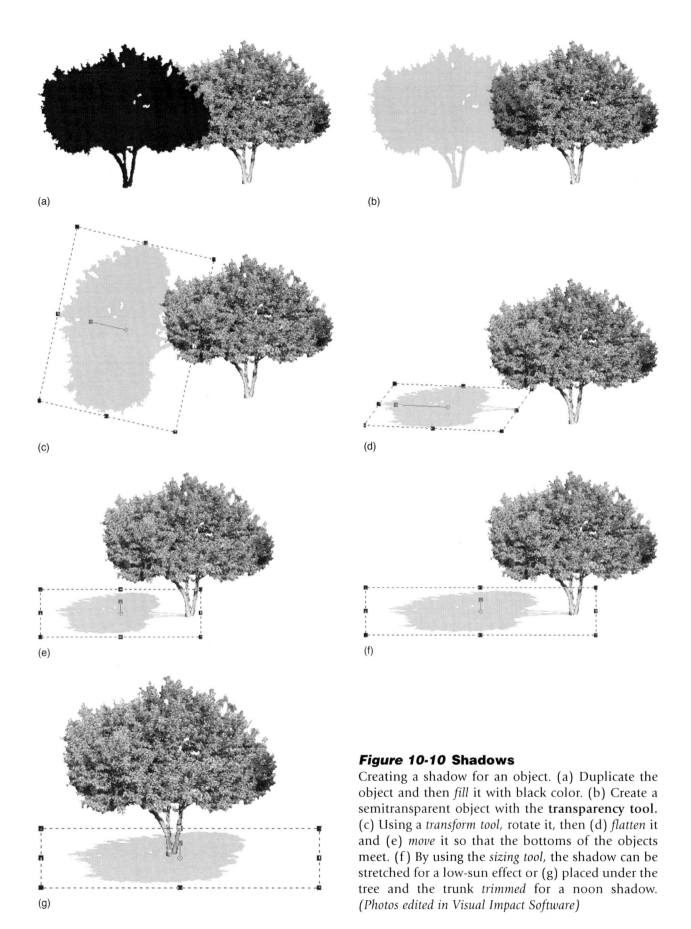

**Figure 10-10 Shadows**
Creating a shadow for an object. (a) Duplicate the object and then *fill* it with black color. (b) Create a semitransparent object with the **transparency tool.** (c) Using a *transform tool,* rotate it, then (d) *flatten* it and (e) *move* it so that the bottoms of the objects meet. (f) By using the *sizing tool,* the shadow can be stretched for a low-sun effect or (g) placed under the tree and the trunk *trimmed* for a noon shadow. *(Photos edited in Visual Impact Software)*

***Figure 10-11* Object Perspective**
As objects appear farther back in the image, reduce their size with the *sizing tool* and dampen the detail by darkening it with the *brightness contrast tool. (Photos edited in Visual Impact Software)*

(a)                                                  (b)

***Figure 10-12* Defining and Filling Area with Texture**
(a) Applying turf to the ground plane by first outlining the front yard. (b) This area can be *filled* with a *texture* (turf). *(Photos edited in Visual Impact Software)*

- Ground plane perspective is a sub-head of this one
- Painting with texture

## Defining and Filling an Area with Texture

With the mouse, use a defining tool to enclose an area and *fill* with a selected texture (Figure 10-12). Textures can be anything. The image database usually carries numerous textures of turf, pavers, concrete, and mulch. With an area selected, the **fill tool** is activated and the desired texture is selected.

Some programs create a perspective effect by making the texture appear finer toward the top of the defined area, thus making it appear farther away.

(a)

(b)

(c)

### *Figure 10-13* Ground Plane Objects

Using an object to create the driveway. (a) The driveway object is selected from the library. (b) The object is manipulated to fit the area by using the distort function. (c) The distort function is used until the object fits. *(Photos edited in Visual Impact Software)*

# Ground Plane Objects

**Ground plane objects** are found in an image database just as trees and shrubs are. The library may be organized to contain a section of walks, driveways, and lawns. Let's look at driveways as an example of how this works (Figure 10-13).

There may be several different types of driveway materials and shapes that appear as objects. Like other objects, one is selected and loaded onto the design. Chances are, the driveway is not going to fit the design. In this case, the object will need to be transformed. By using distort functions, the corners of the driveway can be moved independently until the object fits.

## Ground Plane Perspective

When objects such as a flagstone pathway are placed over the sidewalk, the image can appear flat because it is uniform in texture (Figure 10-14). Create a sense of perspective by *pinching* the top of the object (farther away from the observer), so that the texture is finer and coarser at the bottom (near the observer).

(a)

(b)

(c)

(d)

***Figure 10-14*** **Ground Plane Perspective**
(a) Objects such as this flagstone can have perspective applied to them by (b) *sizing* them so that the top appears pinched and smaller. (c) In this example, the object is placed over a defined area that acts as a cookie cutter (d) to fit the flagstone in the path. *(Courtesy of Joe Gibson: Photos edited in Visual Impact Software)*

## Painting with Texture

Textures are selected as discussed in the "defining:filling". A **painting tool** is used to apply the selected texture (Figure 10-15). The cursor now becomes a "paintbrush" and, whenever the mouse is clicked and held, the texture will be painted on the image.

## The Finished Product

Figures 10-16 through Figure 10-19 illustrate steps to a finished product.

Once the design is complete, saving it as a JPEG will create a small file that can fit on a floppy disk. The file can also be e-mailed to clients, so that they can download and view it.

In most cases, the image is going to be printed on a standard $8\frac{1}{2}'' \times 11''$ piece of paper from an inkjet office printer. Printers with at least 300 dpi (dots per inch) will give satisfactory results, although increasing the dpi capability will increase the photo quality. It is important to use high-quality paper to get the best print. Do comparisons with various papers to find out the best print quality.

***Figure 10-15* Painting Texture**
Texture can be applied to the ground plane by using the cursor as a "paintbrush" with the selected texture. *(Photo edited in Visual Impact Software)*

(a)

(b)

***Figure 10-16* Sidewalk**
(a) The sidewalk is added as an object, (b) then *distorted* to fit. *(Photos edited in Visual Impact Software)*

# Plan Drawing Software

Plan drawing can be done quickly using software to drop in symbols and labels. Computer-aided design has been around much longer than design imaging because of AutoCAD.

Plan drawing software has been developed to appeal to the landscape designer who wants to create plan drawings quickly and easily without having to purchase special equipment. The software is much easier to learn as well as cost-efficient. Many programs have the added feature of an export function that will transfer all the plant material to an estimator list (which will be discussed later).

**Figure 10-17 Plants**
Plants are added as objects from the library. *(Photo edited in Visual Impact Software)*

**Figure 10-18 Mulch**
Mulched beds are added by *defining area* and *fill* with mulch texture. *(Photo edited in Visual Impact Software)*

# Scale

The scale is set at the start of the drawing by selecting the scale, either *architect* or *engineer*. Some programs can simply set the scale to a determined length of line.

**Figure 10-19** **Shadows**
Shadows are added to a few of the plants. *(Photo edited in Visual Impact Software)*

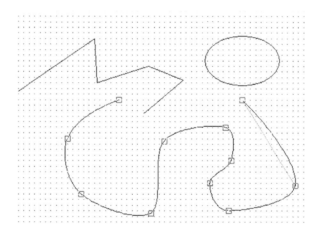

**Figure 10-20** **Lines**
A line tool can draw lines in any shape or angle.

# Line

One of the most basic functions of plan drawing software is the ability to draw **lines** (Figure 10-20). These lines can be quite simple. There are numerous ways to draw lines, depending on the software. A **pen-shaped mouse** helps you draw smoother lines because the instrument fits better for drawing than the standard mouse (try signing your name with the standard mouse!) (Figure 10-21).

# Site Plan

The site plan can be either drawn with the *line tool* or scanned from the original plan. Scanning a site plan can make transferring site information much easier (Figure 10-22).

***Figure 10-21* Pen-Shaped Mouse**
This tool makes it easier to draw lines. *(Photo edited in Visual Impact Software)*

The image of the site plan is *imported* as an object, similar to the way images of trees and shrubs appear as objects. It will serve as a template, so that the property lines and house can be quickly traced onto the drawing with the line tool. Once the tracing is complete, the site plan image can be deleted, leaving behind only the tracing lines.

If a site plan is not available, on-site measurements can be drawn with the line tool.

# Dimensions

A **dimension tool** can be used to automatically specify distances for layout (Figure 10-23). Because the program has a set scale, dragging a dimension line from one point to another will automatically label the correct distance on the plan.

# Ground Plane

Using the line tool, the ground plane can be defined into areas such as the lawn, mulched beds, and hardscapes (Figure 10-24). Using the line tool to enclose areas **(forms)** can open up other tools.

Enclosed areas can be filled with color or texture if desired for presentational quality.

# Objects

Plant symbols are placed on the plan drawing similar to how objects are placed on the imaging software. The image database often contains a collection of symbols that can be dropped onto the design (Figure 10-25). These symbols can then be sized and transformed like any object to the correct scale. Properties can also be assigned to the symbol. These can include, but are not limited to, the plant name, planting size, price, and inventory number.

## Duplicating Symbols

The symbols can be duplicated quickly with a copy command that places the same symbol with every click (Figure 10-26). The important thing is that all the properties be assigned to the symbol beforehand so that they are copied along with it.

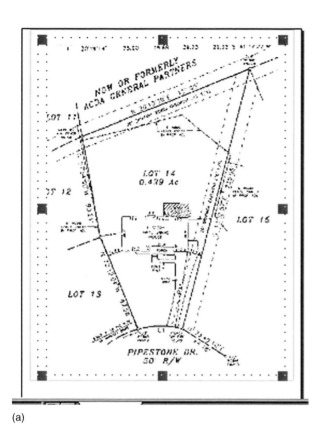

(a)

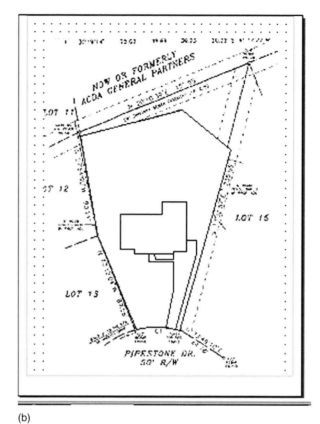

(b)

(c)

### *Figure 10-22* **Tracing Site Plan**

(a) The site plan has been scanned as a GIF and imported as an object. (b) A *line tool* can be used to trace the property lines, house, and concrete. (c) When finished, the site plan image can be deleted, leaving only the traced lines. *(Edited in Visual Impact Software)*

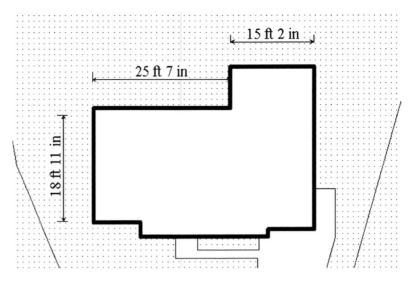

**Figure 10-23 Dimensions**
A *dimension tool* can be used to automatically specify measurements that would help create a planting plan. *(Edited in Visual Impact Software)*

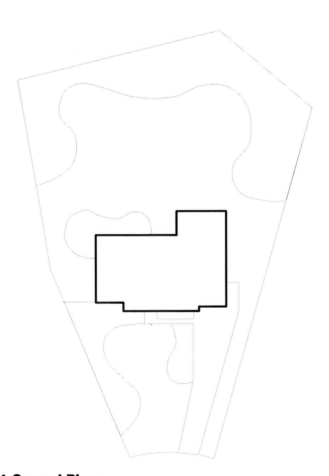

**Figure 10-24 Ground Plane**
Using the *line tool* to draw the sidewalk and bedlines. *(Edited in Visual Impact Software)*

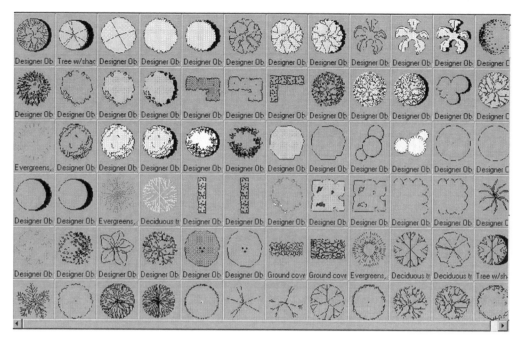

***Figure 10-25* Symbol Library**
The database of images has a collection of symbols. *(Photo edited in Visual Impact Software)*

## Labels

When all the symbols are placed, the design can be quickly labeled (Figure 10-27). Most programs have an automatic labeling command that will place the name of the symbol on the label without having to type it again. Because the properties of the symbol contain the name, the command can automatically assign the name to the label. This makes labeling an easy process that is completed in seconds.

# Area and Volume Estimation

The square footage of the lawn area can be estimated along with an estimate to sod. The square footage of a mulched bed can be estimated as well as the cubic feet required to install it 3″ deep. The depth of mulch can be changed to recalculate volume (Figure 10-28).

# Color

Texture can be added to the ground plane or, for presentation, the plan drawing can be colored for presentation (Figure 10-29).

# Cost-Estimator Software

When the plan drawing is complete, all the plants and other materials can be exported to an **estimator**. The estimator organizes all the plants and materials and their assigned properties, as well as square footage and volume of ground plane areas, into a proposal format that can add up the cost of materials for an estimate (Figure 10-30). This software can be customized for your company as a proposal template that can be printed and presented to the client.

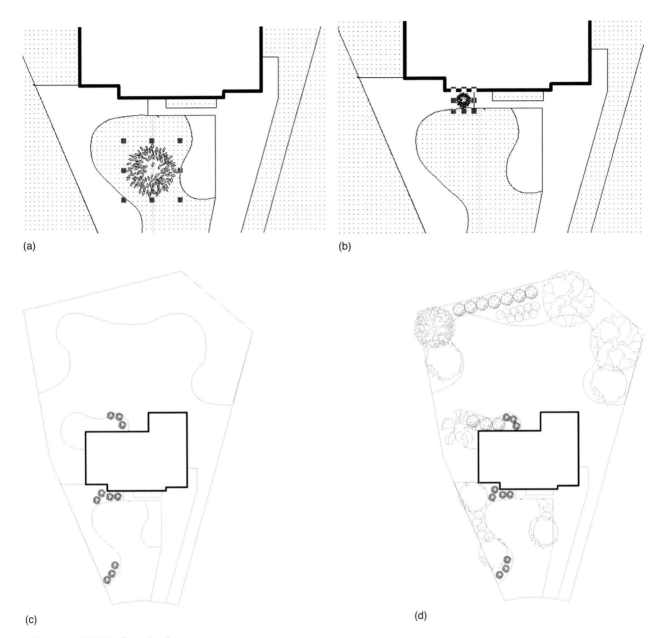

(a)

(b)

(c)

(d)

***Figure 10-26*** **Symbols**
(a) A symbol is selected from the library, (b) *resized* and *moved* on the plan, and (c) *duplicated* to other locations.
(d) Other symbols are placed. *(Edited in Visual Impact Software)*

# Software Products

When considering the purchase of software, shop around at the various retailers listed. Some can send you the fully operational product that will run for a 30-day trial before requiring you to purchase a password to unlock it for further use.

## Design Imaging Group

http://designimaginggroup.com

## Drafix Software, Inc.

http://www.drafix.com

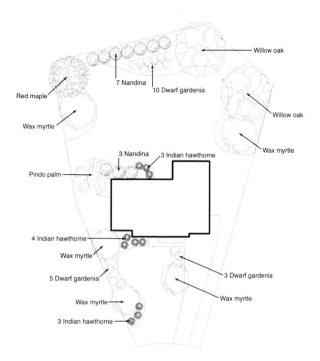

### *Figure 10-27* Labels

Symbols are quickly labeled using a *labeling tool* that automatically picks the name of the symbol that was previously assigned to it. *(Edited in Visual Impact Software)*

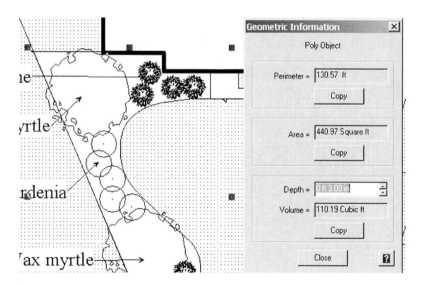

### *Figure 10-28* Area

For materials estimation, area is quickly calculated from areas such as the beds, turf, sidewalk, or driveway. *(Edited in Visual Impact Software)*

## Visual Impact

http://www.visualimpactimaging.com

## Eagle Point Software

http://www.eaglepoint.com

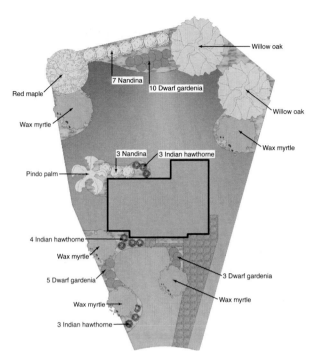

Willow oak

Red maple

7 Nandina

10 Dwarf gardenia

Willow oak

Wax myrtle

Wax myrtle

3 Nandina

3 Indian hawthorne

Pindo palm

4 Indian hawthorne

Wax myrtle

5 Dwarf gardenia

3 Dwarf gardenia

Wax myrtle

Wax myrtle

3 Indian hawthorne

### *Figure 10-29* Color Plan

The plan drawing can also be colored for presentation. *(Edited in Visual Impact Software)*

**Pelican Landscape Designs**

**Date 5/27/2002**
**Invoice # 00000122**

Jon Doe
111 Carolina Lane
Charleston, SC 29111

Tel: (843) 555-1212
Fax: (843) 555-1212

| Name | Qty. | Price | Size | Tax | Total |
|------|------|-------|------|-----|-------|
| Dwarf gardenia | 17 | 12.00 | 3 GALLON | 12.75 | 216.75 |
| Indian hawthorne | 10 | 12.00 | 3 GALLON | 7.50 | 127.50 |
| Nandina | 10 | 12.00 | 3 GALLON | 7.50 | 127.50 |
| Pindo palm | 1 | 45.00 | 4' BB | 2.81 | 47.81 |
| Red maple | 1 | 55.00 | 15 GALLON | 3.44 | 58.44 |
| Wax myrtle | 5 | 25.00 | 5 GALLON | 7.81 | 132.81 |
| Willow oak | 2 | 55.00 | 15 GALLON | 6.88 | 116.88 |
| | | | | | |
| Tax Total | | | | 48.69 | |
| Grand Total | | | | | 827.69 |
| | | | | | |

### *Figure 10-30* Estimation

All the materials can be organized into a proposal. *(Created in Visual Impact Software)*

## LSI Software Inc.

http://www.lsisoft.com

## Dynascape

http://www.gardengraphics.com

### Software Republic

http://www.softwarerepublic.com

### Landmark

http://www.nemetschek.net

# Summary

Landscape design software can make the design process more time-efficient as well as more effective in communicating the concept. Professional-grade software has become easier to learn for the landscape designer. Imaging software utilizes a database of images, such as trees, shrubs, concrete, and mulch, which can be blended onto a digital image of the design site. As a result, clients can visualize the proposed design with the use of photo-quality images. Plan drawing software uses symbol objects from the database to create the plan. Once the site plan is built, the symbols can be placed, sized, assigned attributes (name, size, and cost), and labeled. When finished, all the materials in the plan can be exported to a estimator program that will organize and format the list for estimates.

# Key Words

**AutoCAD:**  allows the user to draw lines, arcs, and circles; for the landscape designer, it lacks a symbol library.

**BMP:**  Microsoft Windows' native image format that will open in the Paint program, which is part of Windows; the files are very large.

**Brightness contrast:**  this tool manipulates the light and dark quality of the image.

**Cloning:**  this tool can be used to erase existing plants or other objects in the image.

**Cropping:**  this tool allows you to select a portion of the photo and delete the rest.

**Customized library:**  organizes the image database with the most frequently used objects and textures.

**Digital images:**  pictures of an object or site that can be captured with a digital camera and downloaded to a computer; also a photograph that is scanned.

**Dimension tool:**  a tool used to automatically specify distances for layout.

**Distort:**  change the proportion of the object; it is often used to create perspective on ground plane objects.

**Duplication:**  this tool can be used to quickly copy an object numerous times.

**Estimator:**  organizes all plants and other materials and their assigned properties into a proposal format that can add up the cost of materials.

**File formats:**  various ways images are stored and read by the computer.

**Fill tool:**  tool used to fill an object or area with color or texture.

**Forms:**  using the line tool to enclose areas for estimating area and volume.

**GIF:**  format of a digital image that requires sharp boundaries, such as lettering or line drawings; the files are relatively small.

**Grabbing:**  clicking and holding on an object in order to move it.

**Ground plane objects:**   objects that appear in an image database just as trees and shrubs do; the library may be organized to contain a section of walks, driveways, and lawns.

**Image database:**   most programs have a collection of objects and textures to place into the design.

**Imaging:**   creates the proposed design with the aid of plant images and ground plane textures on a digital photo of the site.

**JPEG:**   format of digital image good for saving photo images of the site or people; the files are relatively small.

**LANDCADD:**   evolved from AutoCAD to include numerous symbols and applications related to landscaping.

**Layers:**   objects stack up like layers one on top of another; the objects can be moved from back to front so they appear either behind or in front of each other.

**Library:**   see *image database.*

**Painting tool:**   tool used to apply selected textures or color with the cursor.

**Pen-shaped mouse:**   helps draw smoother lines than the standard mouse.

**Sharpness:**   used to improve the quality of the image by making lines and edges more defined.

**TIFF:**   standard format for the computer-based publishing industry; the files are very large.

**Transparency tool:**   tool used to change the degree of object transparency.

**Trimmed:**   the trimming tool acts as an eraser to remove portions of an object.

**Zoom box:**   tool used to drag a selection box over an area to enlarge it for viewing.

**Zoom tool:**   tool for enlarging or shrinking the image.

# Appendices

# A ⎯ Portfolio

Never throw away any of your projects. Even designs from classroom projects should be used to develop a *portfolio*.

A portfolio is a collection of your design work that includes all drawings and photos of the project. By creating an organized, portable portfolio, you will be able to present your past work to prospective clients as well as to prospective employers.

## Project Files

At the beginning of any project, start a file with the project name. Smaller projects can use a small manila folder, but, as projects get larger, expandable folders should be used to hold several files of the same project.

The file should contain

- Site plan (and any other surveys)
- Interview notes
- Site observations
- Pictures
- Contract
- Reduced plan drawing (once project is complete)

The original drawing (24″ × 36″) should be stored in a cabinet (flat storage) or bin (rolled storage) and properly labeled.

## Photography

### Digital Camera

The advantages of a digital camera include the ability to

*Take plenty of pictures.* Shoot as many pictures as you can on-site. You can always delete them later at no cost.

*Improve photos.* Using software, photos can be sharpened and cropped to improve the quality.

*Print hardcopies.* Photo-quality pictures can be printed on your own computer and stored in the project file.

*Store project electronically.* The project can be stored on the hard drive and backup disks, taking up little space.

*Send photos electronically.* Pictures can easily be stored on a CD or hard drive or sent via e-mail.

*Software design.* Photos can be used to build your design and present an actual photo of the design to send electronically (see Chapter 10).

You should look for the following features in a digital camera:

*Zoom:* at least 3× to shoot different photos without moving

*High resolution.* Most midrange cameras have acceptable resolution. Always shoot photos at the highest resolution; you can always reduce the resolution if you need space.

*Amenities.* Extra set of rechargeable batteries for replacement on site and extra memory cards (if required)

## 35mm Camera

Photography with a standard camera works well; however, with each project you have the expense of film and developing.

*Fully automatic cameras.* Automatic cameras, called "point and shoot," are cost-efficient and can produce quality photos without having to understand f-stops and apertures.

*Film.* A 200-speed film will create good photos during bright or cloudy days.

*Development.* Use a reputable film developer. Beware of some one-hour photo establishments that produce lower-quality prints.

*Storage.* Once photos are developed, they can be stored in the project file as well as scanned into a digital image to use on the computer. In fact, many film developers will provide your pictures as computer images on a CD along with your photos for an extra fee.

## Photographing the Site

Take plenty of pictures of the project. Take as many pictures as possible to record various angles and help in the design process.

### Before Pictures

During the site visit, shoot all the possible angles of the project to avoid having to make a trip back. Always include one shot of the entire front of the house and property, which is the angle most people are concerned about. Be sure to mark the spot where you take photos, so you can return to that same spot for *after photos*. It is much more effective to show before and after photos when they are shot from the same angle.

---

### *Tip Box:*  Mark a Before Spot

Be sure to remember a spot where a before picture is taken. This will commonly be a picture of the front of the house. When you return for the after picture, it is much easier to compare pictures that are shot from the same angle.

---

### After Pictures

Return to the site after installation and shoot several photos from the same spots where you shot the before photos. At this point, most of the plants will be very small and the design will not closely resemble the design that has been envisioned.

Return to the site after the installation has had at least one year to establish. In most regions, plants are well established and filling in the design by the third year. This should more closely resemble what the design was intended to look like.

---

***Tip Box:*** **Third-Year-After Picture**

In most regions, plants are well established and filling out the intended design by the third year.

---

# Copying the Plan Drawing

## Blueprint

You will provide the client with a copy of the design. Have a copy reduced to an $8\frac{1}{2}'' \times 11''$ size to store it in a three-ring binder or manila folder.

Instead of a hardcopy of the design, you can get a digital file to store on the computer. It will be the original $24'' \times 36''$ size stored as a TIFF file. This way, you can print out a copy of the design at any size or crop portions of the design for printing. It can also be sent via e-mail.

## Photographing the Plan Drawing

The plan drawing can be photographed with 35mm film.

*Use Proper lighting.* The easiest approach is to photograph the plan drawing outside on a clear day. If you shoot it indoors, you will need to have appropriate lighting.

*Use low-speed film.* Better resolution will result from using 100-speed film.

*Mount plan drawing.* Use a foam board and mount the plan drawing so that there are no wrinkles. Orient the drawing so that it faces full sun.

*Mount camera on tripod.* A tripod will keep the camera still. Focus the camera to photograph the entire plan drawing.

# Assembling a Portfolio

Use a three-ring binder to organize projects. This is a compact way to carry several projects. The binder will fit in a briefcase and the projects can easily be reorganized.

*Use dividers to separate projects.* This way, you can turn to each project quickly.

*Reduce plan drawings.* Include other drawings, such as elevation, if they were created.

*Include before pictures.* Include notes of analysis from each view underneath each picture (in essence, what needed to be accomplished in this area).

*Include after pictures.* Place after pictures with the before pictures that are shot at the same angle next to each other. This makes it easy to see the result of your design.

# B | Student Design

This appendix is a collection of student designs for study. The border, title block, and plant list has been omitted so that the drawing is more legible. There is a short critique with each one to point out some of the strong and poor techniques. The following are the most common weaknesses in most designs.

1. *Lettering.* Although all lettering techniques improve, it is the most overlooked aspect in the design. It is difficult to change your natural writing to conform to a landscape style. This is probably because many people have poor handwriting to begin with. Most beginning designers overlook the basics of lettering. They fail to use guidelines, spacing, and consistency. Even if the style isn't great, pay attention to the basics.

2. *Line weight.* Getting a variety of line weight throughout the drawing will improve it dramatically. However, this is often overlooked. In most designs, all the line weight is the same. Pay attention to where heavy to light line weights should be used.

3. *Labeling.* There are often errors in labeling. Remember to include the number of plants in the label. Pay attention to the key and be consistent. And don't mess up a great drawing with leader lines that fly all over the design. Keep them consistent. Another important shortfall is the lack of labels. For instance, the symbol in the front yard is labeled, but the same symbol in the backyard is not because the one in front has a label. What if you start looking at the backyard? You will have to scan the whole design to find the same symbol with the label. If in doubt, always label the symbol.

4. *Plan balance.* The balance of space is overlooked. The design is squashed up against the border and a tiny plant list is pasted in the middle of a lot of white space. The same applies to the title block where the information is not balanced. Pay attention to visually balancing the drawings and information with the blank space on the paper.

5. *Too many textures.* In an effort to make the design appealing, there are too many different textures on the ground plane. This especially applies to patterns that aren't consistent or the line weight is too heavy. They make it look confusing. Keep it simple.

## Preliminary and Master Plans

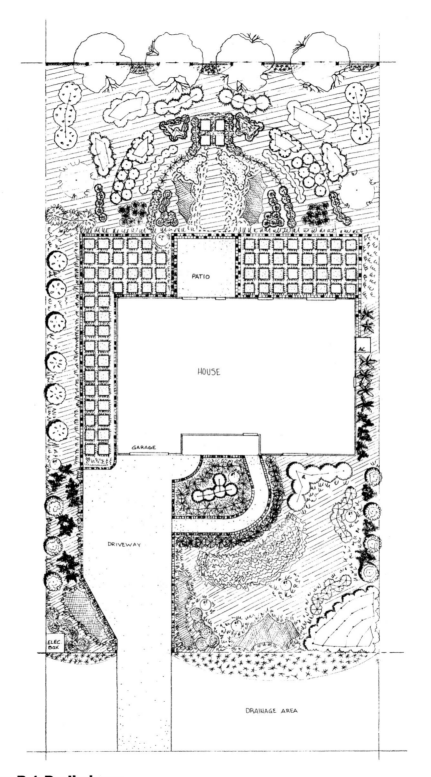

*Figure B-1* **Preliminary**
Line quality is good. Shadows need to fall to the bottom of symbols. Because there's so much mulch, use something besides a pattern. Makes it busy. *(Design by Beverly Thompson)*

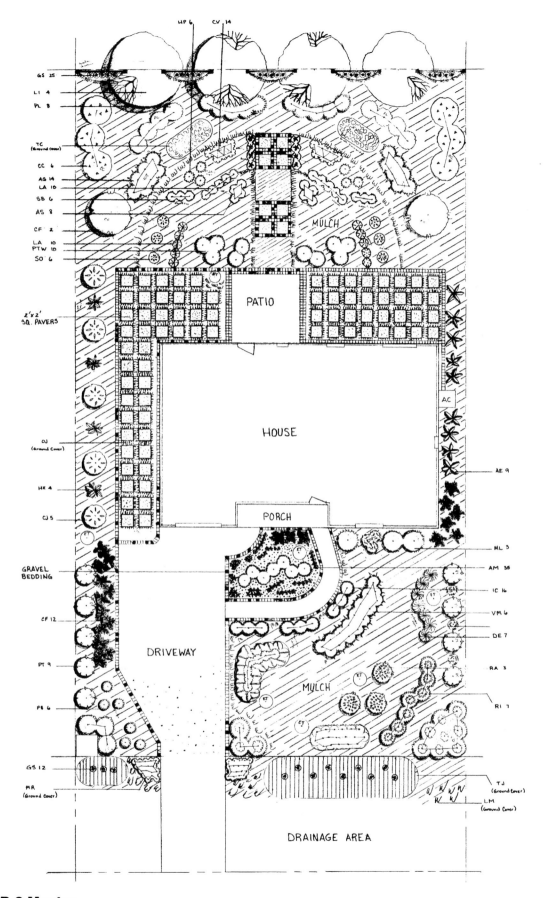

**Figure B-2 Master**

Lettering is decent. Would like to see heavier line weight on house. Still feel the same about the pattern used for mulch. *(Design by Beverly Thompson)*

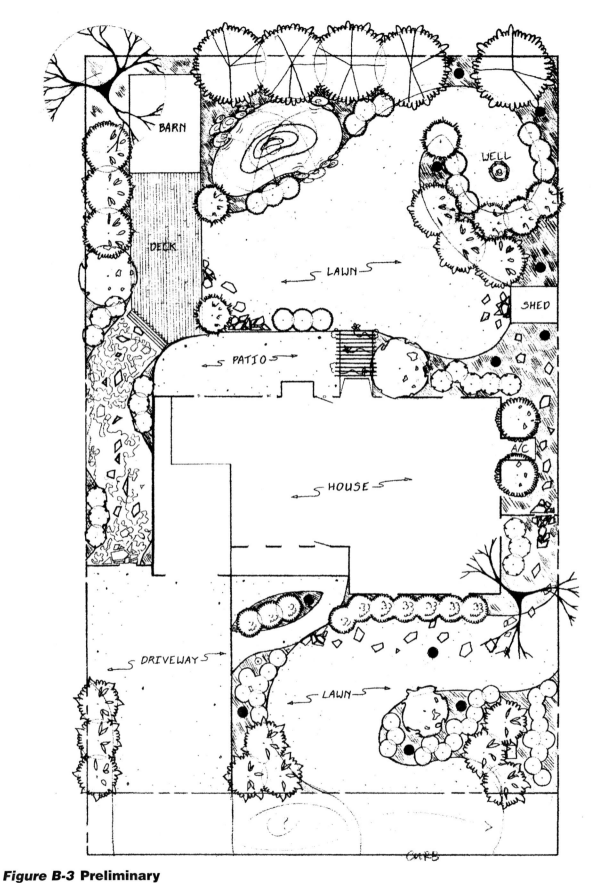

### *Figure B-3* Preliminary
Line quality is very good. Plan reads clean. Texture for pond needs improvement. *(Design by Gabrielle Justice)*

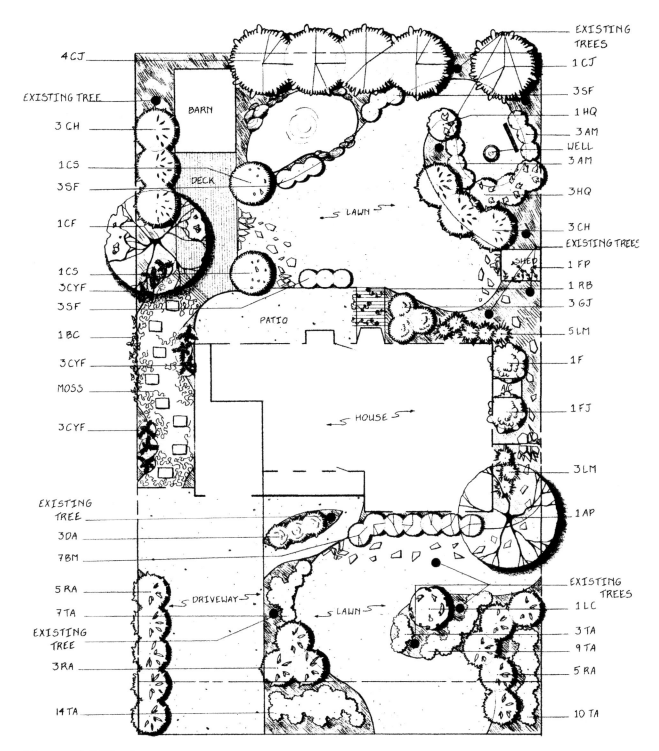

*Figure B-4* **Master**

Line quality even better. Makes a great print. House needs heavier line weight. Lettering is good. *(Design by Gabrielle Justice)*

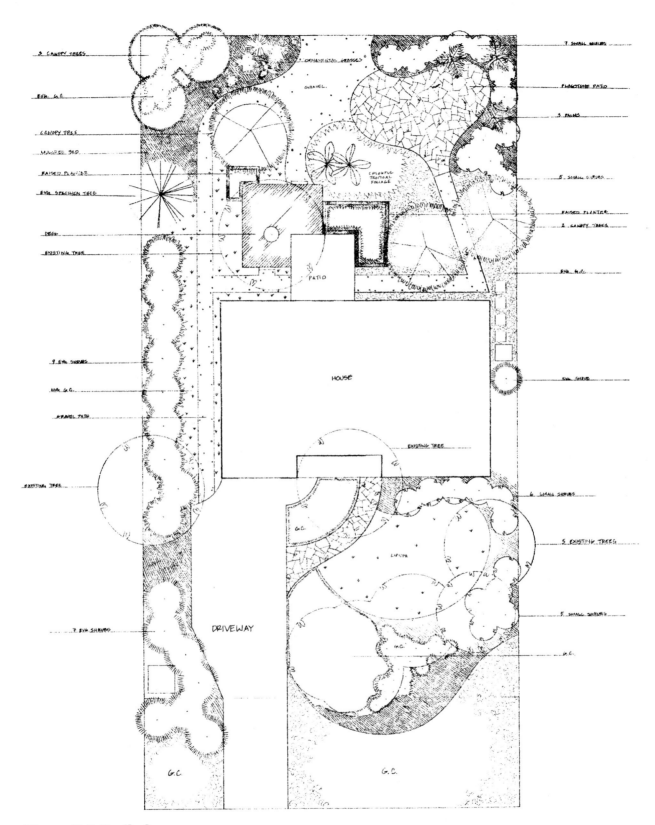

### *Figure B-5* **Preliminary**

Line weight is weak. Great graphics. Good lettering, but put labels at *end* of leader line, not on it. *(Design by James Herndon)*

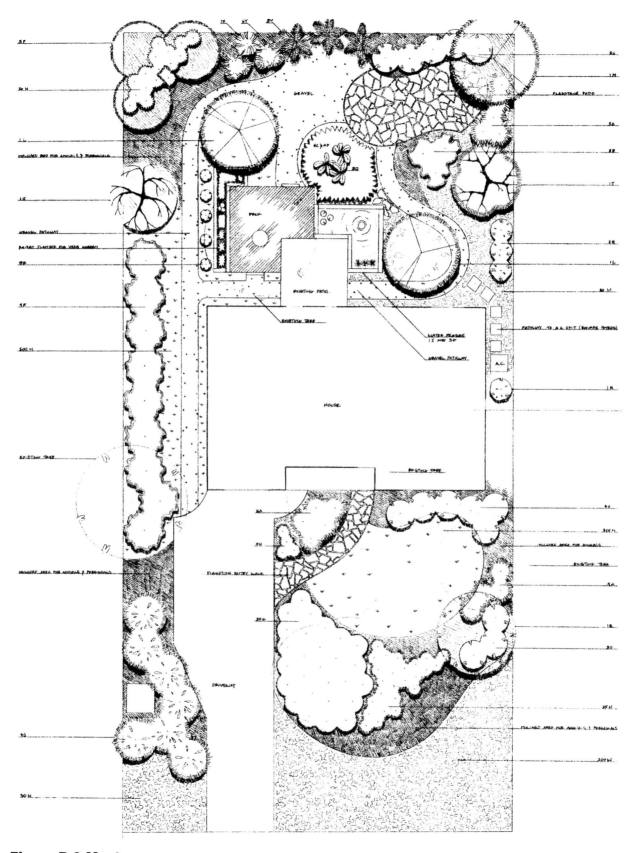

## *Figure B-6* Master

Line weights greatly improved! Still need heavier line weight on house. Great graphical technique. Love the overhead canopies! See comment on preliminary about labeling. *(Design by James Herndon)*

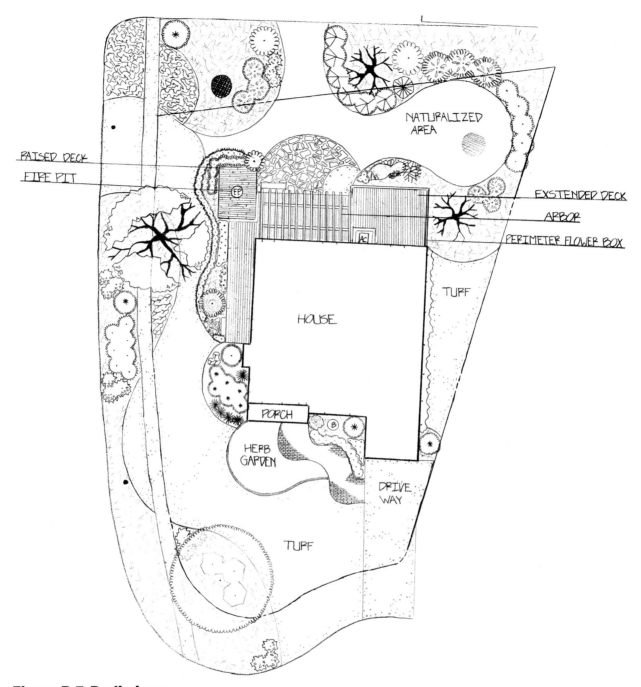

RAISED DECK

FIRE PIT

NATURALIZED
AREA

EXSTENDED DECK

ARBOR

PERIMETER FLOWER BOX

EP

AC

TURF

HOUSE

PORCH

B

HERB
GARDEN

DRIVE
WAY

TURF

### Figure B-7 Preliminary
Great detail and balance. Very good line weight variation. Lettering is acceptable. *(Design by Sarah Thornby)*

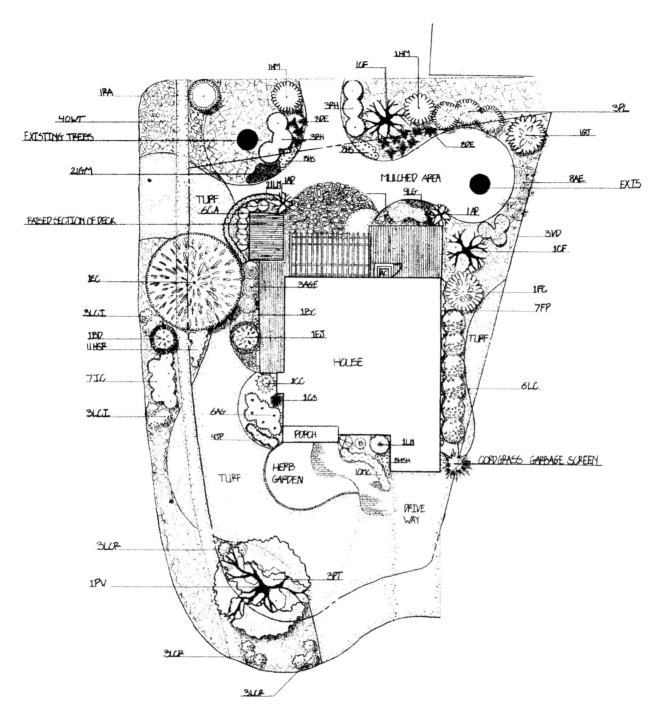

**Figure B-8 Master**

Clear and visually interesting. Notice how the absence of line weight on driveway weakens that part of the drawing. *(Design by Sarah Thornby)*

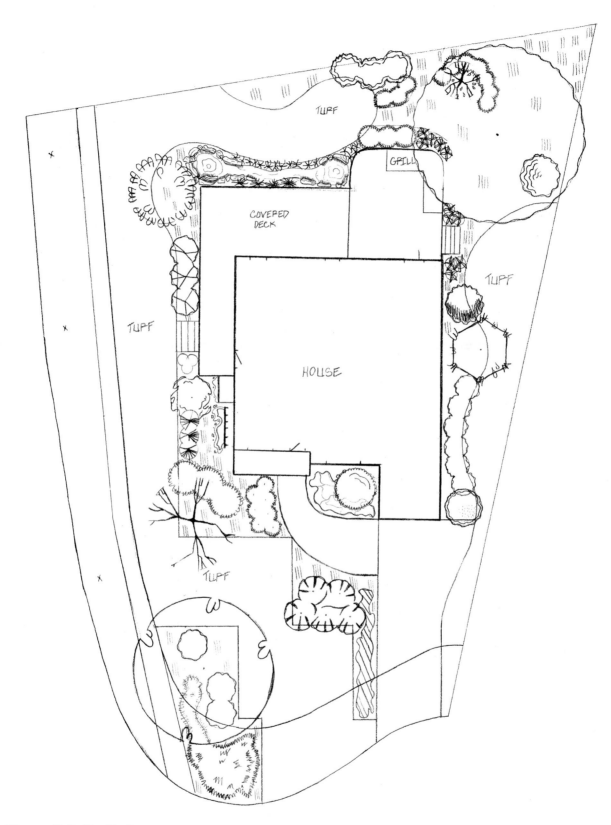

**Figure B-9 Preliminary**
Good, clean drawing. Easy to read. Improve by adding ground plane texture. *(Design by Jay Culbreath)*

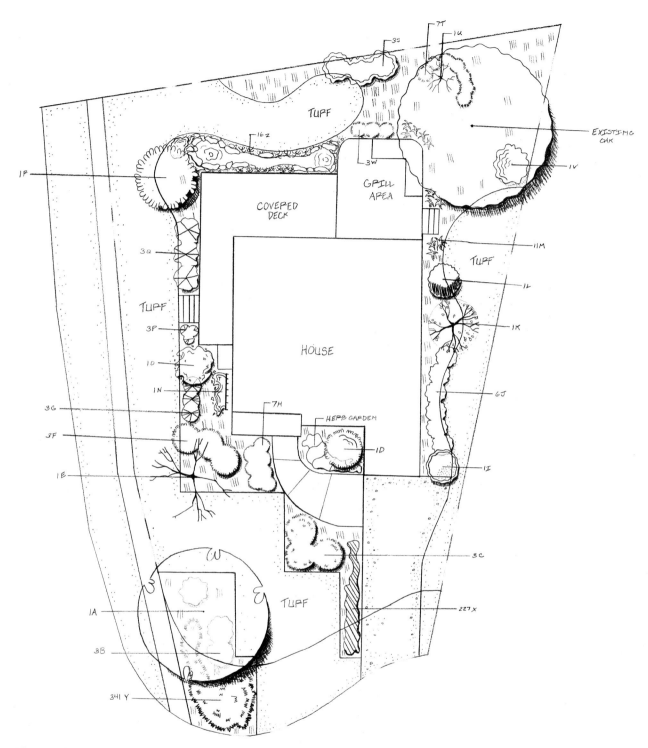

## Figure B-10 Master

Still good line quality. Mulch texture acceptable, not good. Great effect on overhead canopies. More line weight on house! *(Design by Jay Culbreath)*

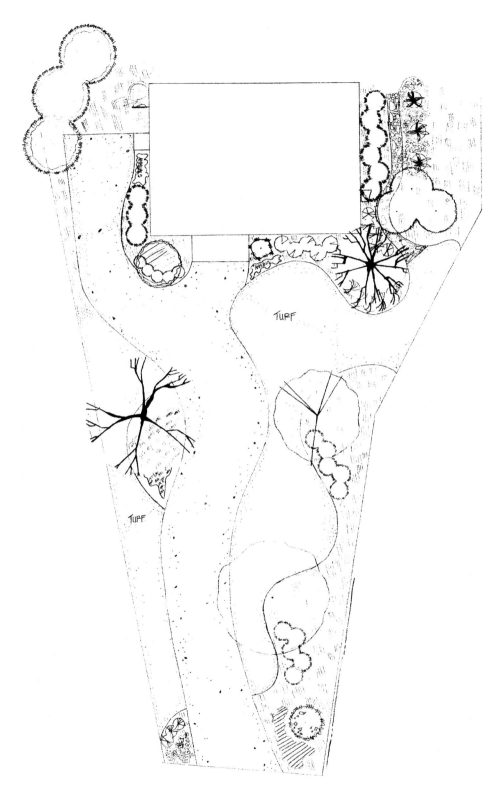

**Figure B-11  Preliminary**
Symbols decent. Line weight very weak. Poor pint. *(Design by Jay Culbreath)*

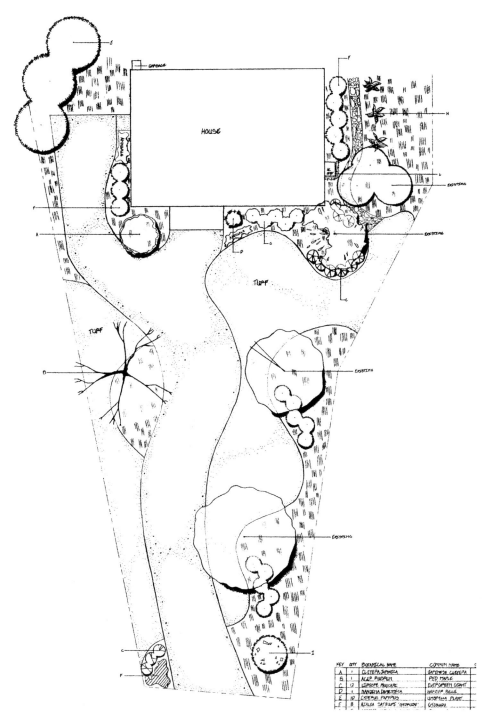

## Figure B-12 Master

Much better symbols. Line weights much, much better (except house). Mulch texture acceptable, not good.
*(Design by Jay Culbreath)*

# Master Plans

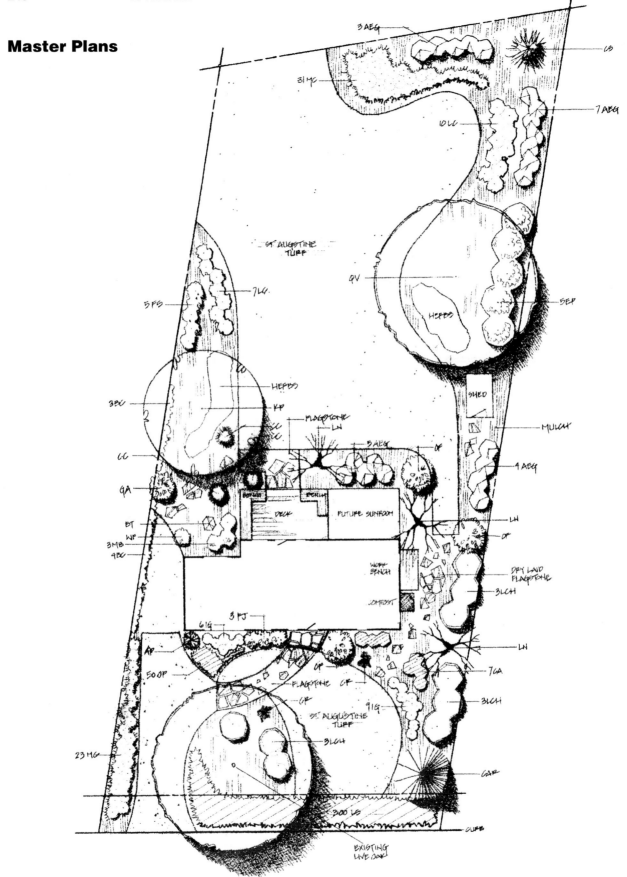

## Figure B-13 Lovering Project
Good line weights. Nice sample technique. Decent lift on overhead canopies. Good lettering.

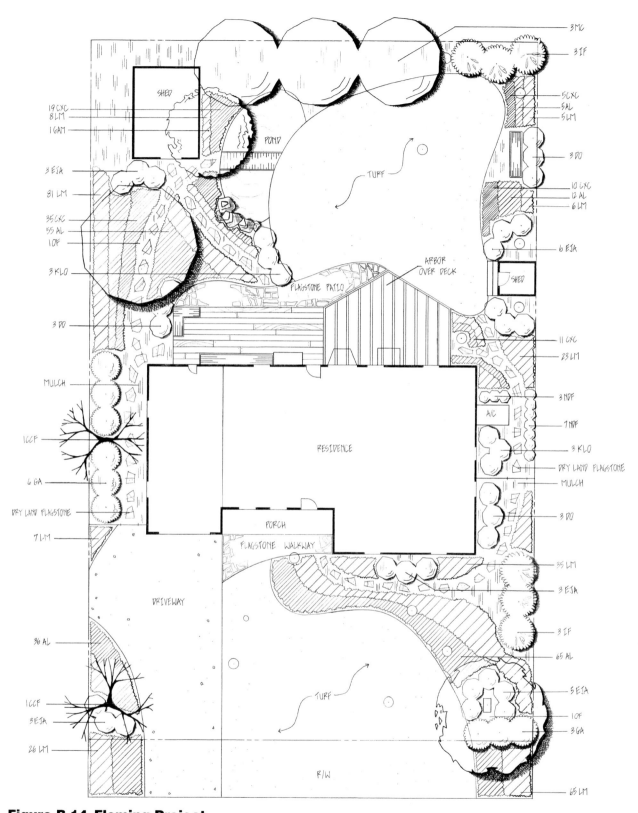

## Figure B-14 Fleming Project
Great line quality! Excellent print. Very easy to read. Lettering good. *(Design by Melinda Altovilla)*

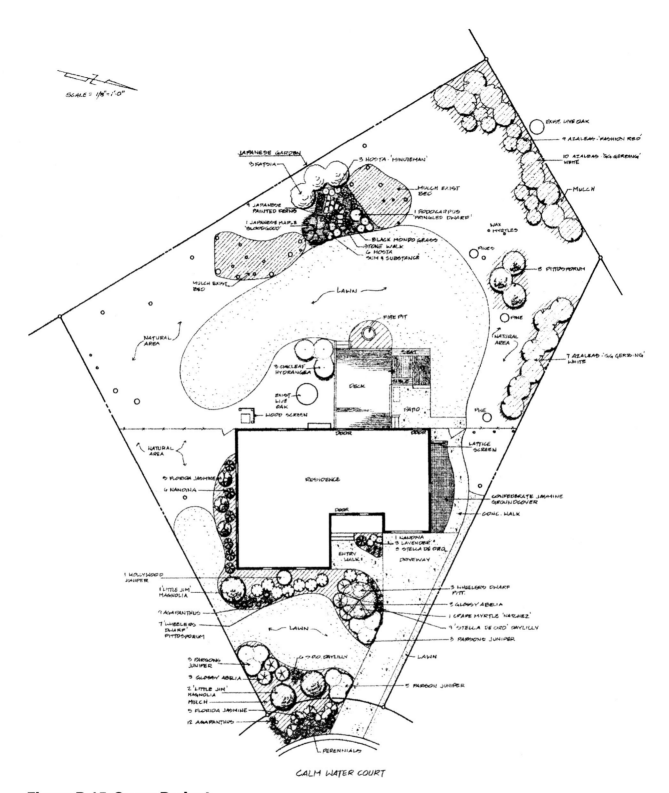

SCALE = 1/8" = 1'0"

CALM WATER COURT

## Figure B-15  Green Project

Very good line quality. That's what house and property line should look like. Lettering is very good. Easy to read.
*(Design by Sandy Plance)*

# Index